A Double-Edged Sword

Maritime Currents: History and Archaeology

A DOUBLE-EDGED SWORD

The Biography of Commodore Jesse Duncan Elliott, 1782–1845

DAVID F. LONG

The University of Alabama Press
Tuscaloosa

The University of Alabama Press
Tuscaloosa, Alabama 35487–0380
uapress.ua.edu

Typeface: Minion Pro

Cover image: John Neagle (1796–1865) artist, portrait of Commodore Jesse Duncan Elliott, May 1824; courtesy of George B. E. Hambleton, Charleston, SC
Cover design: Terrell Harris

Cataloging-in-Publication data is available from the Library of Congress.
ISBN: 978-0-8173-2258-8 (cloth)
ISBN: 978-0-8173-6240-9 (paper)
E-ISBN: 978-0-8173-9588-9

To my wife, Susan, whose acts of kindness and energy on my behalf and on behalf of so many others have made all of us feel more alive and appreciated

Commodore Jesse Duncan Elliott standing in front of USS *Constitution*. Artist unknown. Courtesy of Cheri J. Griffin.

Contents

Illustrations

Foreword

David Foster Long was a long-serving historian and one of the most prolific and respected authors of late eighteenth- and nineteenth-century naval and maritime history who taught American history and history of foreign relations at the University of New Hampshire. Originally from Cleveland, Ohio, he received his AB at Dartmouth College and his PhD from Columbia University and ultimately took a teaching position at the University of New Hampshire. During his career, Long had the honor to serve as a Fulbright lecturer in Sri Lanka, New Zealand, Australia, Uganda, Hong Kong, and Korea and also spent two semesters teaching history with the Semester at Sea Program. His success as a Fulbright lecturer and as a teacher abroad derived from his productivity as a prolific scholar. Long published four naval biographies, including studies of Commodore David Porter (1780–1843), Commodore James Biddle (1783–1848), Captain "Mad Jack" John Percival (1779–1862), and Commodore William Bainbridge (1774–1833), as well as the important book that combined naval history and foreign policy titled *Gold Braid and Foreign Relations: Diplomatic Activities of U.S. Naval Officers, 1798–1883*. At the time of his death, in January 2001, Long had spent the ten previous years working on a biography of nineteenth-century American naval officer Jesse Duncan Elliott (1782–1845), which he titled *A Double-Edged Sword: The Biography of Commodore Jesse Duncan Elliott, 1782–1845*. Completing the manuscript before his 2001 death, the project sat on his library shelf in his home he shared with his wife, Susan.

During the two-decade period after his death, Mrs. Long worked to find someone to shepherd the project through to publication. During the summer of 2022, Michael Verney, a University of New Hampshire PhD graduate who teaches at Drury University and also writes about naval history, contacted me. He said at the time that Mrs. Long was looking for a publisher for a biography of Jesse Duncan Elliott. Indicating to Michael that I edited a series on maritime history, he put me in touch with William Paine, a descendant of Elliott, who, while conducting genealogical research, had received the manuscript from retired professor Alan Belovarac of Mercyhurst University, who in turn had received the Elliott manuscript years earlier from Mrs. Long. Shortly after our conversation, and with the considerable help of Bill, the manuscript was submitted to the University of Alabama Press series Maritime Currents: History and Archaeology.

A Double-Edged Sword is a study of an American naval officer who was involved in several highly questionable events, including the War of 1812's Battle of Lake Erie where Elliott hesitated to bring his ship, the Brig *Niagara*, into the battle, which resulted in creating a lifelong feud between Oliver Hazard Perry and Elliott. He also served as James Barron's second in the fatal duel between naval officers Stephen Decatur and Barron, where Decatur died. Additionally, as commander of the Charlestown Naval Yard, Elliott oversaw the successful rebuilding of "Old Ironsides" (USS *Constitution*) and later the infamous "beheading" of the Andrew Jackson masthead from the USS *Constitution* prior to a diplomatic mission to Europe to fend off an impending war with France in 1835. His time as commander of the flagship *Constitution*, during which he commanded the Mediterranean Squadron, ended with his court-martial; it would later be suspended. After being removed from service, Elliott penned a narrative of his life during his ouster from naval duties before being reinstated and receiving his final command as head of the Philadelphia Naval Yard before his death in 1845.

Throughout this detailed project, Long investigated every aspect of Elliott's life, and as a result, his manuscript is somewhat revisionist since most naval historians had focused on the negative qualities of Elliott's life and personal characteristics. Long maintains that the highly storied naval officer Elliot aspired to serve his country patriotically while seeking approbation from his superiors and other influencers in his ultimate quest for distinguishment.

Since Long's death in 2001, naval and maritime scholarship about Elliott is sparse. One notable recent contribution is Benjamin Armstrong's *Small Boats and Daring Men: Maritime Raiding, Irregular Warfare, and the Early American Navy* (volume 66 of Campaigns and Commander Series). Armstrong describes Elliott's leadership role in the capture of the British ships *Detroit* and *Caledonia* on Lake Erie in the War of 1812. However, most modern research does very little to affect the interpretation that Long had developed about Elliott's life. Long's book will again reveal the abundance of primary and secondary sources that researchers and readers can quickly uncover for projects and also recognize that those sources truly illustrate Elliott's contentious behavior as well as his meritorious service. Ultimately, this study of Elliott will fill a gaping hole in the naval history of the pre–Civil War

United States. It will also enhance Long's reputation as a naval historian and historian of American foreign policy.

Two individuals deserve to be singled out here for special acknowledgments. Larry Moberly was both a student of Long and his longtime research assistant, including for Long's book *Mad Jack*. Moberly assisted Long in many of the tasks related to the research and drafting of *A Double-Edged Sword*. Most significantly, he assisted Long with proofreading, editing for clarity, deciphering Elliott's handwriting, and acting as a devil's advocate for Long's arguments and conclusions. Long could not have found a better candidate for such endeavors than he did with Moberly. Since his graduation from UNH, Moberly has been teaching history in various public-school systems and is presently teaching in Anchorage, Alaska. His primary interests include fishing as well as sharing his passion for and knowledge of history with his students.

Finally, a special note of thanks is due to William Paine, the Elliott descendant who learned about the existence of Long's manuscript form during the course of his own genealogical research. On a trip to the Erie Maritime Museum and Brig Niagara, Paine followed up on his interest in Elliott and the Battle of Lake Erie and contacted a local historian about items of genealogical interest. What he thought was going to be a journal article about the Battle of Lake Erie turned out to be Long's biography of Commodore Elliott. After locating both Mrs. Long and Moberly, he contacted several naval maritime authors/historians, ultimately leading to the Maritime Currents series at the University of Alabama Press. Paine, more than anyone, helped navigate the final voyage for Long's fifth biography of a US naval captain and to bring it to fruition.

Gene Allen Smith,
Series Editor

Maritime Currents: History and Archaeology

Preface

SHOULD WE BEGIN by stating that, because of our several-year study of Commodore Jesse Duncan Elliott, we are presenting the definitive account of the pre-battle, battle, and post-battle of the Lake Erie story, as well as unraveling the mysteries of the Elliot–Commodore Oliver Hazard Perry controversy, the longest in US naval history? Of course we should!—If we wished to become the instant laughingstock of the American naval history establishment.

Our aim is immeasurably more modest, namely, to cast some illumination on previously inexplicable episodes of Elliott's life through maintaining a sharp focus on his career and character, for the battle itself occupies only one of our thirteen chapters.

From our first days of nineteenth-century naval research, we constantly ran across Elliott in a variety of works describing him in the most uncomplimentary terms. In my own publications I have called him "a man of violent likes and dislikes, erratic, suspicious, jealous, and voluble," and have described him as having "inexcusable behavior," as "the early Navy's most malignant officer," and as being "underhanded and generally loathsome."[1] Readers may wonder why sometimes we—David F. Long and M. Lawrence Moberly (research assistant; see mention of Moberly in the series editor's foreword)—use the singular pronoun "I" and sometimes the plural pronoun "we" in the preface and subsequent chapters. The reason is that I had started and been working on this biography of Commodore Jesse Duncan Elliott for more than a decade prior to Moberly's joining me. This, however, is of no importance, for Moberly has rapidly caught up with me and in some areas outdistanced me. We have both read several times every page of the manuscript until we have reached agreement between us as to locations and emphases. But, as we burrowed deeper into our sources, we discovered that we had omitted quite different aspects of Elliott's life heretofore generally overlooked that he was a remarkably industrious, efficient, and cost-conscious administrator, as well as a diplomat scoring conspicuous successes abroad—and these were recognized by the Navy Department by rewarding him with assignments hotly competed for by other officers.

An additional spur to write Elliott's biography was furnished by Leonard F. Guttridge and Jay D. Smith's *The Commodores*. Ever since its appearance, I have referred to it in my publications as the seminal work for those writing about early nineteenth-century American naval officers. Previously, authors had presented portraits of impeccable heroes and aimed their harshest attacks upon them along the lines of "he had flashes of quick temper but soon got over them." Guttridge and Smith have turned them into recognizable human beings. Indeed, when I first read *The Commodores* years ago, their analysis of Elliott caused me to file it away in the back of my mind. Yet, that prospect had to be put aside to complete other scheduled books and articles.

Careful readers should notice eventually the strange sequel in which Elliott, despite widespread knowledge of his questionable conduct, starting in the mid-1820s, was awarded one important and much relished assignment after another. He commanded warships on diplomatic cruises to Argentina and Brazil, 1825–27, and to Mexico and the Caribbean, 1830–32, in addition to commanding the Boston Navy Yard, 1833–35, as well as making two short voyages to Europe in 1835. During this period navy secretaries had to admit that half of their officers rusticated on half pay or none.

We feel that we are justified in calling this biography of Elliott a revisionist work, seeking to balance his credits and debits in order to equalize better his heretofore quite ignored abilities, as opposed to his almost universally admitted delinquencies.

Acknowledgments

MORE THAN TO any other authority, let me accentuate my indebtedness to Gerard T. Altoff, chief ranger/historian, National Park Service, Interior Department, South Bass Island, Put-In-Bay, Ohio. He has provided clear-cut insights about the Battle of Lake Erie, September 10, 1813, as well as to the growing enmity between Commodores Perry and Elliott, his second-in--command, during the interminable aftermath of that conflict.

Altoff's long article "The Perry-Elliott Controversy" is not only some rich mine of information per se, but his additional editing of Samuel Hambleton's diary of that navy purser and probably Perry's closest friend; and the Oliver Hazard Perry papers contain material that can be found conveniently nowhere else. The diary is the property of the Maryland Historical Society; and the Perry papers of the William L. Clements Library at the University of Michigan. Extensive citations must have the permission of the respective owners.

Using the above, however, presents difficulties for the researcher, and Altoff admits that his "transcription is not professional." A few letters are partial only, and apparently, some are missing altogether. Occasionally no solid differentiation is made whether Hambleton's diary is recording Perry's own opinion or telling him what others have said about him, derogatory though they may be. To a lesser extent the Perry papers reflects the same observation. The saving grace is that context can often decide the matter.

Among the host of histories covering 1812–15 consulted, two significantly stand out. Reginald Horsman's *War of 1812* is somewhat dated and is succinct at 286 pages. It is still, however, the one first consulted for varied aspects of that conflict, especially the naval aspects. Horsman's work is researchable with space allocations sensible, writing style readable and accurate, and judgments perceptive. A longer, more modern, and more comprehensive work is Donald M. Hickey's *The War of 1812*, a most impressive production at 457 pages. (Editor's Note: Donald Hickey's *The War of 1812: A*

Forgotten Conflict, Bicentennial Edition was subsequently published in 2011.)

With respect to Elliott's own writings, the following are highlighted:

> *Speech of Commodore Jesse Duncan Elliott, USN with Appendix and Addenda, Delivered in Hagerstown, Maryland, 14 November 1843.* The speech was actually presented in 1844 and surveys his life and naval career from his birth in 1782 until shortly before his death in 1845.
>
> The *Speech* must also be evaluated in the context of an earlier work, written under the pseudonym "A Citizen of New York," who was, beyond doubt, Russell Jarvis, a run-of-the mill journalist from Philadelphia: *Biographical Notice of Com. Jesse D. Elliott: Containing a Review of the Controversy between Him and the Late Commodore Perry; and a History of the Figure-Head of the U.S. Frigate Constitution.* Elliott, braggart personified, at least had enough sense to realize that if *Biographical Notice* had been published under his own name, public rejection of it would have been immediate and lasting; Jarvis necessarily was forced to serve as his front man. Hence, the errant designation of him as the author should appear as an alleged biography or some such qualification.

Even if incorrect in this assumption, it makes little, if any, difference. Neither the *Speech* nor the *Notice* could have been produced without frequent consultations between Elliott and Jarvis, the commodore's insistent inclusions and assiduous proofreading, and the opening of his incredibly voluminous files to his partner. Conceding that their style is literate, if florid, many readers may be repelled—as I have been so often—by their examples of limitless egotism, an inability to admit any judgmental error, and a loaded, even a jesuitical, interpretation of the facts.

I want to acknowledge the writings of Alexander S. Mackenzie, George Bancroft, Benson J. Lossing, Theodore Roosevelt, Alfred T. Mahan, William N. Dobbins, James C. Mills, Charles Dutton, Richard Dillon, Michael L. Palmer, and Frederick C. Drake, with apologies to those overlooked.

Special gratitude must be expressed to five colleagues, without whose assistance this biography would have been gravely crippled. . I believe Altoff's knowledge of the Battle of Lake Erie and the Perry-Elliott feud to be unexcelled. William M. P. Dunne, of the Long Island University's Southampton Campus, provided invaluable suggestions and criticisms over several years; I much appreciate his perhaps overly complimentary remark that I have a flair for evaluating the interpersonal relationships among the early USN officer corps. Commander (ret.) Tyrone G. Martin is an expert extraordinary on USS *Constitution*, and I am proud that I helped set his career in motion, enabling him to conclude his *A Most Fortunate Ship: A Narrative History of "Old Ironsides,"* a first-rate production.

A special thanks is owed to Richard E. Winslow III, the foremost New England naval historian, who has, over the past few years, sent an abundance of pertinent material from the Portsmouth (NH) *Journal.*

Finally, let me hail the scholarly achievements in the first volume of *The Naval War of 1812: A Documentary History,* volume 1, *1812,* edited by senior historian William S. Dudley and several associate editors. This is singular in its convenience and coverage. This was followed by volume 2, *1811;* volume 3, *1814–1815,* may not appear for some years, as restraints of money and time have compelled their restriction to selected documents, but so capable have been Dudley's choices and organization of them that the final volume will be eagerly anticipated. (Editor's Note: volumes 3 and 4, covering 1814–1815, were published 2002, 2023, respectively.)

Chronology

Birthplace: Hagerstown Maryland	July 14, 1782
Death: Philadelphia Naval Yard	December 10, 1845
Dickinson College (Law School), Carlisle, Pennsylvania	1804
Dickinson College (Trustee)	1831–33

US Navy (Rank)

Midshipman	April 2, 1804
Lieutenant	April 23, 1810
Master Commandant (Commander)	July 24. 1813
Captain	March 27, 1818

Naval Service (Ship/Principal Assignment)

First Barbary Wars—Mediterranean, *ESSEX, VIXEN*	1804–6
CHESAPEAKE with Barron and capture by British *LEOPARD*	1807
Norfolk Station, *ENTERPRISE*	1808
JOHN ADAMS	1809–10
War of 1812–15, *ARGUS*	1811–12
Capture of British brigs *DETROIT AND CALEDONIA*	1812
Capture of York, Upper Canada, *MADISON, CONQUEST*	1813
Battle of Lake Erie—second-in-command, *NIAGARA, SOMERS*	1813
Commodore Chauncey's Lake Ontario Squadron, *SYLPH*	1814
Second Barbary (Algerian) War in Mediterranean, *ONTARIO*	1815
Board of Engineers and Coastal Survey, Barron—Decatur Duel	1818, 1820–22
Command Brazil Squadron and South American Coast, *CYANE*	1825–27
Recruiting, Carlisle, Pennsylvania	1827–28
Command West Indies Squadron (commodore), *PEACOCK, FAIRFIELD*	1829–33
Command Charleston, South Carolina, Naval Station and Norfolk, *NATCHEZ*	1833
Boston Navy Yard Commandant, "OLD IRONSIDES" restoration	1833–35

Command Mediterranean Squadron (commodore), *CONSTITUTION*	1835–38
Suspension	1840–43
Reinstatement; Philadelphia Naval Yard commandant	1844–45

A Double-Edged Sword

One

Origins, Boyhood, and Initial Naval Career

Compared to my other naval biographies (David Porter, William Bainbridge, James Biddle, and John "Mad Jack" Percival), material about Jesse Duncan Elliott and his ancestors is annoyingly elusive. The Elliotts, with varying numbers of *l*'s and *t*'s, were prominent in both Europe and America. A common difficulty, however, for their genealogists is to connect a family's progression from often noble forebears in the British Isles to its first emigrants to America, since the vast majority of them were from the middle and lower classes. A genealogical research firm that had given me some information about the Percivals could provide nothing useful in this instance.[1]

Elliott, who churned out a mountain of data concerning most aspects of his career, had little or nothing to say as to his British origins or early predecessors in America, including Robert Elliott, at least until his father's death in 1794. Vague references in secondary works reported no more than that Robert had migrated to Pennsylvania from "Donegal, Ireland." I had no direct confirmation of this until Elliott was commanding USS *Constitution* in the Mediterranean, 1835–38. At Malta he met a British officer named Elliott and wondered if he were a distant cousin, for he came from the same Irish town as his father, "Fincastle, County Donegal."[2]

Finding so little about this topic from American sources, I made repeated attempts to learn more about Elliott's ancestry from Irish documentation but was frustrated totally. Two letters, about a month apart, to the County Donegal Historical Society remained unanswered. After four months of correspondence with the major Irish genealogical center—Office of the Chief Herald, State Heraldic Museum, in Dublin—and a sizable payment, I received an inapplicable list of Elliott first and surnames, with no dates and no connections drawn to the Robert/Jesse branch of the family.

Eventually I was able to make contact with a direct lineal descendant of the correct Elliott line. Robert E. Dunkel of Westerville, Ohio, reported that John Elliott, born c. 1715 in Donegal, was his "4GGF" (fourth great--grandfather), and the first of the family to migrate to the colonies. Presumably he arrived some twenty or so years later and settled in Cumberland County, Pennsylvania, in a district called Path Valley, close to the Maryland border. He died in 1794 after marrying twice, and "his son, William Elliott (Dunkel's 3GGF) was a half-brother of Robert, Jesse's father, thereby uniting the two Elliott branches.[3]

Returning to the Robert/Jesse branch, the father may have been the same Robert Elliott who had been a militia officer in the Seventh Pennsylvania Regiment of the Continental Army, March 29, 1777–July 1, 1778.[4] There is evidence to support this assertion, for the places and dates are applicable, and, more to the point, Jesse's monument to him, erected some time later, was inscribed: "In Memory of the Late Col. Robert Elliott."[5]

As to Robert's wives and children, we found an unsubstantiated allegation that he had been married to both Jean Wilson and Ann Duncan. Later this was confirmed by Dunkel in the same letter cited above. Robert wedded Jean on July 6, 1773, and she gave him four of his ten children: Patience (Mrs. Callender Irvine), William, Robert, and Wilson. I cannot specify when Jean died, but all of her offspring by Robert must have come in rapid succession, a matter complicated by the source's failure to provide the birth dates of any of them, with the exception of Jesse—easily confirmed as July 14, 1782.[6]

Turning to Robert Elliott's livelihood, he seems to have been one of those enterprising go-getters, dabbling in several occupations, who flooded into the West prior to, during, and after the American Revolution. Although Robert may have farmed, and there are suggestions of land speculation, his only early identity was as a "merchant." A Hagerstown newspaper said that he had established there a "fulling mill" in 1791.[7] By then he had moved his family from Franklin County, Pennsylvania, a short distance south into Hagerstown, Maryland, where he occupied a house on the same plot originally purchased by Jonathan Hager Sr., the town's founder.[8]

By this time Robert had found his métier by going into partnership with Elie Williams to provide supplies to the distant northwestern country, an almost insurmountable task where transportation of goods usually had to rely on rivers and forest lanes. Evidently the partners had something of a monopoly for such service. Although there was a so-called US Army commissariat, correspondence listed no other private contractors. Hence the army of the early 1790s was compelled to hire Elliott and Williams for delivering all the necessities to upward of two thousand officers and men in wilderness campaigns against the Native Americans. Food, clothing, munitions, and other materiel of war had to be toted on the backs of horses and men, although where the rugged terrain permitted, wagons could be used. From 1791 to

1794 the United States conducted hostilities against the Miamis, Shawnees, Delawares, and other tribes who inhabited the extensive tracts south of the Great Lakes, east of the Mississippi, and north of the Ohio River, with military actions concentrated in what is now eastern Indiana and western Ohio.[9]

Robert had been employed during the summer of 1794 in his mandatory duties, but early in October, he went back to visit his family at Fort Washington (Cincinnati). But just as he was arriving he received a most urgent letter from General Anthony ("Mad Anthony") Wayne that he must use "the utmost dispatch" in returning to the front in order to accompany the rest of the way his "supplies, cattle, etc." The general stressed that "even one day's delay may be fatal."[10]

While hastily preparing to return on October 5, Elliott asked Captain John Pierce, the fort's commandant, for a military escort "through a wilderness infested with hostile Indians."[11] But Pierce had to respond that he could spare no more than "one sergeant, one corporal, and twelve men to escort two hundred pack horses, twenty-five wagons, three hundred cattle, and three hundred sheep. . . . Could I furnish one hundred I would do *it with* pleasure."[12] Despite the urgency of Wayne's order, Robert's decision to depart on the sixth without waiting for the promised military detail, small though it was, must be called reckless to the extreme, and he immediately had to pay the ultimate price for it. Attended only by his "servant Damon," within two or three days Robert was "waylaid by the Indians and killed."[13]

According to an editorial in Elliott's hometown newspaper, "that zealous patriot and truly respectable citizen" lived just long enough to realize that his wound was mortal, and "his native tendency and presence of mind prompted him to desire his servant [Damon] to leave him and fly for his own safety—which reluctantly the servant did."[14] Very likely Elliott was fortunate in dying as quickly as he did. His death was certain, but he was spared the prolonged and agonizing tortures that were a trait of the eastern forest tribes, inflicted on most captives, white and Native American alike.

Jesse eventually gave details about the immediate aftermath of his father's death: "His servant escaped unhurt, and brought in the horse rode by the contractor, at the time he was shot. The Colonel, being somewhat advanced in life, wore a wig. The savage who shot him, in haste to take his scalp drew his knife, and seized him by the hair. To his astonishment, the scalp came off at the first touch. The wretch exclaimed in broken English, 'dam lie!' In a few moments the surprise of the party was over, and they made themselves merry at the expense of their comrade."[15]

The loss of Robert to his wife and offspring was almost inevitably a staggering blow and particularly so from Robert's sudden demise. Almost a half century later Jesse reminisced: "The distressing event, which made me an orphan [*sic*], brought with it also the evils of poverty, upon a devoted mother [Ann] who in her widowhood had to struggle for the support of those [ten children] who were left her, in infancy and in childhood."[16] He exaggerated, for at least one or two were adults in 1794.

Around 1800 Ann had moved from Hagerstown to Carlisle in Cumberland County, Pennsylvania. There may have been other reasons for her choice, but surely, one was to provide a more adequate education than in Maryland for Jesse and St. Clair, two of her three youngest offspring.[17] There was a grammar school in Carlisle that eventually evolved into Dickinson College where the Elliott brothers attended classes until 1804, planning to become lawyers. The fact that Jesse served as a Dickinson trustee, 1831–33, suggests his earlier association with it. However, a phone call to Special Collections at the college library brought the unwelcome news that all the records pertaining to his years of attendance have disappeared nor is any local church documentation extant.[18]

But prospects for Jesse's and St. Clair's legal careers vanished when President Jefferson, deciding to exceed in value the "2,000 already allocated to the family, as partly in consideration of the services and sacrifices of their father," offered both brothers appointments as midshipmen in the US Navy.[19] Secretary Robert Smith sent commissions to Jesse and St. Clair on April 2 and they were accepted on the fourth. Smith stipulated that they must complete their mathematical studies at Carlisle prior to reporting for active duty, remaining on half pay until then.[20] Any delay must have been slight, for later that same year they were aboard different men-of-war in their lowly stations.

This opportunity gave them a profession that lasted until their deaths but with far different results. The ill-starred St. Clair had a short and lackluster service of little more than a decade. He was on furlough for a mercantile voyage when he was impressed into the Royal Navy for two and a half years, obviating any opportunity to demonstrate prowess in combat. Alcoholism soon contributed to his demise in 1815.[21]

As Jesse's whole life is the subject of this book, only remarks about a quirk in his *personal* makeup seem appropriate this early in the text. Almost all people can recall the year of their birth. Yet his "biography" asserts that when his father was killed in 1794, Jesse was "in the ninth year of my age." Actually born in 1782, he was twelve, and he kept on repeating this error throughout his life.[22] For instance, when he received his commission he was not nineteen but almost twenty-two, a little older than most of his fellow midshipmen. As his initial years of naval duty unfolded, other phases of his persona begin to emerge, such as persecutions to which he thought he was subjected and follow-ups to constant personal feuds.

Jesse's first assignment was to the frigate *Essex* commanded by Captain

James Barron with whom he would form a close association. St. Clair went to the frigate *President* under Captain Samuel Barron, James's brother. Soon both ships sailed for the Mediterranean and remained there from 1804 to 1806, circling from port to port while the Tripolitan War was winding down.[23]

Though the first naval activities of the Elliott brothers were so inconspicuous, in 1801 Jusuf Karamanli, bashaw of Tripoli, irate that his fellow Barbary rulers of Algiers and Tunis were receiving more American tribute than he, declared war on the United States. For the first two years American naval efforts against him were so desultory that momentum could not pick up until the advent of Commodore Edward Preble with victory clearly in sight.[24] But in October 1803 the disastrous grounding and surrender of the frigate *Philadelphia* in Tripoli Harbor hamstrung the achievement of a victor's peace; 306 captives could have been massacred during an American storming of the city. The treaty ending the conflict on June 5, 1805, hailed though it was as an American triumph, was in fact a standoff. The Barbary menace against American and European shipping was not over until punitive expeditions by the US Navy in 1815, and a combined Anglo-Dutch armada a year later finally dispersed this centuries-old threat.

As far as we know, only three letters of Elliott have survived from his initial years in the service. Late in 1807 he set the tenor of much of his correspondence with the Navy Department by protesting to Secretary Jacob Crowninshield about recent promotions from midshipman to lieutenant that had bypassed him, even though "for some months [I] have been as Acting Lieut." In general, he objected to those upgraded who were younger than he (he was twenty-five at the time) or those with commissions dated later than his, but this carping did him no good; he had to await his promotion until 1810.[25] Elliott was by no means alone in this concern. All officers viewed the date of their commissions with absorption. Seniority usually determined who would get desirable active duties in warships or navy yards; their juniors were more apt to be placed on long leaves of absence or furloughed for the merchant marine at half pay or none.

A year later Elliott's second and third letters spotlighted another lifelong characteristic: he was a grudge earner of the first water. Learning in 1808 that Midshipman Fitz Hugh Babbit, with whom he had served in *Vixen* in 1805 and two years later in *Chesapeake*, would be appointed lieutenant in the new sloop *Argus*, he objected about it to the secretary with vehemence. He said that Babbit had stolen clothing and even a "toothbrush!" from his messmates, and after admitting his guilt, he then brazenly denied the charges. Elliott fumed that his enemy was "a perjured villain" whom he could "neither countenance as an Officer or a Gentleman." He went on to harry his prey by eliciting written testimony about it from two other midshipmen and claimed that he had forwarded this evidence along with his own to the secretary.[26] But clearly the department took no action, for Babbit was promoted to lieutenant at the same time as his accuser.

As the major responsibility of a biographer is to keep his or her subject in the foreground as much as possible, the well-known Anglo-American crisis over the *Chesapeake-Leopard* affair may be well pared, except where Elliott is concerned.

During July 1807 Commodore James Barron had been ordered peremptorily to sail in *Chesapeake* to assume command of the Mediterranean Squadron and could only obey although that frigate was unprepared for any hostile action. Because of Captain Charles Gordon's sloth while in charge of the ship for five weeks prior to Barron's takeover, *Chesapeake*'s decks remained littered with a jumble of unassorted stores and munitions. Off the Virginia Capes lay Royal Navy captain Salusbury P. Humphreys and his frigate *Leopard*. Knowing that four Royal Navy deserters were in *Chesapeake*, he intercepted her, demanding the right to board and search for them. Barron tried to stall, but broadsides from *Leopard* poured in until the US flag was hauled down. After removing the deserters, Humphreys permitted the battered ship to put back into port with three killed and eighteen wounded, Barron among the latter. American fury over this atrocity brought the two countries to the verge of war, but it soon had to abate because of America's woeful lack of sea power.[27]

Barron had to be selected as the essential scapegoat to atone for his country's humiliation. Early in 1808 a court-martial found him guilty of having his frigate unready for action and suspended him from the navy for five years without pay, which we deem overly harsh, although some other historians vehemently disagree. At least to us the discrepancy between Barron's sentence and that of the indolent and inefficient Gordon is unconscionable. Although found "negligent" by the court, it was a comparative tap on the wrist that he received only a private verbal reprimand from the secretary, thanks in large part to Gordon's naval and political connections at the highest level.[28]

Elliott had been aboard during *Chesapeake*'s abasement, and his friendship with his commander had commenced when both served in *Essex* in 1804, making him Barron's strongest advocate, an opinion he maintained thereafter. While still recuperating from his wound, Barron singled out Elliott as the one officer whose conduct during the crisis entitled him to special commendation: "Had not Mr. Elliott been in the division, I have reason to believe that there would not have been one man remaining."[29] During Barron's trial, Elliott testified that his division had never been provided with "powder, horns, matches, cartridges, sponges, or rammers." By implication this damned Gordon's indolence while commanding the frigate for more than a month before relinquishing her to Barron.[30]

Initially several other officers came to the captain's defense, among them the same Babbit whom Elliott so despised. According to Barron's biographer, on the day of *Chesapeake*'s surrender, Babbit had "spoken in the most favorable terms of Commodore Barron's conduct." But shortly after Elliott had expressed his admiration for his beleaguered friend, Babbit told him that "he'd better be silent until he knew which way the thing turned."[31] Even worse for Barron, Babbit testified that as the enemy broadsides were hammering home, the commodore shouted to his men, "Keep down or we shall all be cut to pieces!" When interrogated whether he thought that the order emanated from fear, he responded, "Whether it proceeded from fear or any other cause I cannot say," although his implication was reasonably clear.[32] When the question came up concerning Babbit's sudden conversion from pro- to anti-Barron, he denied under oath that he had ever warned Elliott to be quiet until he saw "which way the thing turned," but he was flatly contradicted, and in view of Babbit's well-documented willingness to perjure himself, Elliott comes off distinctly the better.[33]

To return to 1807, following a leave of absence, Elliott was appointed acting lieutenant in the sloop *Enterprise*, engaged in trying to enforce the Jeffersonian-Madisonian embargo and Non-Intercourse Acts of 1807–9 by utilizing economic coercion to compel the belligerents, Britain and France, to respect neutral maritime rights. It was a failing endeavor, due in large part to the American insistence upon the impressment issue, on which the British would not give an inch.[34]

Promoted to his lieutenancy on April 23, 1810, Elliott soon left on the aforementioned dispatch-bearing voyage to London in *John Adams*. He sailed with apprehension that somehow his country would become embroiled with the European combatants: "It appears to me that our affair with the belligerent[s] have taken a rather gloomy appearance [of] War & I believe in the order of the day at least so says the Government"[35]—adding a refreshing dash of cynicism.

Little is known about Elliott between his return from Europe in 1810 and his appointment to the Great Lakes in mid-1812, save that during this interim he said in the most offhanded manner that "shortly afterward he married" without naming to whom.[36] This furnishes another example, so dissatisfying for his biographers, of his silence about the family members most closely related to him. A periodical carrying frequent articles about the navy came up with a modicum of enlightenment about his wife. On April 5, 1812, he wed Frances Caln Vaughan of Norfolk, Virginia, daughter of that city's multiterm mayor.[37]

If Frances remains a cipher, at least their union was reasonably prolific. She bore six children, one son (Washington Lafayette) and five daughters: Sarah Ann, Mary (Jacobs), Harriet (Robinson), Catherine Howell (dead at fifteen on October 16, 1839), and Frances Rebecca—born sometime after Elliott had filed his "Last Will and Testament" on August 29, 1829. The birth and death dates of the other daughters are not given, and the only one mentioned in a later context is Catherine Howell.[38]

Jesse and Frances had only a little over a month together before war with Britain commenced on June 18, 1812. The *Port Folio* described their parting in saccharine prose: "Fortune, that capricious goddess, as if to try the strength of his attachment to arms, immediately compelled him to relinquish the sweets of domestic intercourse, and the calm delights of conjugal affection, for the hardier scenes of danger and battles: War was declared against England."[39]

Elliott wrote that upon receipt of the news he left at once to rejoin *Argus* but just missed his ship. Hearing that the sloop was with Commodore John Rodgers's squadron in Chesapeake Bay, he hired "a small pilot Boat," only to arrive once again too late.[40] He went home to await new orders that directed him to report to the Great Lakes where, for what he would accomplish over October 8–9, 1812, he would explode into national attention for the first but by no means the last time.

Two

The War of 1812

First Encounters

To STATE THE obvious, this is a biography, not a monograph about the second war with Great Britain; anyone searching for an analysis of that conflict must look to histories of it. Concentration here has to be those engagements in which Elliott participated, namely:

(1) his capture of the enemy brigs *Detroit* and *Caledonia* near Buffalo, October 8–9, 1812, which first brought Elliott to his country's notice and therefore merits much longer treatment than the other two instances combined;
(2) the abortive assault on Kingston, Ontario, November, 10–12, 1812;
(3) the American storming of York (Toronto) and the destruction of its public buildings, April 27–May 1, 1813, as well as its brief repossession that July.[1]

CAPTURE OF THE ENEMY BRIGS *DETROIT* AND *CALEDONIA* NEAR BUFFALO, OCTOBER 8–9, 1812

Lieutenant Elliott may have felt a pang of disappointment at missing adventures in the Atlantic where ship-to-ship action could result in an officer's individual luster and handsome prize money. Yet the Great Lakes was a strategically important area where American wartime results would occur. Thrilling to the public as morale boosters though the triumphs of their frigates and brigs might be, the Royal Navy's maritime supremacy could be no more than ruffled by them. The oft-quoted statistic is that in June 1812 the US Navy had seventeen men-of-war, the opponent some eight hundred. Had the high seas been the only arena of combat, undoubtedly the country would have lost the war and been stripped of extensive tracts along the Canadian border, at least temporarily. But the victory of the Perry-Elliott tandem on Lake Erie in 1813 and the culminating mastery of Commodore Thomas Macdonough on Lake Champlain in 1814 enabled the United States to boast about "not one inch of territory lost or ceded" after the Treaty of Ghent.

The realization that the British could be mauled only in adjacent Canada had been basic to the brash American decision to challenge the mightiest naval power on earth. The "war hawks" in Congress airily forecasted that its annexation would be no more than a "matter of marching," as Jefferson put it, while Henry Clay promised to conquer that vast colony with the militia of Kentucky alone.

These dazzling expectations were dashed by American debacles in the Northwest during the summer of 1812, among which only General William Hull's astonishing surrender of Fort Detroit justifies any comment here. Hull had left his post strongly fortified and packed with arms and provisions to advance timidly into what was then Upper Canada (Ontario) with about 2,200 men. When confronted by the top-notch British general Sir Isaac Brock, he scurried back to Detroit. Brock, using psychological warfare, for he had only two thousand troops, many of them Native American auxiliaries, talked him into surrendering on August 16. Hull was sentenced to be shot for cowardice but spared because of his age and because of his American Revolutionary services.

The resultant national despair was dispelled partially on the nineteenth when his nephew, Captain Isaac Hull, in *Constitution*, sent to the bottom HMS *Guerriere*. But for those who esteemed strategic over tactical objectives, Elliott's brilliant seizure of the British vessels on Lake Erie would prove to be a much more significant achievement.

Both Washington, DC, and London had recognized early that ruling the lakes on the northwestern frontier could be the key to victory, and a prewar naval race had been launched there. For both sides it was a formidable problem, as all nonwooden necessities had to be supplied by water to Lakes Ontario and Erie. America's went from Pittsburgh or more remote New York City (although sometimes wilderness trails could be taken), Britain' s from England, via Halifax, and up the St. Lawrence River. Of course, sails, guns, shot, provisions, and other things were mandatory but even more critical were the carpenters wielding axes on timber for the combatants, as their warships had to be constructed from bottoms to spars on the spot.

As for Elliott's career in 1812, he would be instructed to concentrate on

Lake Erie, thereby avoiding participation on Lake Ontario where Commodores Isaac Chauncey and Sir James Yeo sparred in something of a minuet on water, each fleet advancing and retreating while matters would eventually be settled on Erie and Champlain.

On September 7 Chauncey sent Elliott his orders for duty in a long letter, but its essence is in the "Commodore's Abstract":

> 7th Ordered Lieutenant. Jesse D. Elliott to proceed to Head Quarters of Genl [Steven] Van Rensselaer at or near Buffalo and consult with him as to the Best Site to repair, build, and prepare for service such Vessels or Boats as may be required to obtain command of Lake Erie; gave him permission to purchase and to commence their equipment immediately; directed him to have timber sawed for plank for decks and bottoms for 2 Ships of 300 Tons each [by] consulting with Mr. [Henry] Eckford to build 6 boats 40 feet by 10 feet wide; to have quarters prepared for 300 men; a temporary magazine built; to learn the force of the enemy on Lake Erie, and their temporary rendezvous &c [and] to transmit to me general information on roads, sites for building, provisions, &c.[2]

Elliott must have been heartened by Chauncey's conclusion: "Knowing your zeal for the service, and your discretion as an officer, I feel every confidence in your industry and exertions to accomplish your mission in the shortest possible time."[3] Elliott was an extremely efficient naval officer, despite errors of judgment in the 1830s. Hence, we have quoted at length Chauncey's letter to him above and his response to it below. Here is the first instance of his executing a large number of scattered responsibilities with energy, dispatch, and initiative. Elliott sped to Van Rensselaer and engaged himself in hectic activity. Only seven days later he was able to notify Chauncey that

> I have consulted with General [Peter B.] Porter who has agreed to build me 4 of the boats and have them ready in a few days. I have contracted for a sufficient quantity of Plank to deck and bottom 2 ships of 300 tons. The British have a force of considerable moment. One ship of 20 guns [drawing] 10 feet water badly manned [with poor personnel]; one brig of 10 guns and 2 schooners of 10 guns; some other vessels unarmed say 4 in all. We have only 6: A Brig of 90 tons; the others are schooners of from 40 to 80 tons; all good vessels and in the intended place for a navy Yard. . . . The carpenters have not yet arrived. I have by the Express ordered them to Gennessee [*sic*] Falls [Rochester, New York]; and will set out in the morning myself. . . . Should arming these Vessels meet your approbation, the ordnance had

better immediately come on to that place together with the officers and men, our movements at this place will go on as if attended to myself.[4]

Meritorious though his first days in Buffalo had been, Elliott soon fell prey to youthful bumptiousness and suffered a well-deserved rebuke. Early in October he told Sailing Master Daniel Dobbins at Presque Isle (Erie, Pennsylvania), who was intimately acquainted with conditions on Lake Erie, that "it appears to me utterly impossible to build Gun Boats at Presque Isle [as] there is not a sufficient depth of water on the Bar to get them into the Lake, should there be water the place is at all times open to the attacks of the Enemy." He vowed that Sacketts Harbor at Lake Erie's northeasternmost point was the only locale "convenient" for that purpose.[5]

Dobbins promptly became the exasperated schoolmaster. He asserted that there was plenty of water for an American squadron to anchor but not enough to support a British assault. "I believe I have as perfect a knowledge of the lake as any other person on it and I believe you would agree with me if you were here."[6] That settled the question insofar as Lake Erie was concerned, although later requirements would move the American base to Put--in-Bay, far to the west.

About noon on October 8 the Americans at Black Rock espied two vessels coming into nearby Fort Erie (for identifications, see below). At once Elliott perceived an audacious and successful opportunity to seize them that very evening. In retrospect, this was the best day of his forty-one-year service in the US Navy. For snatching up the two, Elliott enjoyed promotion, medals, swords, and money from the national and state governments, the press, and through it the laudations of the American people. As a result, he was seldom out of the people's eye thereafter. Unfortunately, for his lasting reputation, later derogatory aspects of his career never approached his initial triumph, leaving him today and surely into the future a flawed rather than a gifted character in the American naval annals.

When Oliver Hazard Perry and his Newport contingent showed up, the new commodore threw himself with his usual verve to ensure the safety of Presque Isle and to hurry along the completion of his own flotilla. Aided by Elliott and abetted by the crack naval constructor Noah Brown, Perry's intentions soon were attaining their goals. The two American brigs, Elliott's *Niagara* and Perry's flagship *Lawrence* (named after Perry's boon companion James Lawrence, who had just lost his ship and his life when USS *Chesapeake* had been stormed by HMS *Shannon* off Boston), were also making progress. The Americans constructed as well four schooners, a blockhouse, a guardhouse, a mess hall and sail loft, a blacksmith shop, a barracks for fifty men, four camel lighters,[7] fourteen small boats, and approximately fifty gun carriages. A few of them had been begun by Elliott but completed by Perry.

Presque Isle was an excellent harbor but for a sandbar that lay in front of it and the summer had been unusually dry. By September only about five feet of water was available, not enough for the two brigs to go over the bar. Until their little men-of-war had been outfitted for battle, Perry and Elliott lived in dread of a sudden assault by the British fleet, commanded by Captain Sir Robert H. Barclay.[8]

Although they had brought with them a wholly inadequate number of weapons for a sortie into enemy territory, army officers stationed there managed to provide enough for the navy. Soldiers were commanded by Major General Amos Hall, ably assisted by General Alexander Smyth, Colonel William Winder, and, above all, Lieutenant Colonel Winfield S. Scott. They cooperated with the navy to their utmost extent, providing an excellent model of intraservice unity, so often missing in cooperative ventures. Smyth and Scott particularly endorsed Elliott's impromptu plan, the former writing to Colonel William H. Winder: "Be pleased to turn out the hardy sailors in your regiment, and let them appear, precisely at three o'clock this evening. Send also all the pistols, swords and sabers that you can borrow [from civilians] at the risk of the lenders."[9] Two large boats were on hand to provide transportation for the assault.

Scott dispatched Lieutenant Isaac Roach and Sailing Master George Watts to go with Elliott. Roach was instructed to muster no more than fifty soldiers for the expedition. Twenty years later he recalled that under Scott's watchful eye he lined up the men and asked for volunteers. Everyone stepped forward, and finally, he chose sixty because so many had been shouting such pleas as: "Can I go, Sir?" "Take me," "Don't forget McGee!" and "I'm a Phila[delphia] Boy!" Army officers as well accompanied the assault force. "Ensign Stephen W. Pres[t]man was selected because he was a gallant young man."[10] But other officers were outraged at being left behind. Captain Nathan Towson became so insistent that Elliott permitted him to come but only as a " volunteer private" rather than an officer, a decision that years later would spark a raucous controversy between them (see below). Some civilians managed to clamber aboard, and James Sloan, a merchant captain from Black Rock, was appointed pilot.[11]

By four in the afternoon all were assembled and assigned to one or the other of their large boats. Elliott and Roach were in the first, filled with most of the soldiers; Watts and Towson were in the second with the rest of the men. Elliott said that they totaled 100, but a later historian put it at 124, nailing down his accuracy by listing each by name.[12] Toward Fort Erie was hampered by the Niagara River's swirling currents. Moreover, a very light breeze at the day's start would increase during the night to make more perilous the return trip with any captured enemy prizes.[13] The brigs toward which they were aiming were soon identified as *Detroit* and *Caledonia*. The first was two hundred tons and mounting six-pound long guns, three on each side. Apparently a merchant vessel, she had been bought by the US Army for use at Fort Detroit but lost when Hull surrendered her and then sailed to Fort Erie.[14] Commanded by Royal Marine lieutenant Charles Rolette, *Detroit* had on board fifty-eight Englishmen and Canadians guarding thirty American prisoners.[15] The ninety-ton *Caledonia* carried two four-pounder swivel guns and was under the direction of "Mr. Irving," a civilian, with twelve men overseeing ten Americans. The records are confusing about her ownership. At least two historians asserted that she was a North West Fur Company brig, and the evidence supports them.[16]

After an exhausting row, at three in the morning, the Americans closed in to board their quarry. Most of the sources reported that the surprise was complete or, if not, close enough to make any concerted resistance impossible. Elliott could hardly have been more laconic than in his first letter to the secretary about his operation: "At 3 I was alongside the vessels. In the space of about 10 minutes I had the prisoners all secured, the Top-sails sheeted home, and the Vessels were under way."[17]

As Watts and Towson found out, the clamor from *Detroit* aroused somewhat stouter opposition in *Caledonia*. The "valiant Mr. Irving put up a plucky fight with a blunderbuss which he emptied into the crowded boat, but the odds were too great for him and the ship was quickly taken." Elliott reported that those attacking *Caledonia* had suffered the death of one and the badly wounding of four.[18] Towson, however, in a missive to Elliott much later; avowed that these statistics had applied to naval casualties only for one soldier had died and nine were badly wounded.[19]

While their boats had been nearing Fort Erie soundlessly, those left behind at Buffalo and Black Rock waited "with anxiety in the gloom. At three o' clock the sharp crack of a pistol, followed by the flash and roll of a volley of musketry, a dead silence, and the moving of two dark objects down the river, proclaimed that the enterprise had been successful. A shout of joy rang out in the night air and lanterns and torches in abundance flashed light across the stream to illuminate the way for the victors." Of course the din also brought the British scurrying to man their batteries.[20]

Although both enemy brigs had been seized and sailed out from Fort Erie, the American triumph would be flawed should their prizes be unable to return safely to Black Rock. According to Elliott: "Unfortunately the wind was not sufficiently strong to get me up against a rapid current into the lake[,] . . . and I was obliged to run down the river by the forts under a heavy fire of

Capture of the British Brigs DETROIT *and* CALEDONIA, *by Lieut.* J. D. ELLIOTT, *U. S. N., on the Night of the 8th October*, 1812.

No. 1, Buffalo—2, Fort Erie—3, Black Rock—4, British Batteries—5, Sailors' Barracks—6, Artillery Cantonment—7, Squaw Island—8, Strawberry Island—9, Detroit aground—10, Caledonia ashore—11, Navy Yard—12, British Artillery—13, Point of Embarkation.

2.1. *Correspondence in relation to Capture of the British Brigs* DETROIT AND CALEDONIA, *on the night of October 8, 1812*. Philadelphia, 1843.

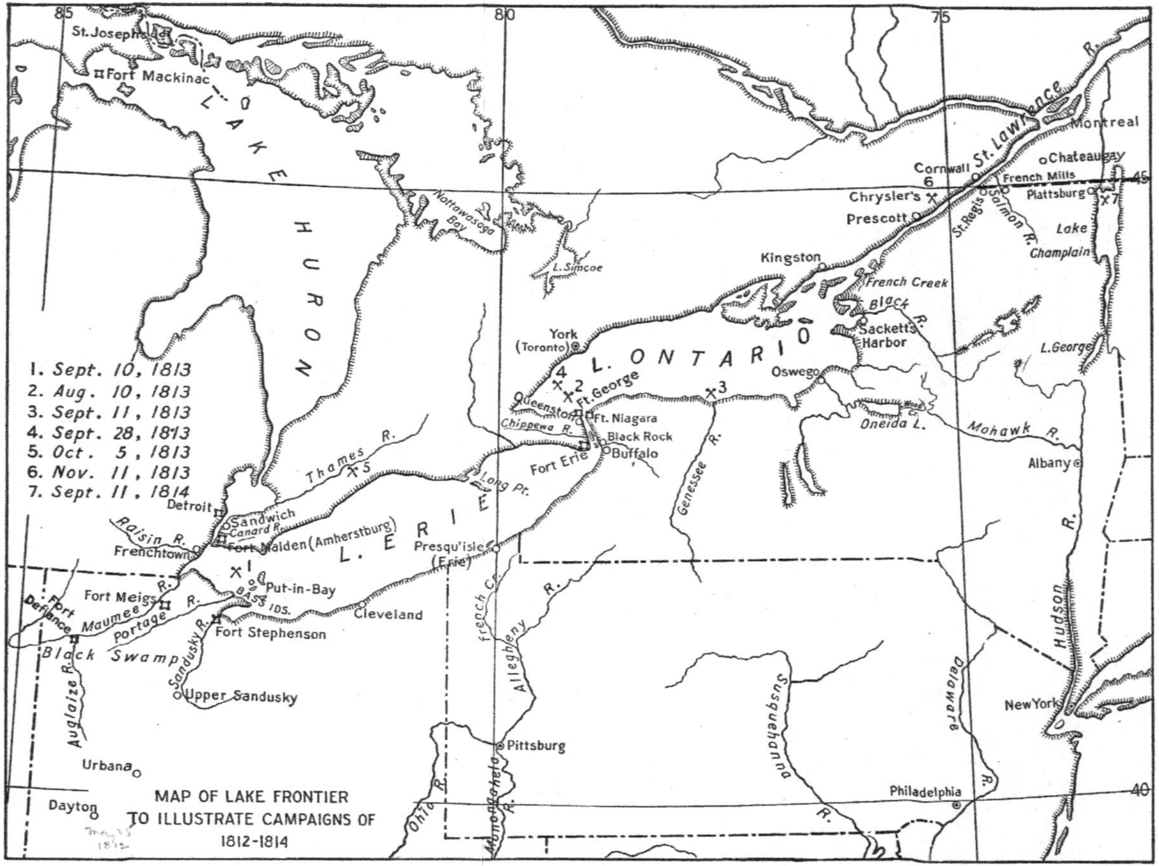

2.2. "Map of Lake Frontier to Illustrate Campaigns of 1812–1814," from Alfred Thayer Mahan, *Sea Power in Its Relations to the War of 1812* (Boston: Little, Brown, 1905)

round, grape, and canister, from a number of pieces of flying artillery, and compelled to anchor at a distance of about 400 yards from two of their batteries. . . . I hailed the seashore, and served to the [British] officer that if another gun was fired I would bring all the prisoners on deck, and expose them to the same fate. But notwithstanding, they disregarded the caution and continued a constant and destructive fire. One single moment's reflection determined me not to commit an act which would subject me to the imputation of barbarity."[21]

Elliott's emotionless account to the department was much enlivened by Roach's exclamatory shouts: "Bang! went my battery of 6-pounders, up helm, Boys! stand by that cable with an axe, but away, and now we get the battery guns on us!"[22]

Breezes too light made *Caledonia* equally helpless against the river eddies. Neither ship could be navigated effectively, but she was lucky, going ashore to safety under the guns of the American naval base at Black Rock. *Detroit*'s exposed position, however, remained under "the penetrating arguments of the Fort [Erie] which kept on firing." Elliott, after moving his six long guns on the side facing the foe, appealed to Americans nearby to warp his ship onto dry land, but their efforts were in vain. He "determined to drift down the river[, and] accordingly I cut the cable, and made sail with very light airs, and at that instant discovered that the pilot [Sloan] had abandoned me."[23] After drifting for ten minutes *Detroit* beached herself on tiny Squaw Island, a few yards from *Caledonia*. While landing his prisoners, Elliott was assailed by forty British soldiers in a long boat, but Scott hastened up in time to ward off the onset and the invaders were repelled "with the loss of nearly all their men."[24]

Yet the grounded *Detroit* still lay immobile, open to the barrages from Fort Erie until her hull was riddled with shot and her sails and rigging "cut all to pieces." About sunset British general Brock led his regulars, intending to renew "the attempt to secure the *Detroit*," but before "the necessary arrangements could be made, the enemy boarded her, and in a few minutes she was seen in flames."[25] Four six-pounders with a quantity of ammunition were recovered eventually from the gutted hulk and used effectively at the Battle of Lake Erie a year later.[26] Elliott, toward the end of his long first report to the secretary, gave only perfunctory praise to those also responsible for his triumph; oddly, in it he mentioned no naval officers worthy of his government's attention, although elsewhere he did laud a midshipman wounded in storming *Detroit*, and that Watts had served "in masterly style." He also admitted "great obligation" to Towson and Roach, as well as six civilians from Buffalo. [27]

Elliott's daring exploit dispelled at least some of the public consternation after the earlier miserable showing of the army along the northwestern frontier. As Scott's biographer pointed out: "It was the first instance [save for *Constitution*'s sinking *Guerriere* three weeks before] that either Government or the public had noted in connection with the war affording an excuse for rejoicing, and both were lavish in their appreciation."[28] Lavish indeed! Fame, a modest fortune, and promotion made 1812 by far Elliott's best year of his life.

Chauncey trumpeted the virtues of his subordinate in two letters to the department; "Lieutenant Elliott deserves much praise for the promptness with which he executed this service," and, "Nothing that I can say . . . will add to the credit to Lieutenant Elliott and the gallant officers and men who accompanied him."[29] Charles W. Goldsborough chief clerk of the navy hailed his friend: "DEAR ELLIOTT; I give you joy! You have fulfilled our expectations! It was well done—done like a naval hero! Heaven be with you always."[30]

Secretary of the Navy Paul Hamilton's response to his first report must have enraptured the new luminary: "I have received with great pleasure your letter of the 9th inst, I have been directed by the President [Madison] . . . to return to you his particular thanks." Hamilton added a postscript about Elliott's reconsideration to expose British prisoners in *Detroit* to their own fire: "Your having restrained from putting your threat into execution is highly approved."[31] Moreover, within a year Elliott was elevated to master commandant changed to commander in the 1830s over thirty lieutenants who had seniority over him, a promotion that must have caused some grumbling and resentment, although we have no documentation to prove it.[32]

If the president and the Navy Department were delighted with Elliott's accomplishment at Black Rock, Congress was little short of ecstatic about it. Clay, Speaker of the House, although he reversed the fate of the two brigs, referred to Elliott's exploit in a speech to the congressmen the next January as "the capture of the *Detroit*, and the destruction of the *Caledonia* . . . for judgment, skill and courage *has never been surpassed* [emphasis added]."[33]

The House and Senate combined to fill Elliott's pocketbook: "Be it enacted, &c., that the President of the United States be, and is hereby authorized to have distributed to Lieutenant Elliott, his officers and companions, or to their widows and children, the sum of twelve thousand dollars, for the capture and destruction of the British brig *Detroit* [nothing was said about *Caledonia*]."[34]

The exact amount that enriched Elliott and his men is not given, but if normal procedures were followed, it is easy to calculate. The system of awarding prize money during this period was: if an enemy warship were taken and brought into port, or if sunk, her assessed valuation be divided into two equal parts, one for the government and one for the victors. The part due to the latter was split into twenty equal shares of which the commanding officer received three—in this case $1,800 for Elliott, a sum roughly equivalent to three full years of his regular pay and allowances.[35]

Substantial donations to Elliott were by no means over. On January 29, 1813, both houses resolved that "the President of the United States be, and is hereby requested to present to Lieutenant Elliott . . . an elegant sword, with suitable emblems and devices, in testimony of the just sense entertained by Congress of his gallantry and good conduct in boarding and capturing the British brigs *Detroit* and *Caledonia*, while anchored under the protection of Fort Detroit."[36]

The government was in anything but a hurry to hire the craftsmen to complete the swords and medals awarded to officers. Elliott had to wait for four years and more until Secretary Benjamin W. Crowninshield sent his sword to him along with a note: "I have a high degree of satisfaction in the performance of this; and at the same time to add the assurance of my personal esteem and respect for your honorable services as an officer, and your character as a gentleman."[37]

Elliott's sword was indeed "elegant": "The blade of the finest *steel* was exquisitely ornamented with *naval* and *military trophies*, and *arabesques* of the most beautiful patterns." One side of it represented the scene of his capture of the British brigs and "the heavy and tremendous fire from Fort Erie." On the other, "*Naval* and *Military* trophies," with a Latin transcription translated as, "Under the batteries of the enemy he boarded the vessels and presented them to his country." The scabbard, polished to imitate steel, was mounted with fine gold; and the golden belt plate "depicted an American eagle,"[38] and a little later Elliott was awarded a gold medal by Pennsylvania's legislature.[39]

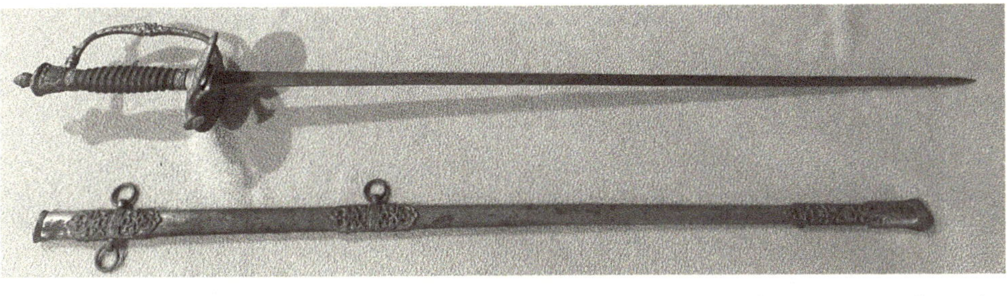

2.3. Replica of sword awarded to Jesse D. Elliott by United States Congress for the capture of British Brigs *Detroit* and *Caledonia*. Courtesy of Cheri J. Griffin.

Despite this adulation, considered only from a tactical viewpoint, Elliott's two captures added up to a bagatelle, but that is not the paramount issue. Strategically his victories had significant consequences and nothing better illustrates them than how instantly British awareness followed. General Brock, tragically for his nation's war efforts in the Northwest, was killed in action at Queenston Heights a mere four days after the loss of the two brigs but lived long enough to recognize their implications; he wrote to the Canadian governor general: "This event is particularly unfortunate, and may reduce us to incalculable distress. The enemy is making every exertion to gain a naval superiority on both Lakes which if they accomplish it I do not see how we can retain the Country. Three vessels are fitting out for war on the other side of Squaw Island which I would have attempted to distroy but for Your Excellency's repeated instructions to forebear—now such a force is collected for their protection as will render any operation against them very hazardous. . . . We have not only sustained a heavy loss in the Vessel *[Detroit]*, but likewise in the Cargo, which consisted of four twelves, a large quantity of shot, and about two hundred muskets."[40]

Even British naval historian William James, whose anti-American bias is flagrant, agreed by implication with Brock when he observed that Elliott's captures "have brought about consequences far more important than the safety of the two brigs."[41]

Perhaps because *Detroit* was the more imposing of the two ships concerned, Britons and Americans alike overstressed her seizure rather than that of *Caledonia*. Although the former had been destroyed, the relatively intact latter was retained to fight for Perry and Elliott at Lake Erie. And when *Caledonia* is mentioned in correspondence almost invariably it concerned her freight. Elliott concluded his first letter about the incident to the department, seemingly as an afterthought: "The *Caledonia* belongs to the N[orth] W[est] Company, loaded with furs, worth I understand 200,000dlrs."[42]

This exaggerated figure was often repeated, but it happened that "unhappily for the prospective sharers of the prize money, this turned out to be not beaver and muskrat as supposed, but merely deer, bear, and buffalo hides, worth less than $ 10,000."[43] Evidently no one ever received a penny for *Caledonia*'s cargo. In 1855 the Senate's Naval Affairs Committee tried to have the proceeds split between Towson and Elliott's widow, Frances. But, since no monetary value of the furs could be agreed upon, nothing could be done.[44]

With Elliott, often the flames of one of his controversies would flicker out within a reasonable time only to have its embers rekindled years, sometimes decades, later. In March 1835 Towson, by this time a militia general, heard of a long article signed only by "B. W." Cambridge, March 4, 1835, (believed to be Benjamin Waterhouse, a pioneer in the field of smallpox vaccination and a Harvard Medical School founder) in a Boston journal adding up to an encomium to Elliott's heroics in taking the two British ships in 1812 without mention of Towson's significant contributions to that end.[45] In a letter dated October 20, 1834, from Waterhouse to Secretary of War Lewis Cass, Waterhouse included similar accolades for Elliott dealing with various problems in the Boston area, citing Elliott's "energy and characteristic promptness." Waterhouse was clearly in favor of Elliott and against the Whig press, which negatively critiqued Elliott partly owing to his allegiance to President Andrew Jackson (see chapter 9).[46]

In July 1835 the aggravated general (Towson) started an acrimonious exchange with Elliott, demanding that he be given proper credit by Elliott's rewriting his official (September 9, 1812) report of the incident to the secretary.[47] Towson said that his opponent could claim full responsibility for planning the enterprise and for boarding *Detroit*, but he had nothing directly to do with *Caledonia*'s capture: "Although but a merchant vessel, she made a gallant and desperate resistance, and it was not until we had two men killed and thirteen wounded (two mortally) that she was captured, while the *Detroit* permitted you to get alongside before you were discovered, and to board her without resistance."[48]

Nothing could have been more certain to enrage Elliott than an imputation that he had behaved with anything short of the utmost bravery. He quickly shot back 1,600 words refusing to alter his report and concentrating mainly upon the fact that Towson, army officer though he was, had relinquished willingly his rank to accompany him: "A small party of private soldiers, without officers, was lent by the general [Smyth]. You went as a private, and your only duty was to report to me, your only superior officer." As to Towson's hint that he had been less than valorous on boarding *Detroit*, Elliott retorted that: "I was assailed by three men, armed with cutlasses, at the moment when I sprung on deck, and the surprise gained us nothing, except a hand-to-hand fight with an enemy superior in numbers."[49]

Towson expended some 2,500 words in a spirited counterattack, charging over the same terrain as to whether he had been an officer or a private twenty-three years before: "No officer of the army, who is worthy to hold a commission, would consent to serve in the *ranks* with his own men, for the purpose of increasing a naval command; such a proposition is too absurd to require." Here Elliott was on solid ground. Unquestionably Towson had to waive his officer status or he would have been left behind.

The general then tossed into their burgeoning quarrel dashes of kerosene, guaranteed to raise Elliott's choler. He remarked that "I do think that you might have made greater efforts to have brought the *Detroit* into harbor before you abandoned her and that the circumstances under which she was burnt . . . did not imperiously require it." The second was much worse, for it applied to Elliott's questionable behavior at the Battle of Lake Erie: "Some years past I was applied to, by a personal friend of Commodore Perry, for a statement . . . to be used to your prejudice, in the controversy then pending between you, but I refused to give it." The fact that Elliott had undertaken "so hazardous an enterprise [at Black Rock] removed from my mind all suspicion of what many of Commodore Perry's friends seemed to suppose, had prevented you from aiding him in the action on Lake Erie, as he expected."[50]

The final allegation drove Elliott into a frenzy. The day after he read it he replied in some 4,500 words (six closely printed pages), most of them on the tiresome subject of Towson's rank vis-à-vis his own in 1812. But in his last half page he made charges against his opponent that have to be judged paranoid: "*You* tell me that you have been tampered with by Commodore Perry's friends. . . . Were *YOU* then, the incendiary that kindled dissension between Perry and me?—that turned our frank friendship into hatred on his part? Were *YOU* the viper that stung? I cannot believe it—it is impossible that one who possesses your reputation could be guilty of this inconceivable baseness. . . . And yet the act was of a class to be done by the creeping, sly, profit-making spirits who hang around commanders, and make private reports of their own brave deeds, and get brevets [promotions] for them. But no—it could not be you."

Elliott's peroration showed how sincerely he meant his last sentence: "But to have done with this. I consider, sir, that you are set on by my enemies to make yourself gain at my expense, and that you pursue your aim in a spirit of determined hostility. "[51]

According to the mores of that era, any man considering himself a gentleman, especially an army or navy officer, who, as Stephen Decatur put it, made "arms his profession," receiving such a stream of vituperation from another had recourse, unless an acceptable apology was forthcoming, only to the dueling grounds. Towson and Elliott knew this as their clash steadily intensified.

Some weeks elapsed without further connection between the two, during which Elliott told a New York journalist that "I have now allowed General Towson twelve days since my last note to him, for any ulterior steps he might choose to take; and as he is silent, I presume he intends to go no further."[52] But six days later Towson returned to the fray by starting a hurried correspondence all crammed into August 17–19, obviously to ensure pistols at ten paces. Towson abruptly informed the other that: "My friend, Dr. Macaulay, waits on you with a proposition from me. If you accede to it, he is authorized on my part to make arrangements."[53] The seconds met later that same day to state "that a meeting was arranged for the following morning at 6 o'clock; all preparations for which have been made—place, distance, time, and arms being specified."[54]

What preposterous make believe is being enacted here? Their duel was scheduled for August 18, the very day that Elliott had been ordered to sail in *Constitution* to the Mediterranean for what would be a long tenure as commodore of the squadron there. "Old Ironsides" was the country's favorite warship, and her movements were closely followed by the press and through it the public; Towson would have known this as well as Elliott. Furthermore, both had opportunities to pull back prior to the ultimate absurdity of a duel on perhaps a commodore's busiest day.

Less than four months before, Elliott had taken that frigate to Europe on a short diplomatic errand for the State Department. Surely he could recall his departure on April 24 and the innumerable responsibilities of a commandant attending to the arrivals and departures of visiting dignitaries, making sure that ship and men alike were in immaculate condition, questioning officers that all personnel and supplies were safely aboard, and, finally, overseeing the pilot in the tricky maneuvering of a large sailer to move out of the crowded and current-ridden New York Harbor.

Somehow, according to the combat terms just set, the commodore and his second would be supposed to sneak off the ship at dawn, proceed to the dueling ground to meet the surgeons and others in attendance, and exchange fire at thirty feet. If Towson's aim was true, Elliott would have had to be carried back to *Constitution* wounded or even dead. This is a script too incredible even to contemplate.

What could have impelled Towson and Elliott to such bizarre behavior? It seems that only their hair-trigger sense of personal honor that so many army and navy officers demonstrate could be explicatory. Elliott had been lauded to the skies for his derring-do in snaring *Detroit* and *Caledonia*. Within a year, however, doubts about his personal courage enveloped him in overt and covert accusations that he had "shown the white feather" in failing to come to Perry's relief at Lake Erie (see chapter 3). Could he have imagined that such a duel would be regarded as evidence of his "true grit"? Towson was also a military man, cognizant that a lasting reputation for valor could be essential for a favorable evaluation of his career, and Elliott had hinted the contrary about his conduct at Black Rock.

Yet both were intelligent. How could either have thought that anyone reading the letters that passed between them could have seen the slightest evidence of bravery whatever in arranging a duel so carefully engineered that it could not be held? We can formulate no rational explanation that is satisfactory to us.

The matter terminated in the lamest of anticlimaxes in a note ostensibly written by Elliott's second: "It may be well to observe, that Col. Canonge, on the receipt of General Towson' s last note, returned on board the *Constitution* during the night [of August 17–18], and advised Com. Elliott that, having done all in his power to bring the affair to an issue, he now had only to go to sea, leaving the farther defense of his reputation to Col. Canonge."[55]

Is it significant that no copy of the above was included among the rival's letters in 1835 but was printed as the commodore's later inclusion in Elliott's *Correspondence*, published in 1843? Does this give rise to a suspicion that perhaps Elliott wrote it eight years later and inserted it, imagining that it might redound somehow to his own advantage?

One might conclude that this termination formed a distinct milestone along Elliott's career. No, it seldom was with his controversies. He had been back from the Mediterranean hardly a year when his dispute with Towson reemerged, this time with James Fenimore Cooper as a leading participant. After brief service as a US naval officer, Cooper had resigned his commission to become a most prolific author who succeeded in several literary fields. His best-selling two-volume *History of the Navy of the United States of America*, first published in 1839 and repeatedly thereafter, had absorbed him in Elliott's activities at Black Rock and his apprehension of the British ships there in 1812. He defended Elliott's rather than Towson's role in their rivalry of 1835.

To be upheld by so eminent a champion thrilled Elliott, and Cooper earned his lasting gratitude in a relationship sometimes embarrassing to the author, as his letters indicate. Possibly two mutual characteristics brought them together. Each manifested a bulldog tenacity for gnawing on the bone of any contention to the marrow, as well as a ferocious delight in discord for its own sake, expressed by Cooper in his penchant for litigation. His life was spotted with lawsuits, most of them inaugurated by himself.

During mid-1829 Cooper noticed a review of his *History of the Navy* in the *New York Commercial Advertiser* referring to the "carrying of the *Detroit* and *Caledonia* . . . by boarding from the shore—which was a military exercise, *projected* and *conducted* by *Captain Towson* of the *Artillery* but as Lieut. Elliott commanded one of the two boats he *assumed* the *whole credit*—and Mr. Cooper *ratifies* his *claim* [Cooper's emphases]." This was enough to impel the author to launch a libel suit against William L. Stone, the paper's editor. Cooper stressed the signal honors heaped upon Elliott from his government and letters from several participants in the engagement, and one is typical of the others. Former army ensign Press[t]man wrote to Elliott that "the planning and conducting of the enterprize unquestionably pertained to *you* and by every role of military service, the credit is your due." As for Towson, once he had realized that his officer's rank "necessarily precluded him, he volunteered TO GO IN ANY CAPACITY

WHATEVER," that is, as a private. Two years passed before Cooper could write jubilantly that on July 18, 1842, the three "arbitrators" had come out squarely on his side. Moreover, Cooper's *History* was "written in a spirit of impartiality and justice"; in short, he had "faithfully fulfilled his obligations as a historian."[56] As for Stone's review, he had "not faithfully fulfilled his obligations as a reviewer."[57]

It may have taken three decades but finally responsibilities at Black Rock had been well decided, in stark contrast to the Elliott-Perry arguments, which are still alive today. In themselves, the details of *Detroit* and *Caledonia* would not require so much amplification here, were they not so revealing about Elliott's makeup.

HMS *ROYAL GEORGE* AT KINGSTON, ONTARIO, OCTOBER–NOVEMBER 1812

In September 1812 Chauncey came to Sacketts Harbor near the St. Lawrence's egress from Lake Ontario to devote himself to a major concern, the presence of *Royal George* at nearby Kingston, Ontario. She was the largest man-of-war on the lakes at 340 tons, according to the British mounting twenty guns, although the Americans listed her at twenty-six.[58] The commodore decided to assault Kingston, which was heavily fortified and was the kingpin locale along enemy supply lines from the Atlantic to the lakes. *Royal George* and her escorts would be seized if possible, but if not, immobilized in port, for the fast approaching winter would soon end operations on the inland seas. During offensive preparations, Elliott had busied himself in purchasing seven tiny schooners while overseeing the construction of his new command, twenty-four-gun *Madison* at 580 tons, to be launched on November 26 but still unavailable for immediate service.[59]

Meanwhile on the eighth Chauncey went along with his little fleet in sixteen-gun *Oneida* toward Kingston, and Elliott, eager for action, changed to the two-gun *Conquest*, one of his new schooners. According to Cooper, on the tenth she led the others "in handsome style" and during the afternoon had closed on the batteries there. Soon the British ships had retreated to the shore, and Chauncey was preparing to storm them, but at nightfall, "the wind blew so directly in and the weather looked so threatening, that the pilots declared their unwillingness to be responsible any longer for the vessels."[60]

In one of his few surviving letters written during this period, Elliott thumped his own drum, avowing that his had been "the van ship" and "largely responsible for chasing into port and assailing *Royal George* at her anchorage," although this would have been quite an accomplishment in an onset lasting almost three hours for a vessel whose "martial thunder" consisted of two guns! In the commodore's long report to Secretary of the Navy Hamilton, listing his casualties as two dead and nine wounded, however, he made no mention of *Conquest*. This leads to an inescapable conclusion that Elliott's contributions had been minimal at best. At least everyone could agree that a threat from *Royal George* had been eliminated. To confuse matters, she was soon renamed HMS *Niagara*, and assigned to Sir James L. Yeo on Lake Ontario, using the same name as Elliott's command at the Battle of Lake Erie. By 1814 she was "dilapidated" and scheduled for repairs on Lake Huron but then disappears from the records.[61] As Kingston still stood, the operation to take it had miscarried, while its success might well have shortened the struggle for mastery of the Great Lakes by many months.

In connection with *Royal George*, five years later another example of an outstanding Elliott trait reappeared. No partial vindication on allegations questioning his valor would satisfy him; such must be completely so and on his own terms. By 1818 his imbroglio with Perry had become common knowledge, and he ran about to find support attesting to his courage during the Kingston campaign and found several of his colleagues willing to assist, at least to some degree.

Army lieutenant Wolcott Chauncey observed that "your volunteering from the ship *Madison* to the schooner *Conquest* was considered as deserving more notice than was taken by the Commodore in his official report."[62] Lieutenant J. S. McPherson, USN, responded: "Your ship drawing too much water, could not get into action, and I know you volunteered to take command of a schooner, which you did, and to the best of my knowledge, you were one of the first in action." [63] It is unlikely that either of the above gratified him, but it was the best that he could do at that time. Yet it did not end there. No less than twenty years later he wrote in vain to Cooper, asking that in the next edition of his popular naval history he would correct his account of this occasion to show that Elliott had not remained on shore because *Madison* was too deep drafted to participate in it, but, rather than missing it, he had insisted on taking his tiny schooner into the fray.[64]

Even then Elliott was not through with his quest for testimony proving his heroism. A little less than two years before he died he elicited a letter from a sailing master who recalled that "you resumed the command of the US schooner *Conquest*. This vessel under your direction was worked to windward, against a strong wind, and brought to abreast of the flag-staff and batteries, within short range, and I have every reason to believe rendered very efficient service on that occasion." He ended on a plaintive personal note: "Nearly thirty years have rolled by since these events transpired, and you have deservedly attained the highest rank in the service, while I most undeservedly remain in one of the lowest."[65]

AT THE AMERICAN CAPTURE OF YORK (TORONTO), APRIL 28–MAY 1, 1813, AND ITS BRIEF REPOSSESSION THAT JULY

COINCIDENTALLY WITH THE battle to control Lake Erie, US military strategy should have concentrated on a new stroke against Kingston. Unfortunately, the ever cautious General Henry Dearborn and John Armstrong, the inept secretary of war, were so discouraged by an enemy sortie on February 22, investing Ogdensburg, New York, on the St. Lawrence that they opted for an easier but far less productive attack at York, the capital of what would become Ontario. That British holding was ripe for harvest. Its defenses had been so neglected that its cannon could hardly pivot and the town was garrisoned by no more than seven hundred to eight hundred regulars and militiamen and some forty to fifty Amerindians.

Under the command of General Zebulon M. Pike, about 1,700 troops had been amassed at Sacketts Harbor and arrived off York on April 25.[66] The navy had come up with thirteen ships to transport them there; all small schooners save Elliott in *Madison* and *Oneida* under Lieutenant M. T. Woolsey.[67] About eight in the morning the boats headed for shore, impeded momentarily by a stiff breeze, which blew them off course, but protected by the heavy fire from their fleet, the men managed to slog through the mud onto solid ground. The outnumbered British could only retreat from oncoming bayonet charges, their morale lowered by the detonation of one of their battery magazines, in which thirty died. Yet a much higher toll was exacted from the invaders when the town's main magazine exploded with devastating effect, killing about forty and wounding over two hundred. Pike was crushed by a large stone and, according to Elliott, was carried to his own quarters, "and on my cot, expired with his head upon it." The wounds suffered by the Americans from the blast itself and falling rocks were memorable. One surgeon "described doctors who waded in blood, cutting off arms, legs, and trepanning heads." On his part the commentator "cut and slashed for 48 hours without food or sleep."[68]

While the carnage continued, Elliott casually tossed off to a naval surgeon the story of an episode that, if true, is perhaps his most astonishing feat—his own amputation of a smashed leg! "From exhaustion the doctor was no longer able to save the life of a gallant soldier. You watched whilst I amputated with my own hand the leg of a Kentucky volunteer. But the primary loss of blood only enabled him to live long enough to expire while grasping my hand." Elliott attempted to authenticate this from a letter of "an experienced young medical officer," but it may be significant that he failed to enclose it.[69] Unhappily, despite orders to the contrary, rambunctious American soldiers paused long enough from chasing the foe to torch the public buildings, as well as private ones, including Parliament House, the lieutenant governor's home, some of the soldiers' quarters, the navy yard where a sizable warship was being constructed, the "possessions" of the officer commanding the Native Americans, and the government printing press. More important strategically, the British lost essential naval equipment and food supplies earmarked for their squadron on Lake Erie that would be sorely missed at the battle there.[70]

Retaliation for the arson was not long delayed. When the enemy sauntered into Washington, DC, in August 1814 what had transpired at York gave them a precedent for their incineration of the Capitol, what would be known as the White House, and all governmental establishments except the Patent Office. A new frigate almost ready for active duty went up in flames along with the rest of the navy yard.[71]

York's surrender terms on April 28 may be summarized in two points: "All public stores, naval and military, shall be immediately given up to the commanding officers of the army and navy of the United States"; and "all private property shall be guaranteed to the citizens of the town of York." Elliott had been granted the honor of sending the British flag to Madison and was the only US naval officer to sign "the Capitulation of York."[72]

Chauncey's fleet and ground forces had been evacuated in early May, but in July, the Americans temporarily raided York again to nab what replenishments had been made. By that time Elliott had returned to Fort Niagara near the British Fort Erie, which fell on May 27 when he had been sent off already on an abortive errand, thereby writing finis to the York expeditions. Chauncey honored him when "the town surrendered by capitulation, and [he was] to see that the articles were carried into execution on the part of the navy."[73]

Despite Elliott's usual tailoring to the greatest extent any occasion to prove that pluck was his constant companion, in the case of York he had sense enough to recognize that only army operations had resulted in its captures and put his inkwell aside.

THREE

The Battle of Lake Erie, the End of the War of 1812, and the Algerian War

THE STAGE IS set for the Battle of Lake Erie, with initial examination of Oliver Hazard Perry, commander of the American naval fleet on Lake Erie, together with a focus on the military planning of both the American and British governments. Combat action through Perry's capture of the British fleet and Elliott's role as his second-in-command introduce the narrative of what later becomes the Perry-Elliott feud, which is the principal design of chapter 4. Subsequent battle engagements complete the War of 1812 chronology, followed by events in the 1815 Algerian War (Second Barbary War) to complete this third chapter.

PERRY'S BACKGROUND

Perry was a Rhode Islander, born and brought up near Newport, his state's premier seaport, and always affiliated with it as a member of one of the town's loftiest families, socially and economically. Christopher Perry, his father, had been a combatant in the American Revolutionary Navy and a British prisoner and became one of the first captains commissioned when the Constitutional Navy was created in 1798. Christopher cruised through the West Indies during the undeclared Naval War with France, 1798–1800.

Oliver, born on August 23, 1785, was the eldest of eight children, five sons (all of whom became US naval officers) and three daughters (two of whom married into that service). Matthew Calbraith, his brother, became the most famous of the siblings after helping Japan to open itself to the world during 1853–54. When Oliver was seven years old his father moved to Newport to secure better educational and cultural advantages for his offspring. Henceforth, Oliver considered Newport his home, and from there, he served several tours of duty. In fact, he seems to have managed to return to that vicinity after each cruise. He married a Newport woman, Elizabeth Champlin

Mason, on May 5, 1811, and all his children were born there. Consequently, that town had good reason to claim him as its own.

As to Oliver's professional rise, he became a midshipman under his father at the age of thirteen, being promoted to lieutenant at twenty-one, and to a schooner command at twenty-three. He was appointed master commandant [retitled commander in the 1830s] in 1812, and after two Mediterranean cruises during the Tripolitan War, 1801–5, he oversaw the building and operations of some Jeffersonian gunboats at Newport.[1]

There was, however, one blot on his otherwise impeccable record. On February 8–9, 1811, Perry was commanding the schooner *Revenge* when she grounded in fog and heavy surf off Newport and went to pieces, although all made it safely to shore. A three-man court of inquiry acquitted Perry fully of "all the blame, while it extolled his coolness and judgment."[2] The panel did find delinquent *Revenge*'s Lieutenant Jacob Hite, although Perry tried to whitewash Hite's role in the disaster. This is highly significant, for it spotlights Perry's admirably generous but dangerous tendency to support his subordinates, no matter what errors of omission or commission they might have committed. When Perry did the same for Elliott just after the Battle of Lake Erie and for a time thereafter, Perry soon bemoaned his laudatory letters about Elliott to the Navy Department as by far the worst mistakes of his life, and most surely, they were.

Many factors had been involved in Perry's advancement in the service. He was physically attractive, extroverted, intelligent, adaptable, and deferential to his superiors without sacrificing a willingness forthrightly to offer contrary opinions. He had served with distinction under such eminent captains as Edward Preble, Isaac Hull, James Barron, and, above all, John Rodgers the elder, who made Perry something of his protégé. Deft in his chosen field, especially in gunnery and navigation, and known for his incessant training of his men in mock battles, Perry became someone that his higher level officers would keep in mind.

Moreover, from 1798 to 1815, the seagoing arm was much more open to rapid promotions than that of succeeding generations when secretaries of the navy complained that often they had to keep idle on half or no pay scores of worthy officers until openings for them were created by the resignations, promotions, or deaths of those above. Only then could midshipmen and lieutenants move up to posts in navy yards or, even more desirable, to assignments afloat.

Similar to many of his colleagues, Perry did not rely solely on his own talents to climb the ladder. He endeavored constantly to enlist political support from local, state, and national organizations. It should not be forgotten that naval and military officers enjoyed high rankings in the small coterie of politicians, land speculators, bankers, planters, early industrialists, major personages in the arts and sciences, and others who controlled the United States during its initial period. The Perrys, Rodgers, Goldsboroughs, and a few other families dotted the navy rolls for generations, and they tended to support one another; Perry was a recipient of such favors.

Perry had another strong resemblance to most of his fellow officers, a craving for combat experience, in the last analysis the single most important credential for advancement, no matter how impressive were such qualifications as excellent administrators of navy yards or diplomats notching significant accomplishments abroad. And of all battle opportunities, the most cherished were chances to score single-ship victories resulting in instant fame and sometimes thousands of dollars in prize money. Unfortunately such desires for individual successes were sometimes at the expense of more prosaic opportunities to affect favorably the course of the war itself.

While Perry was directing his gunboats at Newport, he bombarded the department for blue water service in the Atlantic, only to be rejected as most of such assignments went to veterans of the Tripolitan War, called Preble's Boys. John Rodgers, among others, pointed out that there was sure to be repeated actions along the northwestern frontier.

Chauncey, commanding US forces in the lakes, responded to Perry's appeals and offered him the Lake Erie fleet, which was accepted at once, especially in view of the offer's wording: "You are the very person I want for a particular Service where you may gain honor for yourself and reputation for your Country."[3]

Among the plethora of works about Perry, we found five particularly valuable: Alexander Slidell Mackenzie, *Life of Commodore Oliver Hazard Perry: A Commodore in the United States*, 2 vols.; Frederick L. Oliver, "Commodore Oliver Hazard Perry of Newport, Rhode Island"; William Dudley, ed., *Naval War of 1812: Documentary History*, vol. 1, *1812*, and vol. 2, *1813*; and John K. Mahon, *War of 1812*, which is almost five hundred pages and offers many useful details not found easily elsewhere.

BRITISH AND AMERICAN PLANNING FOR THE BATTLE OF LAKE ERIE, SEPTEMBER 10, 1813

How to conduct naval warfare in a remote wilderness, bereft of almost all necessities save wood, was a staggering responsibility for Perry, Elliott, and their British counterpart, Royal Navy commander Robert H. Barclay. Ships were clearly the most essential, and it would be hard to match the improvisations that had to be made for hostilities on the Great Lakes. They had to be craft unlike anything afloat in the US or Royal Navies—even Jefferson's flimsy gunboats were more seaworthy than they. But since men-of-war on the lakes were "a compromise between delay and security," durability lost out to the need for the utmost speed in launching and equipping them for combat. Hence they could be built of unseasoned wood, shallow-drafted for operation near shore, and only sturdy enough to avoid capsizing when their heavy guns were fired. Unlike ocean-going warships, they could dispense with water casks, heavy ballast, and carry little food supplies, as well as far fewer spars, canvas, and naval stores mandatory for cruising in the Atlantic, which might have to last for many months.

BRITISH PLANNING

Barclay was the newly arrived and temporarily the British naval commander on Lake Ontario, before being superseded by Yeo, who headed the Royal Navy forces on the Great Lakes. Barclay was a heroic, tragic, and already badly wounded officer. He had lost his left arm in 1808 while serving aboard the frigate *Diana* off the coast of France, rather than at Trafalgar, as has so often been repeated. He had served several European postings before being sent to America to aid in operations along the northwestern border.[4]

Furthermore, the war had spread to involve action in the Ohio environs in the western part of Lake Erie. There British general Henry Procter at Amherstburg, near Windsor, Ontario, confronted General William Henry Harrison's Americans. Procter had a chance to control Lake Erie by storming Fort Meigs, the US stronghold where the Maumee River enters the lake, but mishandled it. When Procter was unwilling or unable to protect some Kentuckians, he earned the lasting contempt of the great Amerindian chief Tecumseh who arrived near the end of the massacre and is reported to have shouted at him, "Begone! You are unfit to command; go and put on petticoats!"[5]

Theodore Roosevelt emphasized the difficulty of finding accurately the comparative gunnery of both squadrons on the eve of the Battle of Lake Erie. He lists them in his *The Naval War of 1812*.

American	
Lawrence	20(guns)
Niagara	20
Caledonia	3
Ariel	4
Scorpion	2
Somers	2
Porcupine	1
Tigress	1
Trippe	1

	54
British	
Detroit	19 (guns)
Queen Charlotte	17
Lady Prevost	13
Hunter	10
Little Belt	3
Chippeway	1
	63[6]

Although the British carried more guns, Perry's predominance lies in the weight thrown by two broadsides. He had forty-two thirty-two-pounders and four twenty-four-pounders. The British had seventeen twenty-four--pounders (nothing higher than these twenty-four-pounders).[7]

Barclay's logistical advantages, owing to better water transportation, might have been decisive, but actually, they were not. "He had only a minority of naval ratings [officers], plus American Indians who had no stomach for 'Walking-on-the-Water' fighting, and the Canadian militiamen were not, as he said, 'worth their salt.'"

Since no guns for *Detroit* had arrived, he had to make do (with ordnance dismounted from the fort at Malden /Amherstburg). "As the back-country thereabout was largely wilderness, little or no food could be obtained, and the many thousands of Tecumseh's tribesmen encamped around the base consumed most of the rations. Barclay could fain have waited, if possible for reinforcements [and resupplies] but a serious shortage of necessities forced him out, fatally, on 9 September to meet Perry's vessels."[8]

Barclay continued to blockade Perry's squadron on and after July 17 and realized the great importance of holding the Americans in port, but at the end of the month, he lifted his blockade "with all his vessels and sailed [away for a few days]." In his absence Perry succeeded in floating his ships across the bar during three nights in early August. His smaller vessels had preceded them and guarded the harbor entrance, while the two brigs had their guns taken out before being carried over. One commentator (with a degree of hyperbole) considered this "a tedious, backbreaking, and ingenious accomplishment—all things considered, the most decisive naval accomplishment of the war on the lakes!" [9]

The equipment of Barclay's squadron was so deficient that the guns of *Detroit* and the others had no portfires (devices for setting off explosives), and pistols had to be snapped over loose powder piled in the vent holes—yet they seemed to have operated well enough during the battle. There was a shortcoming even worse. Barclay wrote Yeo, September 12, 1813, "to get supplies of Provisions, and Stores of every description so perfectly destitute was the Post of Provisions that there was not a days Flour in Store, and the crews of the squadron under my command were on half allowance of many things."[10]

Furthermore, adequate personnel was also missing: "Manned as the squadron was with not more than fifty British seamen, the rest a mixed crew of Canadians and Soldiers, and who were totally unacquainted with such a service, rendered the loss of officers more sensibly felt—every officer commanding Vessels and their seconds were either Killed or Wounded as severely as to be unable to Keep the Deck."[11] Under these abominable circumstances, all hats should be doffed to Barclay and his people for fighting so stoutly and coming so close to victory on Lake Erie.

The set was ready and the cast assembled for what was to be the Battle of Lake Erie, September 10, 1813, which, in retrospect, may be seen as the most momentous day in the lives of Elliott and Perry.

AMERICAN PLANNING

The situation on Lake Ontario was to be settled by and large by the perhaps faulty decision of Chauncey and Pike to alter their assault on vital Kingston in favor of Britain's secondary base at York (Toronto), well to the west. Had Kingston been conquered and kept permanently (by no means a surety), the enemy would have been defeated along the entire northwestern border. As to naval action on Lake Ontario, many historians, I among them, have savaged Chauncey and Yeo for their reluctance to follow up temporary successes with a strike to obliterate the foe. Yet each had to recognize that should such an effort boomerang upon them, the abandonment of the Canadian-American frontier—in effect, the loss of the war—could become their nation's fate.[12]

Reverting to Tecumseh's maledictions, this occurrence spotlighted the pluses and minuses of the British-allied tribesmen. Most of the tribes sided with them, recalling well the rapidity with which American settlers, following the Battle of the Fallen Timbers in 1794, the ensuing Treaty of Greenville a year later, and its aftermath, had inundated portions of the present states of Ohio, Indiana, Illinois, Michigan, and Wisconsin. Most of the areas taken had been promised to the Amerindians by treaties with the US government, ostensibly in perpetuity. The newcomers had leveled trees, killed off or driven off game animals, and plowed up the earth, crippling the centuries-old American Indian way of life while ignoring the above treaties.

The main adhesive binding the tribesmen to the Union Jack was their reliance upon British pledges to ally themselves with Tecumseh and the other chiefs that together they would create a huge homeland for them in the Northwest, potent enough to fend off American encroachments. But the tribes had been cozened, for the English became appalled by the large numbers they had to support. By 1814 London dropped precipitously their allies and withdrew permanently to Canada. The fate of the Native Americans east of the Mississippi and south of the Great Lakes was sealed.

Returning to Elliott: "Since [Perry at] Erie would supersede [Elliott at] Black Rock the latter was reduced to little more than a way station for supplies: Elliott found himself a supernumerary. Nominally Lake Erie's commander before the transition, he suddenly discovered his power base usurped, his role considerably diminished, and reason to resent anything related to Presque Isle. Transferred to Lake Ontario a short while later, Elliott was reduced from a potentially significant independent command to just one more fish in a large pond of junior lieutenants."[13] Since he had been already the nation's foremost hero on inland waterways in 1812 by abducting the two British brigs near Buffalo, Elliott's ever present suspicion that injustices were being perpetrated upon him had to have been reinforced. Although Elliott knew that Perry was in dire need of "the most qualified and healthy seamen," he arbitrarily culled for his own brig *Niagara* the same sort of people. "Perry wished nothing to disrupt the harmony of his new command, so he diplomatically and perhaps foolishly allowed Elliott's lack of courtesy to pass without comment."[14]

On February 17, 1813, Perry received departmental instructions to report to Chauncey at Sacketts Harbor near Buffalo, at his immediate convenience, and bring with him his very best men from the Rhode Island flotilla. Perry simplified matters for himself by keeping practically all of his volunteers from Newport and its environs, rather than forwarding them to Chauncey.[15] Perry promptly began sending off his contingent in three batches between February 17 and 20. Still threatened by winter snows and ice, the men tramped to Albany where Perry met Chauncey, who had just arrived from Washington, DC. Perry pushed on to Presque Isle (Erie, Pennsylvania), reaching there on the twenty-seventh.[16]

Apparently the get-together of the two officers was affable enough, but underlying tension came to the fore over the allocation of manpower, a question equal to that of supplies. Each had to have a different priority; Chauncey must concentrate on Lake Ontario, Perry on Lake Erie. As commanding officer Chauncey retained for himself some of Perry's Newporters and thereafter would relinquish only small detachments from time to time. Perry let his dissatisfaction show, and Chauncey's retort was so sharp that his sensitive underling asked to be relieved of his Erie assignment. Chauncey, however, made something of an apology, and the navy secretary in essence ordered Perry to stop sulking and get on with his job. Elliott's rebuff by Perry's original appointment over him on Lake Erie meant that a possible second chance to assume the Erie command had gone by the boards.

A recent valuable article deals with the alliance of the army general

William Henry Harrison and Perry before and during the fracas at Lake Erie, melding army-navy cooperation. This was accomplished, despite a problem created by Chauncey in regard to Perry's shaky self-confidence, caused primarily by the latter's lack of combat seasoning. "Perry's great problem was [not set in motion by] Harrison, but rather Chauncey . . . who refused to provide him enough soldiers and sailors to man his flotilla."[17]

"In a famous exchange, Perry called the few men who remained to him in July [1813] a motley set, blacks, soldiers, and boys," to which Chauncey responded, "I have yet to learn that the colour of the skin or cut and trimmings of the coat, can affect a man's qualifications or usefulness." Seemingly this defense of tolerance had an impact on Perry, for we find little or no later evidence that he voiced similar remarks as to his lower rankers.[18]

In the midsummer of 1813, a US naval officer worried about the composition of Perry's available manpower. The force was composed primarily of "all the refuse of Commodore Chauncey's fleet, with at most 100 able seamen, 13 soldiers furnished by General Harrison, and about 60 militiamen were [en] listed at Erie out of the Militia & therefore little better. Our men were worn down by disease while those of the enemy were in good health. Under these circumstances . . . our success was great."[19]

A mere three weeks before combat would be joined, Perry still agonized about the grievous lack of officers and men, but to his jubilation, he received a providential letter from Elliott that "he would arrive almost immediately with 89 seamen & several officers. Perry was electrified & . . . declared that he had not been so happy since his first arrival: that now he had a commander [Elliott], just such a one as he wanted for *Niagara*, as he was at ease & would sail as soon as they arrived."[20] Here is a case study of how a judgment may be totally reversed by forthcoming events.

Toward the end of one of his many meetings with his officers, Perry issued his most compelling dictate: "Regardless of positioning [determined in prebattle planning], the Commodore's orders were specific when he directed that 'Commanding officers are particularly enjoined to pay attention in preserving their station in the Line, and in all cases to keep as near *Lawrence* as possible.'"[21] In this same vein Perry also ascribed to each vessel's commander, "Engage your designated adversary [in Elliott's instance, *Queen Charlotte*] in close action, at half cable's length."[22] There is a clear-cut ambiguity in these instructions (which had preference) remaining close to *Lawrence*, or fighting your British opponent, when during combat ship locations necessarily became scattered.

One of Perry's most perceptive commentators uses the above to upbraid Elliott: "Elliott's delay after *Caledonia* slowed to fire is inexcusable. Orders are orders, and even though circumstances rendered these orders conflicting [maintain station in line or engage designated adversary in close action] the fluid tactical situation dictated common sense initiative, particularly when Elliott could plainly observe *Queen Charlotte* closing *Lawrence* and clearly appreciated the eventual outcome if his guns weren't employed. If he didn't wish to display initiative it was a simple matter of which of these conflicting orders to obey, maintain station or engage. Elliott for his own reasons chose the former!"[23] Off and on this judgmental error would haunt him thereafter.

The excerpts below are from Gerard T. Altoff's "The Battle of Lake Erie." This segment's prose has been criticized as "florid," but I suggest that "vivid" is a more appropriate word, and I defer to Altoff's superior combat depiction by appropriating it for myself, with due credit to Altoff. "Blood streamed in crimson rivulets along the seams of the stricken ship's gouged deck. As their lifeblood flowed from ghastly wounds, tortured seamen writhed in agony, their heart-rending screams and moans competing with the roar of cannon and musketry. The broken and maimed bodies lying on deck or stretched out in the surgery below far outnumbered the exhausted and mentally stunned sailors still on their feet. Thick clouds of dirty white gun smoke drifted across the restless lake, its rancid, sulfurous smell pervading every corner of the ravaged vessel, stinging the eyes and nostrils of the ship's dazed crew. Like walking zombies they stumbled about their assigned duties, brains refusing to register the horror surrounding them."[24]

"The little twenty-gun brig (*Lawrence*), battered and beaten, shuddered under the impact of each British cannonball, as if in sympathy for the wretched men bleeding on her deck. Her gun ports were mostly silent, only a few of the giant thirty-two-pounders still capable of disgorging their deadly iron spheres. Shredded strips of canvas flapped helplessly in the wind, all that remained of the ship's once majestic sails. Rigging hung limply from her spars and trailed in the water alongside, not unlike a stately willow after a hailstorm. Her tall, heavily punctured frame resembled a bull's-eye after a long day of target practice."[25]

"By 2:30 P.M. . . . *Lawrence* was a defenseless hulk. Pride welled in Perry's chest at the superb performance and superhuman sacrifice manifested by his incomparable crew, which he could not mock by ignominious surrender. . . . Perry realized that he had no choice but to . . . abandon his precious ship. . . . He manned the amazingly intact cutter [with four men, all untouched], and pulled for *Niagara*. Straining at the oars the already exhausted sailors were spurred on by the incessant splash of British shot. . . . The little skiff disappeared . . . only to reappear unscathed. . . . Finally, after a journey of about fifteen minutes, the frail cutter and its soggy occupants gratefully slipped under the protective sheer of the looming *Niagara*."[26]

When Perry abandoned his shattered flagship, he told one of his officers to make his own decision as to surrendering *Lawrence*, but within a short time, Perry conquered the entire British squadron. The disposal of these fighting men-of-war was for a long time ignoble. *Lawrence* and *Niagara*, along with the enemy's *Detroit* and *Queen Charlotte*, were scuttled at Misery Bay in Erie, Pennsylvania, during the early 1820s.[27]

To those Americans who retain even a fleeting memory of the Battle of Lake Erie, the sketch of Perry's abandonment of his stricken *Lawrence* in a rowboat to reach Elliott's *Niagara* is probably the most retentive: moreover, it turned out to be the climactic moment of that lake's engagement. What occurred at the post-battle meeting of the two officers differs almost entirely from Elliott's version to that of Perry: "I looked over the stern and saw Captain Perry in it; whom I met as he came over the side, asking what was the result on board his brig. He answered, 'CUT ALL TO PIECES. THE VICTORY'S LOST EVERYTHING GONE! I'VE BEEN SACRIFICED BY THE DAMNED GUN BOATS!' TO WHICH I REPLIED, 'NO, SIR, VICTORY IS YET ON OUR SIDE. I HAVE THE MOST JUDICIOUS POSITION, AND MY SHOTS ARE TAKING EFFECT. YOU TEND MY BATTERY, AND I WILL BRING UP THE GUNBOATS.' 'Do so,' said he, 'FOR HEAVEN'S SAKE!' Returning on board *Niagara*, Captain Perry observed, 'I OWE THIS VICTORY TO YOUR GALLANTRY.'"[28]

As to be expected, according to Richard Dillon, Perry's interpretation of their conversation was quite the opposite: "Reaching the rail of *Niagara* at about 2:45, Perry was met by Elliott who inquired, foolishly, 'How is the day going?' 'Badly enough!' snapped the smoke-grimed Perry. He bluntly demanded to know, 'Why are the gun boats so far astern?' A nervous Elliott leaped at the opportunity. Instead of answering, he said, 'I'll bring them up' [actually they were already approaching their top speed]. 'Do so,' was Perry's curt reply. He wished the gun boats brought up; but he was even more grateful to have the fellow out of his sight."[29] The denouement of the contest was at hand.

"After conducting a survey to determine *Niagara*'s fighting capabilities, Perry rapped out a string of orders. . . . At last the [brig's] earnest and willing crew were about to join the fray. Eyes widened in shock as British officers and seamen viewed the truculent apparition approaching through the dissolving gun smoke. After two hours of blood and suffering they had defeated the American flagship; by rights they should have won the day Although completely wrecked, *Lawrence* had nevertheless succeeded in meting out harsh punishment to her opponents. . . . [Barclay was hit twice], the captain and his first officer of every British ship had been either killed or wounded. Inexperienced junior officers now commanded these complex vessels of war."[30] And again:

> The British were all too aware that only one tactic might preserve them from *Niagara's* fresh broadsides. If they could turn their men-of-war 180 degrees, then the guns on the starboard side, not yet engaged, could be brought to bear. . . . Haste was imperative, *Niagara* was bearing down rapidly. . . . The ravaged British flagship slowly turned with the wind—all too slowly. . . . Inexperienced junior officers who commanded *Queen Charlotte* failed to judge *Detroit's* sluggish movements and pressed on too much canvas, crashing into the other's stern. . . . Now, at the most critical phase of the battle, the two largest British ships were locked together and helpless. Perry thrust *Niagara* midpoint . . . [of the British battle line]. . . . Twenty gun captains jerked twenty lanyards. . . . A mind-numbing blast [erupted], as forty heavy cannonballs sped on their destructive mission. Sponge, load, fire! Sponge, load, fire! . . . Hundreds of deadly wood splinters purged the disarrayed decks. British and Canadian blood flowed freely. . . . Other than death and total destruction only one option was left. *Detroit* . . . fired a gun off her disengaged side, signaling her surrender.[31]

"A couple of Barclay's smallest vessels in vain tried to escape, and understandably disheartened by the cataclysmic change in fortune over the past few minutes, for the first time in its centuries-old naval annals, an entire British squadron had been captured. At first the silence, after three hours of earsplitting pandemonium, was perplexing, but after a few minutes, Perry began to grasp the enormity of his success. . . . Perry had achieved what he set out to do, and in the process immortalized himself in American naval lore.[32]

If it had been a star-spangled day for Perry, it most certainly was not for his second-in-command. An American eyewitness reported that "just as the guns fell silent, Elliott suffered a most embarrassing loss of self-control. He was on board the schooner *Sommers* [*sic*] and behaved, as I was told by officers of that vessel, in a manner altogether unbecoming an officer by beating a Capt'n of a gun severely with a speaking trumpet for laughing when he (Capt'n Elliott) dodged a shot." In addition, "he arrested *Somers* captain [sailing master John J. Almy] for intoxication," albeit his colleagues testified that he was in "a perfect state of sobriety . . . with Almy's feelings much wounded by Capt. Elliott's false report."[33]

A few observations beyond Altoff's description are acute or memorable enough to warrant inclusion in this chapter: "When . . . Perry in *Niagara* turned the conflict into a rout, Elliott must have bit . . . his lip in frustration. If he had meant to sacrifice his commander, all had gone wrong. From abject Defeat Perry had singlehanded-thrashed five [six] vessels. It was awesome. Perry had fled a wreck; now he had wrecked a fleet."[34]

"Perry's dog was locked in a stateroom for the duration of the battle. But the noise of the cannonading, the impact of the British shot, the stench of death and the horrible cries of the wounded and dying terrified the animal. The spaniel growled and barked, then howled piteously as a cannonball smashed a nearby closet of crockery. Yet another solid shot pierced a bulkhead, the dog thrust its head through the hole to yap at its master for help. It was a bit of insane comic relief."[35]

A few words of background information apply at this juncture. Although references to American strategy and tactics dot this text throughout, Theodore Roosevelt made pertinent comments about them, and particularly as to their impingement on the outcome of the war in the Northwest:

> Captain Perry showed indomitable pluck and readiness to adapt himself to circumstances; but his claim to fame rests much less on his actual victory than on the way he prepared the fleet that was to win it. Here his energy and activity deserve all praise, not only for his success in collecting sailors and in building two brigs, but above all for the manner in which he succeeded in getting them out on the lake. On that occasion he certainly out-generaled Barclay.[36]
>
> But it will always be a source of surprise that the American public should have so glorified Perry's victory over an inferior force, and have paid comparatively little attention to [Commodore Thomas] Macdonough's victory [on Lake Champlain in 1814] which really won against decided odds in ships, men, and metal.[37]

Let us reemphasize that Macdonough's trouncing of the British, rather than Perry's at Lake Erie, made sure that the Great Lakes frontier—including Ontario, Erie, Huron, and Superior—would remain partially in the United States.

ON THE NORTHWESTERN FRONTIER, 1813–1814 (POST BATTLE OF LAKE ERIE)

Throughout almost all of his naval life Elliott proved himself to be an efficient and indefatigable administrator—with the exception of this and one other period—when he lapsed into sloth and ineffectuality to a surprising degree. Was it because of his discouragement over the army's inability to trounce convincingly the British when so many factors operated to its advantage? Or because of the pall cast over him by accusations of cowardice about his performance at Erie and the honors the American public heaped on Perry for the victory to which he was not invited to participate? Both seem to have contributed to the same sad result.

Elliott probably concluded that US territorial conquests along the Canadian border had been trifling and would have nodded assent with a newspaper editorial in mid-1814 that, so far, his nation's successes there had been thrown away: "A tenth perhaps a twentieth of the force would have been sufficient to have accomplished without any loss which may now cost many lives. It is exceedingly to be regretted that such is too generally our conduct. We seem to despise to follow up to its conclusion any advantage gained."[38]

This citation is more applicable to land struggles than to the naval clashes on the lakes themselves, for if Ontario could not be cleared of the British, Erie had moved solidly into the American sphere. Furthermore, the above editorial appeared two months before Macdonough would pulverize the British on Lake Champlain, forcing the foe to cancel his advance toward Albany and retreat back to Canada. If that, coupled with the impact of American privateers on Britain's seagoing commerce, is considered, the following is true: "This event, among many others, convinces the British government to seek peace."[39]

In late October 1813 Perry suddenly resigned his command of the Erie Squadron and hurried east, both to secure a blue water command and to revel in the acclaim that awaited him en route from Buffalo to his home in Newport, Rhode Island. Elliott became his successor and failed to perform his duties on that lake. He allowed the hospital at Erie to deteriorate in favor of building a "huge blockhouse" about which navy purser Samuel Hambleton, Perry's close personal friend, observed: "Against which enemy, I have not learned. It is just as likely, I think that the Dey of Algiers will attack us as the British."[40]

Historian Dillon also gives a terse but admirable summary of conditions along the Canadian frontier under the new commodore: "Discipline grew lax, morals collapsed. Drunken tars brawled in Erie, insulted the townsfolk, raided chicken coops." Officers quarreled among themselves, and a few duels resulted, in one of which a sailing master killed Midshipman George Senat.[41] Purser Humphrey Magrath of *Niagara*, long Elliott's ally in the Lake Erie dispute, became mentally deranged and committed suicide, shooting a pistol from his mouth through the top of his head with the expected unpleasant results.[42]

Fleet matters reflected the same collapse. In late 1813 no less than eight of Perry's smaller ships, so triumphant only a little over three months before, "were allowed to run aground" and "put to the torch" in an enemy raid because of "Elliott's seeming paralysis."[43] An unerring summary put it: "In a sense, Perry and Elliott combined to destroy the Erie Squadron, the Commodore by his absence, the latter by his presence."[44]

During April 1814 Elliott was replaced on Lake Erie by Commodore

Arthur Sinclair who informed the department of the atrophy he found, blaming much of it on his predecessor, although gently at first: "I trust, Sir, in doing my duty I shall not make unfavorable impressions as regards Capt. [*sic*] Elliott. He is very young as a commander, has had but little experience, surely none to justify the difficulties he has had to contend with here—they have been many and of magnitude."[45] But within four days Sinclair's estimate of Elliott had hardened: "Timber . . . not only for the use of the fleet but for a public storehouse which Capt. Elliott is finishing . . . has been exposed to pilfer and at the mercy of the waves, and I am told that there are great quantities of 32 pd shot . . . thrown overboard and are covered with sand." He went on to describe how the conditions of the warships at his post had decayed and that supplies of food and alcohol had been allowed to become seriously depleted. In short, a stinging rebuke to Elliott as an administrator, a field in which he had already demonstrated much competence and would do so again.[46]

Elliott was finally able to leave Lake Erie to assume command of the men-of-war on Lake Ontario. Now, excused from the crushing responsibilities that had so disconcerted him, he could look forward to contact with the foe for himself and his subordinates. But the results were somewhat disappointing for the Americans; the best that they could do was to engage in inconclusive small ship actions on May 6, June 19, and July 1, 1814. Elliott was able to win his navy's last victory on the lakes in his schooner when he caught and drove ashore the British brig *Magnet* on July 31.[47] He provided further details about this incident but with a more somber ending: "I found a vacant brig, the *Sylph,* a fast sailor of 20 guns, and by agreement [with Chauncey] I accepted the vessel. . . . Late in the summer we were enabled to take [to] the Lake, proceeding to its head and there intercepting a brig of nearly the same size as *Sylph*. . . . Comm. Chauncey made a signal for me to give chase and attack her, which I accordingly did; but when I thought her to be in my grasp, my laurel was snatched from me; her captain running her on shore, and finally blowing her up."[48]

At least his squadron had ensured that the United States would maintain a rough equality with Britain on Lake Ontario thereafter. Shortly, Elliott was granted a long leave to spend with his family, to wait for the tocsin to sound, this time calling him to do battle in the Mediterranean.

IN THE ALGERIAN WAR, 1815

In comparison with his more vital performances as to the taking of the British vessels in 1812 and to a lesser extent at the Battle of Lake Erie a year later, Elliott's donation to the last hostilities with the Barbary states of North Africa was surely insignificant, with one major exception for any of his biographers—how he used it for self-aggrandizement.

If the US-Tripolitan Treaty of 1805, terminating the war with Tripoli, had chastened the bashaw it most certainly did not the neighboring dey of Algiers, who continued to collect American tribute and snap up American ships and enslave their people. The toll might have been much higher in the Mediterranean had not most of that trade been wiped out by the Jeffersonian and Madisonian commercial restrictions, the embargo especially. During the War of 1812 the dey, the bashaw, and the bey of Tunis practically allied themselves with the British, turning over to the Royal Navy US privateers and their captives.[49]

Finally able to retaliate against his Barbary tormentors with a much stronger fleet in 1815, Madison had Congress declare war on Algiers only two weeks after receiving word that the Treaty of Ghent had been signed. He dispatched overseas Commodore Stephen Decatur with an impressive ten-ship armada, the frigates *Guerriere, Constellation*, and *Macedonian*; sloops *Epervier* and *Ontario*, and assorted smaller craft.[50] Elliott commanded *Ontario*, and in Jarvis's "biography" of him a strange lack of attention is paid to his combat experiences in Algiers, amounting to a mere eight lines in the book, and omitting his creditable action in the swift and overwhelming American victory.[51]

As the expedition peered into Gibraltar while passing, it was indeed fortunate. Algiers had only one potent warship, the forty-six-gun frigate *Meshouda*, and once spotted, her doom was inevitable. *Constellation* was the first to engage under Captain Charles Gordon of *Chesapeake-Leopard* notoriety.[52] The other men-of-war raced up, among them Elliott's *Ontario*, which hammered away from *Meshouda*'s portside while the Algerian was trying to make for the neutral Spanish shore. This created a diversion, permitting Decatur's *Guerriere* to slash to the fore and fire repeated broadsides, one of which cut in two her captain, before additional pounding caused a quick surrender. The war's only other combat was with the twenty-two-gun *Estedio* three days later. She ran into shoal waters too shallow for frigates and sloops to enter and had to be engulfed by brigs and schooners.[53]

After dictating peace terms to the dey, at the "cannon's mouth," as Decatur put it, he went to Tunis before proceeding to his last stop at Tripoli. For the same sort of delinquencies as at Algiers, the bey and basha were compelled to disgorge $46,000 and $25,000 respectively.[54]

Why was Elliott so reticent about his North African sojourn? A strong case may be formulated that he was determined to let nothing interfere with his portrait of himself as a bona fide hero, providing another example of his appalling lack of modesty. At the bey's palace in Tunis: "Captain Elliott performed another public service, which, for daring and desperate valor, as well as for cool, inflexible resolution, exceeded any previous act of his life, and rarely has been equaled."[55]

Decatur had delegated negotiations with the dey about his ultimatum for peace to three of his subordinates, Mordecai W. Noah, US consul at Tunis, and Captains Gordon and Elliott. Noah wrote that when they entered the "hall of audience" two of the ruler's sons "were present and extremely insolent." Their father was angry about Decatur's absence: "Why does not your admiral come on shore?" Noah responded, "He will not land, Sir, until you decide to pay the value of those vessels which you permitted the British to take from us." "The Bey . . . in a tone of uncommon insolence and violence was about to contest the matter," when Elliott intervened. "We did not come here to be insulted. This interview must be cut short. Will you or will you not pay for these vessels? Answer nothing but that." Enraged though he still was, the dey caved in and eventually turned over $46,000 to the commodore.[56]

Significantly, Elliott did not stop here, for he added: "One circumstance of this interview has been omitted by Mr. Noah. While Mustapha, the son of the Bey, was addressing the American deputation in a tone of excessive insolence, about thirty Mamelukes [in this sense, soldiers] entered the room with drawn cymetars [*sic*]. Captain Elliott, at once perceiving that this was either intended to intimidate them, or preparatory to some violent outrage, placed his back against the wall, drew his sword, and declared that he would sell his life dearly. The Bey, finding that the Americans were not to be intimidated, assented to their demands and dismissed them. This affair needs no comment. It was the act of a man, who, in a battle, *could never have been a coward* [emphasis added]."[57]

This explains why Elliott accentuated so much the inclusion of this material, especially when he left out almost every other phase of this Mediterranean tour. One wonders if there were any extended periods during the years remaining to him when he was able to put aside the rumors and accusations against him during and after the Battle of Lake Erie? Ergo, he must always stress any incident to prove that one of his most outstanding traits was intrepidity. Note that his defiance of the Mamelukes rests upon his word alone, for no substantiating evidence about it has been unearthed. Even more damaging, Elliott makes no mention of this dramatic exploit in his *Speech*, published in 1844, leading to the strong supposition that it had been "made out of whole cloth."[58]

Four

The Perry-Elliott Feud, 1813–Present

This material is of the greatest essence, having the most telling impact upon Elliott's life. It has been allocated into six very loose subdivisions, which permit interplay between them, instead of strict adherence to them.

1. Fleet accusations against Elliott for holding back *Niagara* from engaging the British during the first two hours of the Battle of Lake Erie, September 10, 1813, without aiding Perry's flagship *Lawrence*
2. Perry's warmhearted but failing efforts to win Elliott's affection and gratitude by appeasement of him
3. Perry's growing awareness that he had created inadvertently Elliott's ensuing enmity
4. The Perry-Elliott feud widens, 1813, through Elliott's complete vindication at his court of inquiry, 1815.
5. How the US government determined its sizable prize money bestowal for the fleet's officers and men
6. A perceptive Canadian analysis of Elliott and the Battle of Lake Erie

For a man of Elliott's makeup, very likely the seeds of future conflict with Perry had been implanted deeply when he learned in 1812 that he could be no better than the Lake Erie Squadron's second-in-command to his rival.

To be sure, Elliott knew already that Perry's commission had been issued shortly before his, meaning that throughout their careers, all other factors being roughly equal, Perry would have preference. But how could Elliott's ever replenished sense of persecution been able to ignore his own wartime accomplishments compared to his opponent's? While Perry had been waging make believe warfare with his gunboats in Newport, Elliott had stormed the British brigs *Detroit* and *Caledonia* at Black Rock, near Buffalo, October 8–9, 1812 (see chapter 2). This bold strike had restored much of his nation's optimism, plunged into despondency by the army's abject collapse along the Canadian border. Soon Elliott had been able to have been indulged in acclaim, jumped to commander over more than a score of other lieutenants ahead of him on the service roster, and awarded substantial prize money from the government. He would have every reason to hope that Secretary of the Navy William Jones and Commodore Isaac Chauncey would confirm him in the Lake Erie command, only to receive the dash of ice water across the face represented by Perry's appointment over him.

Furthermore, an even worse humiliation for Elliott was in the offing. In the sharpest contrast to the American intraservice collapse of 1812, which was exemplified by General William Hull's craven surrender of Fort Detroit, Elliott's seizure of the British brigs provided the major shaft of light slicing through the pervading national gloom. The US Army and Navy cooperated effectively in 1813. Perry's naval dominance on Lake Erie was matched by General William Henry Harrison's troops who first fought the British to a standstill on Erie's farthest extremity and then invaded successfully southwestern upper Canada (Ontario).

Although many localities held impromptu celebrations of Perry's triumph, it was not until late October that the main event took place at Erie, Pennsylvania, honoring Perry and Harrison who were cheered to the rafters by the witnessing multitude. With the greatest relish, Samuel Hambleton informed Perry that: "No notice was taken by them of Captain Elliott who was also in the house; at which, I presume he was much mortified. A number of newspapers on the table, which he had looked over, were filled with encomiums to Commodore Perry, while his name was hardly mentioned. He complained to Gen. Harrison that . . . he was entitled to an equal share of honour with Capt. Perry, and should have received it, if the former had followed through on a pledge to alter his official account of the battle as reported to the Department. Had Elliott closed for action earlier than had been supposed, Perry would have made 'a supplemental statement,' but he saw no reason to do so."[1]

Such a one-two punch could result in nothing less than Elliott's certainty that he must move to the offensive to garner what be believed to be his rightful place in his country's naval historical annals.

Perry's charitable but doomed sallies to win Elliott's friendship and gratitude boomeranged back on him, for he paid little attention to the objections of his allies, some of whom warned him that his second-in-command was irreversibly hostile. This resulted in Perry's lamentations about his futile course until the day he died in 1819.

"A few years later the Commodore admitted that if he had known of the intrigues of Elliott, he would have preferred charges against him before resigning his Lake Erie appointment to return to Rhode Island. Though he sensed the jealous rage of the man, it would be months before his real character became clear to his superior. When he left Erie[,] . . . Perry designated the command of the fleet to the man who hated him the most."[2]

Nevertheless, Perry led off with his initial complements shortly after the Battle of Lake Erie. He wrote: "At half past two, the wind springing up, Captain Elliott was enabled to bring his vessel . . . gallantly into close action." Without mentioning that he had already personally assumed command of *Niagara*, Perry continued, "In this action he [Elliott] evinced his characteristic bravery and judgment,"[3] which on second reading may be seen to be a two-edged sword.

Appeasement continued when Perry wrote to Elliott: "I am indignant that any report should be in circulation prejudicial to your character. . . . It affords me pleasure that I have in my power to assure you that the conduct of yourself, officers, and crew are such as to meet my warmest approbation. I shall ever believe it a premeditated plan of the enemy to disable our commanding vessel, by bringing their force to bear upon her; and I am satisfied, had they not pursued this course, the engagement would not have lasted thirty minutes." Hardly a week after the combat Hambleton "discovered that a strong party had sprung up in the fleet, particularly on board *Niagara*, hostile to Commodore Perry." Before he could tell Perry this news (on the same day, October 19, 1813), Hambleton learned that the commodore had, "at the earnest request of Capt. Elliott, written him a letter approbatory of his conduct in the late action. On being informed of this cabal, at the head of which was Capt. Elliott, Commodore Perry was highly excited. Notwithstanding, he desired me to say to his friends that he wished them to pursue a conciliatory course towards Capt. Elliott, to which they reluctantly agreed, and suppressed. . . . [condemnatory letters about his behavior on Lake Erie]."[4]

An able modern historian has tried to plumb Elliott's mindset at this juncture: "Perry was in a bind; he simply could not figure Elliott . . . out. . . . But he sensed that there was much more to Elliott, as a problem, than mere stiff-necked irritability. Was it emotional instability? The talk of the fleet was that it was cowardice. Perry did not believe it. But he was halfway beginning to believe worse scuttlebutt; that Elliott had been so blinded by ambition and envy that he had tried to deliberately sacrifice his commander to the enemy. It was hard to believe that anyone in the service should be such a despicable scoundrel. . . . But, naively, Perry put his faith on an English admiral's maxim: 'It is better to screen a coward than to let the enemy know there is one in the fleet' and did just that."[5]

It also appears that Perry had been deeply touched by the manner in which Elliott, just following the slaughter's end, had gone to pieces mentally:

"Meanwhile, hearing what was being said about him, Elliott took to his bed, worn out by nervous energy [or more accurately, perhaps a lack of it]. Dr. [Usher] Parsons, USN, who had attended him, convinced that he was not really ill, nevertheless reported his condition to Perry, who at once visited *Niagara*. He found Elliott in a nervous state, talking wildly, and protesting that he had lost the finest opportunity of distinguishing himself that any man ever had. Perry managed to calm him, but no sooner had he got back to his own ship than he received a letter . . . from Elliott. It had been written *before* his visit," disavowing that he in *Niagara* had been responsible for sacrificing the commodore's *Lawrence*. Even though these last words cast a different aspect on the validity of Elliott's repentance, Perry still plodded on for a time on his conciliatory course.[6]

James C. Mills remarks that Perry had committed "a grievous fault by his charitable approach" to Elliott, "although his motives were generous, cannot be denied." Up to this point we had evaluated Mills as one of our most valued authorities, but here he takes a belly flop off the deepest end. He claims that "Perry's *neglect to arrest Captain Elliott on the day of the battle* [emphasis added] was the greatest error of his life, and he had sufficient cause to repent it."[7]

We deem the above paragraph to add up to total nonsense. Such an arrest could have been done *only* with the permission of the Navy Department and through it the president. How could this have transpired just as the nation was readying itself to bask in the glow of its most momentous naval conquest up to that time? Furthermore, the country would have divided over it at once, and Perry's scintillating modern reputation would have been marred irrevocably. Nor do we know of other sources, including anything from Perry himself, that has echoed Mills's unbelievable conclusion. Finally, even without any such explosive action, the Perry-Elliott controversy rages even today.

Among the first of the post-battle events, five navy and two army officers attached to *Niagara* told the department that they backed most enthusiastically their captain for his combat behavior, realizing that anything derogatory of Elliott might well redound most negatively as to their own naval career prospects: "We are induced by motives of: the warmest admiration and great respect for our commander, Captain J. D. Elliott. . . . We are unwilling to quit the subject without expressing our admiration for our noble commander . . . for his conduct during the action, which was manifested by his cool, brave and judicious deportment, and are firmly of the opinion that his valor could not be surpassed by any; and that in him the American flag has a most zealous, skillful, and heroic defender."[8] Nonetheless, officers from other vessels in the squadron refused to endorse this fulsome acclamation, and because of that, they charged Elliott with hectoring them while commanding the Lake Erie fleet after Perry's resignation and the latter's return to Newport a few weeks later.

As to the feud, almost immediately after the engagement's blood-soaked end, Elliott had commenced his anti-Perry onslaught, surreptitiously at first, but soon openly avowed. Perry was initially so complimentary to Elliott, which had been caused by his generous but ill-considered desire to apportion the glory with as many of his colleagues as possible, but by 1815 had become positive that his second-in-command was a deep-dyed adversary. The sequel was inevitable. Two blocs were formed, one manned by Elliott's partisans and the other by Perry's zealots, and this unspannable bridge between them continues down to this day with no signs of abatement.

Elliott had "assumed a bolder tone," by first "claiming one half of the honor of the victory" and then all of it. He implied "that when Capt. Perry came on board *Niagara*, he was in a state of despair, & but for him would have surrendered the fleet. . . . Some of our officers, aware of his ambition and having a better opinion of his courage than of his morals, suppose that it was his wish to have *Lawrence* sacrificed that he might come up and decide the action himself, and thus secure the honour of the victory. . . . The circumstances of his volunteering to bring up the Gun Boats, of which he boasts might, by an ill-natured person, be imputed to a regard for his own safety. . . . I must say that he has acted towards Commodore Perry in the most ungenerous and ungrateful manner. Gen. Harrison, with whom I conversed while here, observed, 'Commodore Perry has saved his character, for which he will never forgive him.'"[9]

His brush-off at Erie appears to have been basic to Elliott's determination to wrest from his superior credit for the triumph of September 10, no matter what the cost to him personally nor how long it would take. The seed of dissension between Elliott and Perry had been sown to flourish thereafter.

It is frequently illuminating to use outside commentary on American occurrences, in this case Pierre Berton, the leading modern Canadian assessor of the Battle of Lake Erie, who not only writes with élan and competence but asks and answers a rhetorical question. "Why did Elliott not bring *Niagara* into combat? It devolves upon Elliott's known character, his ambitions, his mild paranoia."[10]

"He is nettled at being superseded by a younger man, piqued at being taken out of the van at the last moment, is stubbornly hewing to the letter of Perry's instructions . . . to stay a cable's length from the vessel ahead. . . . Elliott undoubtedly sees himself as the savior of the day; when Perry is driven to strike his flag, he, Elliott, will move in. On *Lawrence*, even the wounded are cursing Elliott. 'Why don't they come and help us? . . . We can expect nothing from that ship,' comes the bitter reply. As far as the public is concerned, Elliott is a hero. Why does he not keep quiet? But that would be contrary to Elliott's temperament; he is a man with a massive chip on his shoulder and an unbridled lust for fame. He is also a man with a guilty conscience."[11]

In a later recollection of Lake Erie, an officer, admittedly hostile to Elliott, claimed that the latter had insisted that because *Lawrence*'s flag had been pulled down, "the squadron's officers and men [including Perry!] were not entitled to prize money as she was a recaptured vessel."[12] To anyone even faintly aware of the merciless pounding that *Lawrence* had had to endure, the demand of Elliott's officers that they were the only rightful recipients of the victor's payments may be termed contemptible to the utmost degree. But justice was accorded to all when both Perry and Elliott, working as one, insisted on judicious allotments to all.

The government in Washington, DC, responded generously to those who had won on Lake Erie. Such accolades were set in motion on December 27, 1813, with Secretary of Navy Benjamin Homan's report to William Lowndes, chairman of the Naval Committee of the House of Representatives: "While the heroic commander of the American squadron justly merits the highest honors which the expressions the National Council can bestow, the second in command on that eventful day, appears to merit particular distinctions for the important and decisive share he had in that glorious event; and it is grateful in the highest degree, that every officer and man on that trying occasion, discharged his duty to the nation with zeal, fidelity, and honor."[13] The House of Representatives followed with its response: "Resolved—That the President of the United States be requested to cause gold medals to be struck, emblematical of the action between the two squadrons, and present them to Captain Perry and Captain Jesse D. Elliott, in manner as will be most honorable to them; and that the President be further requested to present a silver medal, with suitable emblems and devices, to each of the commissioned officers, either of the Navy or Army, serving on board, and a sword to each of the Midshipmen and Sailing Masters, who so nobly distinguished themselves on that memorable day."[14]

In 1814 Congress authorized the purchase of the captured ships at a price of $255,000 in order to add them to the Erie Squadron. From this fund Chauncey received $12,750, the largest sum bestowed on an individual, although he was not even present at the battle. Next came Perry who got $7,140, but Congress, to bring the commodore's payment almost to the share Chauncey got, voted him another $5,000 with Elliott taking in $7,140. In all, 596 persons were supposed to share in the distribution, but only 533, for one reason or another, received any money. [15]

4.1. Remnant of battle flag of the *Niagara* from Battle of Lake Erie, September 10, 1813. Courtesy of Chris Jacobs

Elliott was presented with a sterling opportunity in 1815 to exonerate himself from the onus overhanging him since his questionable refusal to rally to Perry's side at the Battle of Lake Erie. Unfortunately, he botched it, for reasons explained below.

During British commodore Barclay's almost simultaneous court-martial in England for losing his fleet to Perry, Elliott's alleged "biography" devoted much of a long chapter to refute only two words. Barclay had asserted that Elliott's *Niagara* was "making away" from the action on September 10, 1813. He was incorrect, for Elliott personally remained almost motionless during the first two hours of the engagement.[16]

This Briton is worth much more than a single glance. As he stood before his peers, a tragic but proud figure—one arm gone, the other in bandages, a portion of his thigh missing, and five wounds elsewhere, he had immolated his body for his country. Of course Barclay was honorably acquitted of blame for the loss, but he never went to sea again. There is a story, difficult to resist, that in view of his mutilated condition, he offered to release his fiancée from their planned marriage. She replied that if there was enough of him to contain his soul, she would wed him. And she did.[17]

Meanwhile the American naval establishment was closing ranks behind Elliott, not so much to suit his object of confirming his spotlessness as from the necessity of defending the navy's good name from British insinuation. Secretary of the Navy Benjamin W. Crowninshield wrote to Commodore Alexander Murray, court of inquiry president, that "the conduct of Captain Jesse D. Elliott . . . who commanded the brig *Niagara* on that day is misrepresented: justice to the reputation of Captain Elliott, and to the Navy of the United States, requires that a true statement of the facts . . . be exhibited to the world."[18]

Murray and his fellow members hurried to accede to Crowninshield's wishes: "The court of inquiry . . . sincerely regrets that there should have been any diversity of opinion, respecting the events [of September 10, 1813]. The court, however, feel convinced, that the attempts to wrest from Capt. Elliott, the laurels he gained in that splendid victory, as second in command. under the gallant and highly meritorious officer, Capt. Perry, ought in no wise to lessen him in the opinion of his fellow-citizens, as a brave and skillful officer; and that the charges made in the proceedings of the British Court Martial, by which Capt. Barclay was tried, of his attempting to withdraw from the battle, is malicious and unfounded in fact."[19]

Elliott's rejoinder about his so-called flight from Lake Erie was to the point: "It is liable, not only of the general imputation of falsity which is characteristic of British official reports, but likewise to the charge of gross improbabilities, of inconsistencies, and of contradictions by the American officers. Yet this . . . has been quoted against Captain Elliott, for the purpose of convicting . . . him of cowardice or treachery."[20]

An American sailing master, after witnessing what he thought was *Niagara*'s inexcusable delay in joining the action, cited one "Captain Bignall," a British officer, who averred that had Elliott belonged to the Royal Navy "he would have been hanged." Again, the accused turned this to his own advantage by stating that the enemy allegation, "is not improbable, for personal animosity against Captain Elliott seems to have existed among the British officers [while they uttered only compliments about Perry's conduct]."[21]

How much better for Elliott had he dropped his clash with Perry at this point when totally vindicated by a jury of his peers and refused thereafter to be drawn into discussions of it! But instead he must push on for victory completely on his own terms. While commanding in the Mediterranean, 1835–38, he wallowed in a quagmire of his own making by quarreling with his subordinate officers and by other mistakes in judgment. This damned him to the department, leading to his court-martial's sentence in 1840 of an almost three-year suspension from the navy. Moreover, his continuation of his feud with Perry forced him to endure their onslaughts for the rest of his days, and the intermingling of the two proved doubly disastrous for that latter-day Iago's historical reputation.

In a reopening of the Perry-Elliott clash five years after the battle, USN surgeon Usher Parsons gave his "Account of the Battle [of] Lake Erie," leveling his barrage against Elliott. Although some of its contents are presented elsewhere, it is so pertinent as to bear repetition:

> I well recollect that the wounded . . . complained that *Niagara* (commanded by Capt. Elliott) did not come up to her station and close with *Queen Charlotte*, although she had been ordered to by signal, and this complaint was frequently repeated by them till *Lawrence* struck. . . . It was at the same time observed that *Caledonia* was in close action while *Niagara*, a faster sailer, was quite out of reach of the enemy. After the action closed, the censures upon Capt. Elliott were so general and severe, not only among *Lawrence*'s officers but those of the small vessels, that in writing to my friends the day following I did not hesitate to say that Capt. Elliott had disgraced himself in the action, and the same sentiment was expressed in the letters of nearly every officer on board. [But Hambleton] had a private interview with Com. Perry and told us the Commodore wished us to be silent on Capt. Elliott's conduct. . . . He was then unwilling after its happy termination to destroy an officer of his rank and that honor enough had been gained by the action with everyone engaged in it. This request of Com. Perry's was complied with.[22]

Perry continued:

> I have the honor to lay before you copies of a letter lately received by me from Capt. Jesse D. Elliott of the Navy & of certain certificates inclosed therein. . . . The conduct of Capt. Elliott . . . imposes upon me the duty of preferring the charges against him which accompany this letter & request that a court-martial may be ordered for his trial thereupon. I [regret] having mentioned favorably an officer whose conduct had been so reprehensible. Having, previously to the engagement given all the orders that I thought necessary to enable every officer to do his duty, & feeling confidence in them all, I was, after it commenced, too necessarily engaged in the actual scene before me to reflect deliberately upon a cause which could induce Capt. Elliott to keep his vessel so distant from both me and the enemy. And after the battle was won I felt no disposition rigidly to examine into the conduct of any officer of the fleet; and strange as the behavior of Capt. Elliot had been, yet I could not allow myself to come to a decided opinion that an officer, who had so handsomely conducted himself on a former occasion [capture of the British brigs, 1812] . . . could possibly be guilty of cowardice or treachery. The

subsequent conduct also of Captain Elliott, the readiness with which he undertook the most minute services, the unfortunate situation in which he was placed, & which he lamented to me, & his marked endeavors to conciliate protection, all were well calculated to have their effect.[23]

Again:

But still more than all, I was actuated by a strong desire that in the fleet I then had the honor to command there should be nothing but harmony after the victory they had gained; &that nothing should transpire that would bring reproach upon any part of it, or convert into crimination the praises to which they were entitled &·which I wished them all to share and enjoy. . . . If I omitted to name Capt. Elliott or named him without credit, I might not only ruin that officer, but at the same time to give occasion to animadversions which, at that period I thought would be little to the honour or advantage of the service. If the official report of that transaction is referred to, these embarrassments with respect to Capt. Elliott under which I laboured in drawing it, will I believe be apparent. That report was very different from what had been expected by the officers of the fleet but having adopted the course I thought most prudent to pursue with regard to Capt. Elliott, I entreated them to acquiesce in it, & made every exertion in my power to prevent any farther remarks on his conduct & even furnished him with a favourable letter or certificate for the same purpose, of which he has since made a very unjustifiable use [publishing Perry's letter after swearing that he would not]. These Sir were the reasons which induced me at the time not to bring on an inquiry into Capt. Elliott's conduct. The cause and propriety of my now doing so will, I trust require, but few explanations. I would willingly for my own sake as well as his (after the course I had adopted for the purpose of shielding him) have still remained silent. But this Capt. Elliott will not allow me to do. He has acted upon the idea that by assailing my character, he shall repair his own.[24]

Purser Samuel Hambleton, aware of Perry' s admirable motives, spoke for all who abhorred Elliott's negative reaction to his superior when he informed Perry that

Your conduct toward Elliott, merited, I think a very strong reason to believe, dictated by Humanity and Love of Country. In the moment of victory you could not consent to the fall of a man, high in public favour, whom you had the power of saving—nor were you willing that the enemy should believe that the second in command had failed in his duty. That captain Elliott had

> done so (whether correct or not) was the general opinion in the fleet. . . . Whatever the motive the consequences were dreadful! . . . Instead of impressing him with a sense of gratitude, you appear to have planted in his Bosom a most implacable hatred of you.[25]

Late in 1813 Elliott laid down a fusillade against Perry as a commander of an armada: "I am not a, little mortified that our Country should be so wrongly informed of our late action on this Lake, and when the particulars of it are known the promotion of Perry to a Post Captaincy and me to the command of a Lake without an enemy to contend with will be viewed as an ill-judged reward. Perry will make a better second than a principal in a fleet action and nothing but the interest I have for the Service prevents my detailing facts to the public."[26]

Agreeing with Elliott, Theodore Roosevelt led off the supporting critique: "The American fleet came into action in worse form than the hostile squadron, the ships straggling badly, either owing to Perry having formed his line badly, or else having failed to train the subordinate commanders how to keep their places. . . . The attack was made in too loose order, and whether it was the fault of Perry or of his subordinates, it fails to reflect credit on the Americans."[27]

William F. Dudley, one of our most respected modern historians, has commented on Roosevelt's book: It "is valuable for its attention to minor as well as major naval actions. Roosevelt proceeded carefully, comparing the American and British versions of each action. He took issue with his sources on occasion and did not hesitate to express his judgment of officers' actions. He is as critical of Perry for his tactics as of Elliott for his failure to support his commodore."[28]

After mentioning that until recently members of the literati have written more about the maritime aspects of the War of 1812 than naval historians, Dudley states that "naval history writing is moving away from purely operational accounts. Nowhere is the need more evident than in the lack of administrative, logistical, political, social, and technological aspects of the Navy in the most recent histories of the War of 1812. On these subjects, landmark studies remain to be written for most of the US Navy's early history."[29] We hope that this Elliott biography may make a small contribution to the social sphere.

Michael A. Palmer has arrived at approximately the same conclusions as Elliott and Roosevelt. He concurs that Perry, while an excellent tactician, lacked the strategic ability to direct multiship operations in battle conditions. Moreover, each commentator suggests that Perry's instructions to his officers were imprecise, leading to confusion among them as to whether remaining close to *Lawrence* had preference over maintaining contact with their designated British opponents, in Elliott's case, *Caledonia*.[30]

Palmer adds: "My intent here is not to offer a detailed account of the action on Lake Erie nor attempt to judge the contentious dispute that arose between Perry and his principal subordinate, Jesse Duncan Elliott, but to examine Perry's exercise of command before and during the battle using contemporary standards and norms. While Perry was an able and aggressive ship's captain and a man blessed with personal courage, he was nonetheless a mediocre commander. The shortcomings evident in the American squadron during the Battle of Lake Erie are attributable to Commodore Perry. If his subordinates failed to support him, it was because Perry failed to exercise his functions as commander."[31]

This author's next several pages discuss naval signals systems, Perry's early career, his dissatisfaction with the Erie command, and his substitution of his own *Lawrence* for Elliott's *Niagara* to lead the van in the engagement.[32] Palmer then repeats the gist of his thesis: "Perry's responsibility as Commodore, whatever maneuver he adopted, was to ensure that his intentions were understood by his squadron. According to his own report, he 'directed the other vessels to follow,' itself an ambiguous statement that could easily be taken to mean that Perry wanted the ships to follow him in line, not to mimic his movements."[33]

"No matter how assiduous the advanced communications preparations, once multi-ship combatants clashed amid the incessant uproar of cannon fire, the crack of muskets, the splintering of masts and spars glancing off in all directions, the drifting smoke, shifting winds, the crunch of colliding vessels, and the screams and moans of the wounded and dying helped make sure that even through speaking trumpets and sometimes posted signals they used, they were of no avail." Palmer wonders how Perry could "expect to have a verbal order to be passed by trumpet to *Caledonia*—300 to 400 feet distant—if his own orders could not be heard on the deck of *Lawrence* more than ten feet away. . . . And how could Elliott, at least a quarter mile behind, have heard?"[34]

Palmer continues: "Yet at no point during *Lawrence*'s run toward the British did Perry make any signal. Even if we accept the view of Perry's supporters regarding Elliott's behavior, we are left with an image of a commodore so engrossed in fighting his own ship that he made no effort to direct the movements of his squadron for over two hours. The responsibility for Elliott's delay, if that is what it was, must be borne, or at least shared, by Perry."[35]

"No doubt, Elliott could have left the line earlier or directed *Caledonia* to make way and sailed down to assist his Commodore. The very vehemence of Elliott's defense over the decades after the battle is indicative of a man who felt that he had either failed, or at least missed a golden opportunity, the only one that he would ever get in his career, to make himself an 'ornament' in the young U.S. Navy. But for the historian to expect an officer of Elliott's caliber to desert the line, unordered, on his own initiative, is to expect too much."[36]

In general, Palmer's article is well written and to us persuasive, but his occasional interjections of former naval battles (British especially) appear extraneous and even unfair. He uses the strategy and tactics of such luminaries as Horatio Nelson, Admiral Richard Howe, and Captain Philip B. V. Broke vis-à-vis the maneuverings of Perry and Elliott at Lake Erie much to the American disadvantage.

For almost three hundred years the Royal Navy, replete with huge ships of the line (of which the United States had not one until 1815), aided by frigates, brigs, sloops, and other lesser craft, struggled successfully against the Spanish, Dutch, and French armadas, enemies usually with equal and sometimes superior strength. Over the decades, British commodores and commanders gained invaluable nautical knowledge that was passed on to successors from generation to generation. But not until the war was over could any American officer begin to evoke such an accumulated collection of top-level lore.[37] If ever a neophyte had to lead a fleet squadron it was Perry; hence we feel that Palmer's "A Failure of Command, Control, and Communications" would have been an even more persuasive work had these historical comparisons been eliminated.

Returning now to the crux of this chapter, a letter from Perry to Elliott, written prior to the beginning of their rift, gave the latter abundant ammunition to continue the feud. Perry wrote Elliott: "I shall ever believe it a premeditated plan to destroy *Lawrence*. This plan . . . nearly succeeded, for the flagship was captured, and Commodore Perry went on board *Niagara* in despair." Elliott snapped up this statement to lavish glorification upon himself: "What frustrated this plan! Aye! What saved three fleets and General Harrison's army. . . . The skill, the courage, and the constancy of Captain Elliott! His skill, which told him the necessity of changing Commodore Perry's order of battle and ordering *Caledonia* out of the line; and his constancy, which sustained and nerved him under difficulties that reduced Captain Perry to despair."[38]

Pointing out that Perry had raised no objection to Elliott's succeeding him as commandant of the Erie Squadron late in 1813, Elliott averred that "here then is a glaring inconsistency between Commodore Perry's letters of 18 September 1817 and 18 June 1818; and the only mode of saving him from the imputation of deliberate misrepresentation in the one or the other . . . is to consider the first as a frank, sincere, and statement of the case, and the second as the outpouring of a mind diseased by personal enmity."[39]

Three years after the above exchanges, Elliott seized an opportunity to accuse Perry of madness, trying to discredit everything derogatory to himself that his superior had made: "No reasonable doubt can therefore exist in the mind of any person, about the merits of Captain Elliott in this battle," and "it is inconceivable how Commodore Perry could have doubted it in 1818, unless laboring under a species of *monomania*, a degree of animosity . . . which amounted to insanity. If then he could be so blinded . . . in 1818, what reason is there for supposing that he would be more correct in any other case where Captain Elliott was concerned, and consequently what reliance can be placed upon his accusatory statements?"[40]

Some years earlier Captain H. B Brevoort, aboard *Niagara* during the battle, gave testimony that Elliott had to have incorporated with delight: "He says that when Captain Elliott returned to *Niagara*, Commodore Perry shook him by the hand and said: 'I OWE THIS TO YOU!!!' What did he owe to Captain Elliott? The rescue of his own fleet from destruction and the capture of the British! In other words, THE VICTORY OF LAKE ERIE!!"[41]

Adding substance to Elliott's hatred of him happened when the typically self-controlled Perry suffered an embarrassing and even potentially ruinous blow to his naval career while sailing to join the Mediterranean Squadron at Port Mahon in the Balearics during January 1817. His dissatisfaction with the frigate *Java*'s marine captain John Heath, whom he found lazy, inefficient, and insolent, had peaked when the previous mid-December Perry had slapped Heath across the face, "after having been ashore at a party, where he had consumed a considerable quantity of liquor." Soon both adversaries filed charges against the other, Perry for disobedience and contempt; Heath for "oppression." The department handled this untidy affair with kid gloves, amounting to taps on the wrist, by penalizing the two to "private reprimands," from Chauncey, which the supporters of both considered whitewashes.[42] Unquestionably this occurrence was what Elliott had in mind when he wrote, incorrectly: "The whole truth is, Perry drank very hard, and continued to do so until his death, and which I have no doubt hastened it."[43]

Reverting to another look at the Battle of Lake Erie, eventually Elliott provided two explanations of why he had remained so far from the action while the British were pounding *Lawrence* to pieces, a shorter version in 1818 and a longer and more detailed one in 1843. In the first, "he remained in place because 'He had had no *signal* from the *Comodore* to *change* his *situation* [emphasis added].' He complained much of Commodore Perry's injustice to him and said he only regretted that he had not sacrificed the fleet when it was in his power to have done so. . . . He also expressed sentiments to that effect, frequently afterward, at Buffalo as I am informed by the citizens and

Midshipman [George] Senat, who was present when the observations were made."[44] This exemplified Elliott's "mild paranoia," perhaps understandable, as he blurted it out in a moment of highest emotional stress.

In the second, a bare two years before his own expiration, Elliott finally explained at some length in a letter to a colleague, why he did not bring *Niagara* into the action earlier: "On the day previous to the battle, Perry and I were on board *Lawrence*, when all was settled as to the manner and mode of attack. I said to Perry that an Englishman had true bull dog courage—fight him in his own way and get a good hold on him and keep it fast and he would be worried [?] out. He and the Commodore had agreed that if I had a breeze, and I could get clear 100 minutes [it] would determine the battle. In accordance with this plan the signal was made to form the established line of battle [in which *Niagara* would hang well behind *Lawrence*]. Thus Perry attacked [but could not close fast enough]. Hence the long guns of *Detroit* cut him to pieces. I saw this, but I was only *second* in *command* and could not alter the position I had in line without permission—still with a halter around my neck.

"After the two Americans had changed ships, Elliott watched while Perry's *Niagara* cleared a most deadly fire from this new position. The British were cheering along the whole line for Victory. These cheers were soon changed for groans and as the ships rolled to Windward, the blood ran from the scuppers as from the spout of your house after a moderate rain."[45]

After Perry's death in Venezuela in 1819, Elliott lavished upon him an encomium as profuse as it is insincere:

> Permit me now, my friends, to remark. In reference to Capt. Perry that up to the time I went on board my brig, *Niagara*, after the battle had ceased. I FOUND HIM TO BE NOBLE, GALLANT, HIGH-MINDED, AND HONORABLE; AND NO MAN IN MY PRESENCE, SHALL SAY AUGHT AGAINST HIM! THAT HISTORY CONTAINS THE REGISTRY OF UNCEASING PERSECUTIONS, DARK AND INGENIOUS CONSPIRACIES, UNMITIGATED AND VINDICTIVE ASSAULTS UPON ME. BY THOSE WHO PRETENDED TO BE HIS FRIENDS! BUT, SO HELP ME GOD, I DO SOLEMNLY DECLARE, THAT I BELIEVE HIM TO HAVE BEEN THE VICTIM OF THEIR HOLLOW HYPOCRISY, AS I HAVE BEEN THE OBJECT OF THEIR INFAMOUS AND VILE SLANDERS! I TAUGHT MY HEART TO CAST AWAY ALL UNFRIENDLINESS TO HIS MEMORY; AND NOW THERE IS A FULL, DEEP OBLIVION TO ALL THAT HAS PAST, IN MY BREAST! IN RELIGIOUS SINCERITY, I SAY, PEACE, ETERNAL PEACE, TO THE BRAVE AND GALLANT PERRY! AND BEFORE MY ETERNAL

JUDGE, I DECLARE THAT THERE IS NO HAND, INSTINCT WITH LIFE, THAT IS MORE READY TO DECK HIS TOMB WITH LAURELS, THAN THIS SAME ONE, WHICH ONCE GRASPED HIS, WHEN CONGRATULATING HIM ON *OUR* [emphasis added] VICTORY![46]

Was Elliott sincere in his effusive eulogy to Perry, his most outstanding foe? Correspondence between them soon illuminated how ramshackle a supposedly amiable facade had been erected. Once the Perry-Elliott broil became known to the press and through it to the public, it was clarified by the four letters they exchanged in 1818, roughly a year before Perry's death.

The intensity of their hatred is unmistakable. Elliott led off on July 7, employing such choice epithets as calling a Perry missive "a masterly production of epistolary blackguardism," followed by "false and vulgar assertions," "low and ungentlemanly acts," "your most treacherous memory," and "I have the most horrid opinion of your general character." Elliott hurled the ultimate challenge—pistols at ten paces.[47]

Perry's response on August 3, 1818, was shorter and more restrained than Elliott's, but its tenor was much the same: "I have prepared the charges I am about to prefer against you, and . . . shall transmit them to the Secretary of the Navy, and request that a court-martial be instituted for your trial upon them." He vented his true opinion of Elliott, "Mean and despicable as you have proved yourself to be, I shall never cease to criminate myself from having deviated from the path of strict propriety, for the sake of screening you from public contempt and indignation."[48]

Two notes terminated their exchanges. Elliott to Perry, October 3, 1818: "Two months have elapsed since the date of your answer to my invitation to the field [of honor], I have visited the Navy Secretary who told me that he does not know of any transaction [a duel] between us. I am still under the impression that you are disposed to continue your old game of deception."[49]

Perry's retort, dated October 6, 1818, simply stated that on August 10 he had forwarded to the department "charges which I have preferred against you. It is not for me to account for their not having been submitted to the Secretary."[50]

Perry had no desire to face at ten paces a man he now despised so thoroughly. But for naval and military officers, if the public saw no adequate reasons for refusing private combat under the code duello, his esteem would be lowered if not lost. Perry's best option to avoid risking his life, while maintaining his "sacred honor," was to gamble that Elliott would be found guilty on any one of the court-martial's charges and specifications brought against him. If so, his enemy would have been shown to be neither an officer nor a gentleman, an individual so low that as lofty a figure as Perry need not dirty his hands with him.[51] Of course, Perry's diplomatic mission to and death in Venezuela in 1819 settled this interpersonal matter at once.

Thirty years after the engagement, Elliott was still refighting the Battle of Lake Erie. In the spring of 1843 he informed James Fenimore Cooper that "my own affair is now in the hands of [President Tyler] with whom I went over the whole ground, including the Erie affair. He asked me to explain the diagram of [the battle particularly], and [I] put my finger on the exact position which [American vessel] was ahead of *Lawrence* on her starboard beam . . . and he exclaimed with great warmth, I know that there was not a drop of coward's blood in your veins. . . . I suggested to him to lay the whole wrongs [?] before his Cabinet and if there was one of it who did not believe me an injured man, I would return to my plough."[52]

An acute article has been published by the president of the Great Lakes Historical Society and his aide, generally tracing chronologically the Perry--Elliott fallout from the Battle of Lake Erie almost to date. Two applicable quotations are from it: (1) Michael A. Palmer's "Perry was a good ship's captain, officer, and gentleman, but a second rate commander in chief; and Elliott was an average captain who has been judged too harshly by historians" and (2) "Elliott's *Biographical Notice*, supposedly written by newspaperman Russell Jarvis, which was probably written by Elliott himself." How true![53]

Only a little more than two months before Perry fell to yellow fever on August 23, 1819, he wrote to a relative by marriage regarding the current situation:

> [Commodore Stephen] Decatur is truly and sincerely a friend of mine. . . . He informs me Elliott was very industrious, when in Washington last winter, beseiging members of Congress, changing his lodgings frequently, and many other such arts—upon some he made impressions unfavorable to me—others had sense enough to discover his intrigues. . . . Decatur had a long conversation with the President [Monroe], who was, extremely desirous of [settling the seemingly certain approach of a Perry-Elliott duel] and asked me whether his mediation could possibly effect it. D. assured him, a reconciliation was altogether out of the question. The President had great objections to having the business brought before the Public, and it is probable the charges will sleep on the desk of the Sec' y. It is very certain, they understand E. now. I am told he was very much alarmed, at the prospect of a trial, complained that I had waited until all his witnesses were dead, boasts of having challenged me several times on his having won the battle & tells so many and contradictory stories that he has effectively established his reputation for falsehood.[54]

As noted by G. T. Altoff, "although his official career remained unblemished by Lake Erie, Elliott passed the remainder of his days attempting to justify his conduct in the Battle, as attested to by his machinations after the conflict, his request for a Court of Inquiry [1815], his 1835 'Biography' [quotation marks added], and numerous speeches over the years. Nevertheless, despite the number of his rejoinders and the lapse of time, Jesse Elliott was unable to erase the despairing cries of those bloodied men on the shattered decks of *Lawrence*: 'That brig will not help us!' 'Why does she hang back out of the battle?' 'Where is the *Niagara*?'"[55]

Leonard F. Guttridge and Jay D. Smith continue: "The main impression one gets from . . . Elliott's scandal studded career is that every uproar was precisely to his liking. Had he become the lawyer he started out to be, one might have heard no more about him . . . , but instead he entered the Navy for the rest of his life. He ill deserves the imputations of cowardice raised during his lifetime and by some historians since [with a single exception, see chapter 6]. But whatever his motives—and greed, revenge, ambition, and jealousy can be detected at one time or another—it is certain that he relished every controversy into which they pitch-forked him. Let other officers lust after glory and prize money, Jesse Elliott's predominant appetites fed on intrigue and controversy."[56]

Conceding the fact that Elliott's conduct featured some instances bizarre in the extreme, the question must be asked whether they indicate a mind so unbalanced as to be called insane. Samuel Eliot Morison is quite sure that such was the case: "Elliott was a very odd fish, even for a naval officer. His career is studded with quarrels, challenges, duels and courts-martial, and some of his letters and speeches suggest that he had a 'screw loose.'"[57]

This is a most serious allegation, but Morison's comment seems unique. Let me call attention to a thought-provoking article that I read in process and to which I made a small contribution: Lawrence J. Friedman and David Curtis Skaggs, "Jesse Duncan Elliott and the Battle of Lake Erie: The Issue of Mental Stability." The authors have delved into this matter in depth and conclude: "We were amazed to find nothing in our extensive examination of contemporary comments that questioned Elliott's mental soundness. . . . Given the exaggerated discourse of the period, one or two comments on his emotional instability might well have been made. But we found it remarkable that despite Elliott's disputatious career and many disparaging portrayals of him that we uncovered, not one accused him—even implicitly—of being psychologically unfit for naval duty. . . . This is not to say that we accept Elliott's testimony at face value. . . . But we do call into question the judgment of twentieth-century historians who characterize him as an imbalanced figure. Elliott's thoughts and actions commanded serious attention in his day. They were rarely if ever dismissed by nebulous speculation concerning his 'loose screw.'"[58]

Friedman and Skaggs say, "Naval historian David Long is among the many scholars who have questioned Elliott's mental competence and have demanded psycho-biographical evaluations." To this I must plead guilty, but point out that it was made some years before I decided to write a life of Elliott. And my suggestion was adopted that the best way to describe him is "that latter-day Iago."

The editor's comment: "No one would call Iago mentally unbalanced—jealous, devious, duplicitous, yes; mentally unbalanced, no. . . . Like Iago Elliott suffered from professional resentment . . . based upon a sense of injustice in a military rewards system that gave too much credit to one man and not enough to another. Like Iago, Elliott's primary purpose was to reduce one man's reputation [Perry's, for instance] in order to enhance his own. And like Iago, Elliott's scheming eventually did him in. Both Iago and Elliott were left with reputations not of mental instability, but as sordid plotters and architects of deceit."[59]

Christopher McKee, my longtime friend—although here we have to disagree—is the dean of those concentrating on the US Navy's original officer corps, has leveled an accusatory finger at a matter of surpassing interest to anyone trying to fathom aspects of Elliott's makeup. "That Commodore's name brings us to the controversial literature, 'praising, defending, or excoriating Elliott's role in the events of September 1813.' The reason to find such output "dreary to the point of unreadability is because all the tons of thousands of words written fail to get to the heart of the matter."[60]

McKee then launches into the usual early assumption that only psychohistorians possess the means essential for coping with this problem, a hypothesis to which we voice a strong exception: "What Elliott did or failed to do on 10 September 1813 are beyond the reach of customary historical sources studied with conventional historical tools. One fervently hopes that someday a highly skilled practitioner of the psycho-historian's craft will take on the task of mastering the extensive sources respecting Elliott and offer (at last) a convincing and consistent explanation of this fascinating, albeit inscrutable, figure."[61]

We cannot call ourselves true psychohistorians, particularly when some of its members veer toward Freudian analyses. But here let us vent a positive expectation that our almost decade-long probe into Elliott's naval career, character, personality, liabilities, and assets should well outweigh this so-called critical deficiency.

Five

On the Coastal Survey and Naval Fortifications Board

This segment has to include a variety of differing topics describing almost a decade of Elliott's life, and a biography of him must concentrate on, in order (1) his duties and experiences on the Naval Fortifications Board, (2) his connection with piracy in the Caribbean, (3) the travails of his friend Commodore James Barron, (4) the troubles of his enemy Commodore Isaac Hull, and (5) his own pursuit to regain active duty in the service.[1]

After a long post–Algerian War stretch of inactivity, Elliott was eager for new assignments from the secretary. Similar to most of his top-ranking colleagues he preferred a ship command, the larger the vessel the better. Next would be as a commandant of a navy yard or station with much opportunity for decision-making but under closer supervision of the department than the captain of a man-of-war. Perhaps the third would be as a member of a research team with other officers and/or civilians, often for scientific goals and endorsed by the public. The latter was the slot in which Elliott found himself when the Monroe administration named him to the board for "examining the entire coast of the United States, for the purpose of selecting points for permanent dock yards, for fortifications to protect the maritime frontier, and for lighting the coast of North Carolina."[2]

The board's genesis went back to Jefferson in 1807 who recommended and Congress enacted a law whereby "the President . . . shall be, and is hereby, authorized and requested to cause a survey of the coasts of the United States . . . together with such other matters as he shall deem proper for completing an accurate chart of every part of the coasts." Ferdinand Hassler, a Swiss-born "geodetist and scientist of outstanding reputation," was chosen as its head, but funds were not available to hire him before 1811 when he went off to Europe to collect the needed books and instruments. Stranded abroad by the War of

1812, he did not start his work until 1816, but his thorny personality and civilian status gave him time to do no more than "triangulate" New York Harbor.[3]

Hassler was dismissed (until reinstated in 1830), and military professionals served the board under the Navy Department, but during the next year, they went to the War Department under its secretary, John C. Calhoun of South Carolina.

Geodesy expert Weber described surveying operations during the 1820s as a time when "detached surveys" of army and navy operations were conducted, "but no general or connected survey of the coast was attempted during this period." Fellow authorities Joseph Wraight and Elliott B. Roberts have it that service personnel made "detached surveys of rivers and harbors," but "they were generally of mediocre quality, and no attempt was made to connect them into any system." Perhaps readers of the next few pages might agree with us that these evaluations are incomplete and partially incorrect in their conclusions.[4]

From its commencement into the late 1820s the actual direction of the Survey and Fortifications Board was under a Frenchman, General Simon Bernard, an erstwhile engineering officer high in Napoleon's army, but after the Battle of Waterloo, he applied successfully for work in America and was granted a general's title and salary. Before Bernard returned to France in 1831, rising to minister of war twice prior to his death in 1839, he was hailed for his scintillating scientific accomplishments in America not only for its defenses but also for "his extensive development of interior communications by roads and canals."[5]

Bernard presided over a mixture of service appointees, with Major Joseph G. Totten and others upholding military interests, while Commodore Lewis Warrington and Elliott represented maritime concerns. Warrington was almost at the top of the naval career ladder, and it was a distinct honor for Elliott to be his single associate, for he had only gained his captaincy on March 27, 1818. As will be noted below, Elliott's tasks for the board were pretty well completed by 1823, and he could glow with appreciation for his enthusiastic testimonial from the Frenchman December 3, 1823:

> Dear Captain,
> The pledge of national gratitude for your great naval achievements, has become, in my hands, a pledge of our mutual friendship. If your glorious deeds assign you to an elevated rank among American heroes whose courage and genius will be handed down to future generations, your generosity of soul assures you a distinguished place in the hearts of those who are honored with your friendship. . . . Continue to me, dear Captain, all your friendship, and accept all expressions of the high esteem of your most thankful friend.[6]

The labors of even the top-grade officers were anything but armchair operations. In surveying afloat, there were long periods of incessant repetition of the same chores, and employees were often buffeted by winds and waves while sweltering during the summer months or freezing in winters even in the South. Watches always had to be maintained to guard against the sudden approach of gales and other emergencies that sometimes could not be anticipated.

In the latter connection, according to Elliott, the second day of board duty was almost his last. En route in a small steamer amid choppy seas to meet Bernard he managed to fall overboard. A "gallant tar" saw him go and aided by a shipmate with the greatest difficulty cut loose a boat that filled as it went under. The two sailors, frantically bailing with their hats, reached Elliott just as he lost consciousness. Back on his vessel he "disgorged the water I had swallowed, and I do assure you that I have never placed my hands in a basin of water without thinking of that scene."[7]

The land-based surveyors faced considerably less dangerous situations, but their discomfort was heightened by the miserable roads they had to traverse and the substandard food and accommodations they had to use. Elliott came up with one of his infrequent flashes of humor when he described an inn at Tarboro, North Carolina, inland from Albamarle Sound: "I could have slept upon the wretched apology for a bed, had not the bugs which thronged the chamber greeted me as an intruder. While suffering from their visits of ejectment, I determined to make an impression that would cause my hostess to see a little better to her sleeping concerns in future, and accordingly I seized one of my pistols and fired it. The report brought all hands, who in the greatest terror, inquired what was the matter! I answered very calmly, 'Oh, nothing—only shooting bedbugs!' My landlady could not disguise her mortification, and looked daggers and furies."[8]

The Calhoun papers cannot be expected to provide any such light touch as the above. Throughout, Elliott was mentioned solely as a member signatory in group reports of areas surveyed and fortifications recommended, so there is nothing about Elliott's contributions to the board's accomplishments. All of these citations refer to precise locations throughout the nation, of no need in this narration, with one anomaly: the board's interim report in 1821 to prove that governmental appropriations for it had been well spent. See below for amplification.[9]

To digress from the report momentarily: the geodetic authorities Weber and Wraight and Roberts cannot be criticized for excluding any remarks about defense for that was beyond their purlieus of expertise. But when all three authors call the surveying work of Bernard's board "generally of mediocre quality, and no attempt was made to connect them into any system," their statement is simply untrue.[10] Surely they should have known that for some years Calhoun and Bernard had been the basic contributors to the mapping and charting of the country's shores. But it is significant that neither book mentions them in their texts or indexes—mysterious omissions indeed.

The interim report of the board's first three years was signed only by Bernard, Totten, and Elliott (Warrington was otherwise employed). It was most succinct about surveying, but its breadth strongly implied that its people must have been almost perpetually at work: the commission charged with reconnoitering the frontiers of the United States has completed the three most important sections of the maritime boundaries, namely "the coast of the Gulf of Mexico from the Rio Grande to North Carolina, the segment between Cape Hatteras and Cape Cod," and the coast between Cape Cod and the Maine boundary with Canada. "The only section which remains to be examined . . . is South Carolina and Georgia." A distinctive accentuation was devoted to the brief stretch "between Cape Hatteras and Cape Fear," for centuries the "graveyard" for ships.[11] Moreover, this brought Elliott into the center of affairs, if his memory is to be trusted.

In Jarvis's so-called biography of him, Elliott "recommended that light--ships or vessels [be] constructed for the purpose of resisting gales, and provided with lights [which] should be placed upon the extremities of Cape Hatteras, Cape Look Out, and Cape Fear," the focal points for the worst storms howling out of the Atlantic. In a sad example of braggadocio, the captain maintained that he performed "an act of intrepidity and self devotion that would have conferred honor" to anyone "who set his life at nought in seeking the good of mankind." Learning that because of the "supposed danger of locating a light-ship, and occupying it during a gale, no person could be found" to do it; "CAPTAIN ELLIOTT VOLUNTEERED TO LOCATE ONE." He boarded the revenue cutter *Alert* under one "Captain Cahoon," and she towed the light-ship to Cape Hatteras where he "remained on board her" during "three gales of wind!!" Thus he demonstrated "the practicality of occupying . . . light-ships."[12]

In his *Speech, Appendix*, he elaborated upon this occurrence, ending with a portrayal of Captain Jesse Duncan Elliott, USN, as an amateur medical diagnostician and practitioner. He and the unfortunate Cahoon had ridden out the first of three storms: "The violence of the gales . . . came near deluging the vessel[,] . . . but we battled the storm until it abated." Later Elliott left Cahoon alone in the light-ship during a tempest and, when the wind had died, went out to get him. He found that "he, like all other timid men, had taken excessively to liquor to brace his nerves for the trial; so much so indeed that he had become the subject of disease [constipation]. . . . I thought the only means of cure would be evacuation [an enema], and being without any other means, I order[ed] a large sow killed, converting her bladder into a glister pipe, and had the patient relieved before the meat of the slaughtered animal was cold." My dictionary has no listing for "glister pipe," but with a bit of repellent imagination, one may visualize how it was used.[13]

To return to the board's interim report of 1821, it treated its second responsibility of the nation's defense far more amply than the first, although surveying pops up frequently but always in relation to preparations to foil foreign invasions and unnecessary in this context. Elliott's name appears merely as the document's cosigner, but clearly, he had much to do with its content.

The report made six recommendations to answer the paramount question of where to locate forts:

> 1. To close important harbors to an enemy, and secure them for the Navy of the country. 2. To deprive an enemy of strong positions, where, protected by his naval superiority, he might fix permanent quarters in our territory, maintain himself during the war, and keep the whole frontier in perpetual alarm. 3. To cover the great cities against attack. 4. To prevent . . . the great avenues of interior navigation from being blockaded by a naval force, at their entrance to the ocean. 5. To cover the coastwise and interior navigation, and give to our Navy the means necessary for protecting this navigation. 6. To cover the great naval establishments.[14]

The report's next six pages analyzed the details of specific locations throughout the country and may be ignored here. But remembering the ease with which the British had penetrated Chesapeake Bay only seven years before, Philadelphia was named the linchpin of US defensive positions in this area, anticipating the methods used and the directions from which an enemy might attack. Seven strong naval bases, three to the south and three to the north of Philadelphia were judged mandatory: New Orleans, Norfolk, Baltimore, New York, Narragansett Bay, and Boston. Priorities for their construction were set: (1) those to prevent a foe from founding permanent or even temporary establishment on American soil in wartime, (2) to defend our "great naval arsenals," (3) "to protect our chief commercial cities."[15] Particulars were itemized to a ludicrous extent: "That the total expense of completely fortifying the maritime frontier will amount to $17,795,005; and the troops necessary to guard our fortifications, in peace, to 4,690 men, at most, and 37,962 men in time of war."[16]

The report arrived at an effective conclusion: "If to our system of permanent fortifications and naval establishments we connect a system of interior communications by land and water, adapted both to the defense and to the commercial interests of the country, if to these we add a well-constituted regular Army, and perfect the organization of our militia, the Union will be not only completely secure in its territory, but preserve its national institutions from those violent shocks and revolutions which, in every age and in every nation, have been too often incident to a state of war."[17]

Even though Elliott was under the War Department's direction, he was obliged to keep the Navy Department informed about his activities. Some of his letters to the secretary from 1818 into the early 1820s repeat what has been covered already in the Calhoun papers. Others, however, provide evidence of Elliott's interest in most phases of his profession. He was ever cost conscious, estimating that he and his fellow board members had cut in half the normal expenses paid by his government for such surveying duties and boasted that he had been able to purchase for the Treasury Department a seventy-ton revenue cutter for an unexpectedly low price of $500.[18] On the other hand, he thought that the midshipmen attached to the board should get an additional $1.50 a day to equal the pay of their army equivalents.[19]

Elliott's duties while on the board featured periods of arduous but by no means continuous exertions, granting him time to apply to other interests. Astute readers should recall from the previous chapter that his major preoccupation had been his quarrel with Perry over the Battle of Lake Erie, which had reached such a point that pistols to the death may have been averted only by Perry's yellow fever victimization in 1819. Monroe had sent Perry to stem Venezuelan privateers in the West Indies, and this forms a convenient link to another of Elliott's concerns—piracy in the Gulf of Mexico and the Caribbean.

The American maritime community was horrified about what was happening to the nation's trade in these southern waters. By 1815 the Spanish--American colonies had risen against Madrid's restraints, and Mexico, Colombia, and Venezuela declared their independence. Spain not only released its navy against rebel activities at sea but started issuing "Letters of Marque and Reprisal" to almost anyone requesting them.[20]

Mexico, Colombia, and Venezuela promptly followed suit, infesting tropical seas. Most privateers found it simpler and more lucrative to drop any pretenses by becoming de facto pirates, preying upon the commerce of all flags, particularly off Spanish Cuba and Puerto Rico. Elliott complained to the department that Spanish authorities in both colonies refused to adopt any effective measures against the corsairs as they, too, shared in their profits. He wondered whether the outbreak was sponsored secretly by the British to ruin the merchant marine of their major trading rival; not so, for the Royal Navy took the lead in buccaneer hunting.[21]

At the height of these illegalities a Philadelphian asserted that he had kept a meticulous account of piratical assaults in the West Indies from 1815 to

1822 and that they numbered precisely "3,002."[22] This has to be an exaggeration, but undoubtedly, they ran into the many hundreds. Elliott backed up the barbarities of these attacks in a handwritten five-page letter signed by one John (the surname is illegible). It told of no less than eight separate atrocities committed in a mere two months just off the Cuban coast. Number eight is typical of the others: "[Illegible] Jones, master of the brig Leander of New York in from Tenerife [Canary Islands] on 1st Jany [1822] was boarded and robb'd by a piratical Boat with 12 men about 9 miles eastward of Morro Castle [Havana]. Captain and crew badly treated, the Captain's Lady being on board and was taken by the pirates into the stateroom and not only robb'd of all her ornaments and everything but otherwise shamefully and unfeelingly treated."[23]

Washington, DC, did not begin responding effectively to these depredations until March 1822 when Commodore James Biddle took his West India Squadron south. He had some successes, but his warships were too deep drafted to use just offshore, permitting their quarry to vanish inland. The continuation of the Spanish governors of Cuba and Puerto Rico to refuse to Americans the essential permission to chase corsairs into their territories was vital, and Biddle resigned his command in June. Elliott reentered the story when earlier that year he had heard that Biddle was ill and asked the secretary to replace him as commodore in the frigate *Macedonian* but was rejected.[24]

The flamboyant David Porter soon took over, substituting for his heavy frigates smaller craft able to skim over the water almost to the beaches' edges, picking off pirate aggressors coming out of Cuba. But like Biddle, he could not send his men inland. In August 1823 the dreaded "yellow jack" struck. Of the twenty-five US naval officers stricken, Porter was one of the two who survived, although nearing death and then had barely recovered when he caught yellow fever again in February 1824.[25]

Porter returned to Washington, DC, without permission, and this started a series of wrangles with Secretary of the Navy Samuel L. Southard who was supported strongly by Presidents Monroe and Adams, which culminated that November. Although he had not, the commodore claimed that he had been in active pursuit of corsairs when he led his men ashore at Fajardo ("Foxardo"), Puerto Rico. He had erupted into a colony that had been ruled by Spain for some three hundred years. For this excessive behavior in August 1825 Porter was found guilty of "Disobedience of Orders," and "Insubordinate Conduct" toward Adams and Southard, after which he resigned from the navy.[26]

Elliott had sat as one of Porter's judges and voted guilty. As an ardent supporter of Commodore James Barron in the latter's court-martial, almost surely he would have recalled that Porter had been the most aggressive in questioning the accused as to whether he had discouraged *Chesapeake*'s men from a willingness to resist *Leopard*.[27] Lewis Warrington, Elliott's naval companion on Bernard's board, was Porter's successor, and he hammered so relentlessly at corsair ships and shore installations that their activities were sharply curtailed. Two factors available to him but denied his predecessors were indispensable to his accomplishments: landing privileges and better British cooperation. Driven from the sea, the pirates were compelled to carry on forays inside their own Spanish colonies, which forced the local administrations to fall upon them, encouraging Cuban and Puerto Rican governors to grant to the Americans the right to chase them into the bush wherever they pleased. Moreover, efficient joint operations of the US and Royal Navies solidified so that their combined sweeps became overwhelming. By the end of 1825 commerce had been freed to sail in peace through tropical waters although minor depredations recurred but most infrequently. [28]

Long before this outcome, Elliott had immersed himself into other matters that engrossed him: the continuing travails of Barron in the aftermath of *Chesapeake-Leopard* in 1807–8, the quarrel between Commodore John Shaw and Captain Isaac Hull over the situation at the Boston Navy Yard, and his own lively but lengthy quest for a ship command.

Barron, after his court-martial conviction and sentence, had had to endure five years of bleak poverty and loneliness in Europe. Restored to half pay in 1813, he asked the department for active reinstatement, but his letter was never even acknowledged. When he finally came home in 1818 he learned that long since the secretary had read two allegations much to his discredit concerning a mercantile voyage to Penambuco, Brazil, in 1809. One had it that Barron had made anti-Jefferson remarks to the British consul there, confirmed by a US Navy officer on leave and an American businessman. But by 1818, when Barron disavowed vehemently the charge, all three attestants were dead. The other accused him of sailing on a merchant marine cruise under a British license, easily proven false by the US consul in Copenhagen, who swore that Barron had never left Denmark during that period. That is why Smith Thompson had greeted Barron so icily on his appearance in Washington, DC. Finally, and most damaging, the secretary asked him why he had not left Europe once his suspension was over.[29]

Enter Elliott in 1821 when Barron, deciding that only a favorable judgment by his peers could clear his name sufficiently for service reemployment, requested and received permission to have a court of inquiry held.[30] Barron persuaded Caesar Augustus Rodney, Delaware's most eminent elder statesman, to act as his counsel. Elliott, who much admired Rodney, sprang into action, enlisting what support for the defense that he could muster. He gave

Rodney the names of several citizens of the Norfolk area, friendly to Barron, whose testimony might assist, and that of an anonymous eyewitness at Pernambuco who could refute the charges of the accused's statements against Jefferson there.[31] Did Elliott's spurt of activity come up with anything concrete in Barron's behalf at his court of inquiry? It could not. A thorough search of the court's proceedings revealed that none of those mentioned above, including Elliott, were called to testify nor were they listed "in any of the documents." Rodney must have concluded sensibly that since they had only hearsay to offer such would be ruled inadmissible.[32]

By the time the judges had issued their verdict on July 15, they had dismissed the allegation that Barron had sailed under British license during the war and restricted themselves to the other two charges. "The Court is of the opinion that the conversation alleged to have taken place between Captain James Barron and Mr. Lyon, the British consul at Pernambuco, in the year 1809, has not been proven." In regard to Barron's long delay in returning after the war, "the Court is of opinion that the evidence of his inability to return sooner than he actually did is not satisfactory; and . . . that . . . his absence from the United States without the permission of his government was contrary to his duty as an officer of the Navy." So Barron's vindication was only partial and he remained under a cloud.[33]

To look ahead, in 1822 the government finally printed for public consumption the full testimonies and verdicts in 1808 and 1821 that Barron had had to endure. Opinion about him gradually shifted to a favorable view, but for three more years, he was kept on half pay. In 1824 President Monroe restored him to active duty, and sixteen years after his *Chesapeake-Leopard* suspension, he was made commandant of the Philadelphia Navy Yard. Contrary to many erroneous accounts that he was never again offered a sea command, in 1828 he was assigned to *Guerriere* as commodore of the Pacific Squadron but rejected the assignment for personal reasons. He had another billeting at the Philadelphia yard, and when he died in 1851, he had been the senior officer of the US Navy since 1838.[34]

During these months Elliott had kept an eye on developments in Boston where Hull, commandant of the navy yard there, was in trouble. Having never commanded more than one warship at one time, he could not use the courtesy title of "commodore" and urged the department to abolish that imprecise term, thereby infuriating those who bore it, primarily William Bainbridge, James Biddle, and especially John Shaw. The latter charged Hull with complicity in the peculation of a clerk and for overcharging outrageously the passengers in *Constitution* for cross–English Channel trips in 1811 and 1812. Hull had him court-martialed and convicted of "Unofficerlike conduct" after Shaw's evidence was shown to be secondhand and therefore useless.[35]

Why Elliott moved against Hull is hard to say, other than he so hated Navy Commissioner Porter, Hull's ardent supporter, who had made obvious to all his abhorrence of Elliott's behavior during the Barron-Decatur duel in 1820 (for that story, see chapter 6). At any rate, he warmly embraced Shaw's cause. His sentiments were summarized in a letter about him: "I had already observed by the papers that Capt. Hull had made his appearance before a Board of Inquiry. The reason assessed for appointing two of the conspirators [?] on it [was] produced from a belief it was proper he should have a Court of Inquiry unprejudiced and of course such as would make him as smooth as silk. . . . Has it not appeared that [Secretary of the Navy] Thompson should have acted with so much inconsistency in charging you [and two others]?. . . . We are intimately anxious to get your trial, let us have it as early a moment as possible . . . and I am inclined to think it will."[36]

After Shaw's six-month suspension for insulting Hull was over, Elliott, with consummate malevolence by implication, suggested that he entice Hull into a duel and kill him. "Your case should be another Barron's[!]."[37] By this juncture Elliott's responsibilities to Bernard's board had become moribund, and boredom set in. He was still stationed at the Norfolk yard, close enough to his house in Carlisle, Pennsylvania, for frequent visits with his family. Nevertheless, his overweening ambition was to cruise again, although his prospects for that were slim. The postwar stalemate in the navy meant that most chances for quick promotion and riches had vanished after 1815; far more officers were qualified for active duty than openings for them existed. Those furloughed or idle at home considered themselves unemployed, and Elliott was among them. He began peppering the department for a blue water command. The sight of his signature along with those of his competitors for jobs inundated the secretary and must have made him wince for he could accommodate so few. Yet from early 1820 until mid-1824 Elliott applied occasional but intense pressure to gain that end.

In his first request to his higher officials he complained unsuccessfully that his participation in the Algerian War had made it impossible "for an officer of my rank to go on the frigate *Guerriere*," but "I would be pleased in an appointment to that ship."[38] Two years later he lowered his sights to suggest taking over the smaller frigate *Cyane* but to no avail. Undaunted, he was back within a few days to say that he would accept the little frigate *John Adams*, with the same unhappy result.[39] In a letter already mentioned in another context, Elliott aspired to command the flagship *Macedonian* in the West Indies only to discover that Biddle had recovered from his illness and remained in charge. Temporarily discouraged, a bit later he conceded that he would welcome any frigate at all.[40]

Turning at once to a different gambit—an exertion of political pull—he begged Rodney, his ally for Barron in 1821, to come to Washington, DC, and assemble "what friends I had and have" to induce Secretary Southard to give him *Macedonia*; nothing transpired.[41] Reverting to his frontal attack on the department, he wrote, "I have been unemployed since 1817 [and] you will readily excuse the liberty I have taken in presenting my claim for the frigate *Congress*"—another misfire.[42] By late that summer this hope had been dashed, so Elliott darted off on another tangent; he would "have no objection to take over and hold" the Philadelphia Navy Yard as commandant.[43] Rebuffed once more, he focused in vain upon a much less desirable post: "I offer myself to command the Charleston, S.C. [Naval] Station" until a frigate became available at the Philadelphia yard.[44]

Elliott was now desperate enough to fall back on political patronage from Thomas Newton, and once more, Rodney. Newton, for over thirty years the representative of the Norfolk congressional district, had been his confidant and backer and pops up now and then in Elliott's correspondence. Replying to an appeal for aid, Newton sent the secretary a glowing testimonial about Elliott's career and caliber: "He is intelligent, active, enterprising and . . . in management skillful and steady. . . . I recommend Captain Elliott because, I am confident, he will fill the station with ability and of great advantage to the Service. . . . His zeal and patriotism, give him a fair and just [right] to the notice and patronage of his Country."[45]

Late in 1823 the captain was galvanized by the tidings that Rodney would be dispatched as US minister to Argentina and soon sail for his new post. Calling upon their warm personal relationship, he declared that he would have "much pleasure of conveying you to South America. I should like to have a command in the *Fleet*[,] . . . and if that should be impossible, I would then presume to join with my other friends in getting something [off Cuba]." When he discovered that Biddle had been awarded that plum, he must have been plunged into despair.[46]

This was the last of Elliott's beseechments to go to sea, probably because he had learned through scuttlebutt that in the near future he would be offered the frigate *Cyane* and a prestigious appointment to command the Brazil Squadron. There, from 1825 to 1827, Elliott's undeniable administrative and diplomatic talents would have room to flourish.

Six

The Fatal Duel between Commodores James Barron and Stephen Decatur

All of his adult life Elliott was a compulsive writer of holograph letters, a host of others that appeared in print, and incessant published autobiographical commentaries. These covered in detail practically everything about his naval and public, if not his personal, life. But there is one singular departure from this characteristic, namely, his remarkable reticence concerning his participation in the duel in which Stephen Decatur was mortally wounded by James Barron's single shot during March 1820. Apart from Elliott's strangely laggard behavior at the Battle of Lake Erie, this is one of the authenticated instances of his cowardice, certainly moral and possibly physical.

Regarding the Battle of Lake Erie, all that is needed here is to recall that at the height of the melee the cry often went up from the ravaged deck of *Lawrence*, "Where is the *Niagara*?" Intimations that circulated slowly at first but then picked up momentum alleged that Elliott's conduct had been motivated by fear for his own safety or, with greater malignancy, that he had kept away in hopes that Perry would be killed or gravely wounded. This would ensure that Elliott would win enduring fame as the savior of the Northwest and— as his superior would—garner all the outpourings of a grateful nation. Elliott passed the remainder of his days in the loudest denials of these charges, and this text is sprinkled with his own citations that bravery was ever one of his most conspicuous traits and usually such was the case.

The inescapable proof of Elliott's cowardice is, however, that as soon as the duelists had toppled over at Bladensburg, Elliott panicked and fled in the carriage that had brought him and Barron to the scene, leaving his principal soaking in blood on the damp grass during a winter morning. He did not return until bystander David Porter had galloped after them, physically forcing

Elliott, not once but twice, to go back to convey the stricken Barron to Washington, DC.[1]

How could Elliott justify his acting the consummate poltroon? He did so by disregarding it, as confirmed by three points. First, in his many scores of personal and official letters, precisely one referred to the Barron-Decatur duel. On October 27, 1821, he told Caesar Augustus Rodney, Delaware's most eminent elder citizen that Porter did not regret Decatur's death, and that is totally incorrect; while differing occasionally, the two had been long on the most intimate terms, and remained so.[2] Second, in Elliott's *Speech, Appendix, Addenda*, which summarized his entire life, the duel is not mentioned. Third, in what is supposed to be his biography fewer than two full pages are applicable. Although calling Decatur's fate "lamentable," the rest of this source pertains to Elliott as Barron's champion during and after the *Chesapeake--Leopard* encounter in 1807–8 and through Barron's 1821 reinstatement in the navy. Elliott even had the gall to state toward the end that he had "never fled from an enemy nor *abandoned* a *friend* [emphasis added]." He augments further his informed reader's indignation by arguing that because of his intrepid defense of Barron, "a blow has been aimed at his character by the anonymous publication of documents." (It was well known that they had been published by Matthew Calbraith Perry, Oliver Hazard's younger brother.) He concluded that "had Commodore Decatur lived, they would not have seen the light of day."[3] Absurd! By the time that Perry left for his terminal voyage to Venezuela, plans had been finalized for his exchanging fire with Elliott at the Bladensburg, Maryland, "field of honor."

On the night of March 8, 1820, a visitor was rowed out from the lower Chesapeake Bay to where the seventy-four gun *Columbus*, a ship of the line, was swinging quietly at anchor. Elliott clambered aboard and was soon conversing with Commodore William Bainbridge, her commander. Their business was potentially deadly, for they were meeting to draw up the terms of a duel between Commodores Barron and Decatur. This would be the culmination of a sequence that had started on June 22, 1807, when Barron's frigate *Chesapeake* had been mauled savagely by HMS frigate *Leopard*. The humiliated Barron was eventually tried and convicted by a court-martial on the charge of "neglecting, on the probability of an engagement, to clear the ship for action."[4] Captains Bainbridge and Decatur had served as judges of the accused, while Midshipman Elliott had testified for the defense. These three would be implicated; one way or another in the consequences of the affair until Barron killed Decatur thirteen years later. (For Barron's punishment, see chapter 1.)

Apparently Elliott's loathing for Decatur was based upon his "sympathy for Barron's savage treatment by his court-martial and consternation at Decatur's subsequent public debasement of Barron's reputation."[5] Another contributor to Elliott's animus may have been that Decatur was a member of the Board of Navy Commissioners, which had thwarted the aspirations of Barron as well as his own. Decatur had sent his anti-Elliott evidence to the Navy Department, and in 1819, its chief clerk had passed it along to President Monroe. Secretary Smith Thompson was out of town for some time and could claim truthfully that he had never examined these papers. According to naval historian William M. P. Dunne referring to Alexander Slidell Mackenzie's work, *Life of Commodore Oliver Hazard Perry: A Commodore in the United States* "Decatur had a long conversation with the President" who had "great objections to having the business brought before the public; and it is probable the charges will sleep on the desk of the secretary."[6] That is exactly what happened when Monroe pigeonholed them; preferring to bury such evidence of intraservice hostility, as so many other well-publicized instances had been giving affront to the people since 1815.[7]

Perry caught yellow fever in Venezuela and died on August 23, 1819, thereby robbing Elliott of a chance to kill him. But the latter promptly began pipelining some of his endless pool of malice toward Decatur. He proceeded to use Barron as his instrument of retaliation, although Decatur himself would provide thorough, if unwitting, cooperation in bringing about his own demise.

Barron's association with Decatur had commenced in 1798 when both had served in the forty-four-gun *United States* and other warships, and their relations were most cordial, with the younger often commenting about his appreciation of the elder' s benign counsel, especially when Barron had talked him out of two hasty and ill-considered decisions to resign his commission. In 1806, however, everything changed when Barron made an innocent, if thoughtless, remark about Decatur's romantic attachments to which the latter took a quick and lasting exception.[8]

From that moment Barron could only see that he had created an unrelenting enemy. Decatur had condemned publicly *Chesapeake*'s unreadiness in 1807, tried unsuccessfully to be excused from Barron's court-martial as biased against the accused, and voted for his conviction. Once the exile had returned from Europe in 1818, his sparks were fanned into flames by Elliott, who passed along the information that Decatur was not only opposing Barron's reinstatement but advocating that he be dropped from the navy altogether. Any question about Elliott's central casting in the coming tragedy was provided by Barron himself. Without mentioning any name, there can be no doubt as to whom he meant when he wrote years later: "I consulted a friend in whom I had entire confidence, and from whom I learned much which had been circulated to my prejudice."[9]

Barron was thus impelled to write Decatur during the spring of 1819: "Sir, I have been informed that you have said that you could insult me with impunity, or words to that effect. If you have said so, you will no doubt avow it, and I shall expect to hear from you."[10]

Decatur's reply, less than a week later, should have terminated the entire affair: "Whatever I may have thought, or said, in the frequent and free conversations I have had respecting you and your conduct, I feel a thorough conviction that I could never have been guilty of so much egotism as to say that I could insult you (or any other man) with impunity."[11] Barron clearly thought this was apology enough. He responded: "Your declaration, if I understand it correctly, relieves my mind that you had so degraded my character, as I had been induced to allege."[12]

Tragically, Decatur yielded to some kind of an impulse to keep the surface roiled. His next letter would have been hard to ignore by anyone laboring already under a sense of persecution: "I meant no more than to disclaim specific and particular expression to which your inquiry was directed, to wit: That I said that I could insult you with impunity. As to the motives of . . . your informants . . . [they are] a matter of complete indifference to me, as is also your motives in making such an inquiry upon such information."[13] In Decatur's behalf, it should be accentuated that he was convinced wholeheartedly that Barron, especially by his prolonged absence during his country's war even after his suspension was over in 1818, had disqualified himself from retaining a navy commission.

Four months then elapsed without further contact, and Decatur probably imagined that he had put to flight a craven. But during this interim Barron had been ill, and his convalescence was surely enlivened by Elliott's further sowing seeds of animus. An undated and unsigned letter among Decatur's papers has a blank space for the name. It reads: "That [blank] is the sole instigator of the renewal of the correspondence, and will prevent any sort of adjustment if he can do so" and was printed in Mackenzie's Decatur biography, published in 1846, carrying the explanation that the note contains no "odium to any living person."[14] Significantly, Elliott had died the year before. Mrs. Susan Decatur was, as always, forthright in expressing her opinions. Writing in a private letter in 1821, she stated that she wished to expose "to the world the real character of Captain Elliott as some punishment for the base and assassin-like part that he acted toward my beloved husband, in artfully inciting Commodore Barron to the measures he pursued, in urging him on under the assurance that we would have the affair amicably settled."[15]

Not until the following October did Barron pick up his pen, but then, he used it with so much sulfurous resentment that a contest with Decatur became practically a certainty, unless Decatur should express openly regret for charges that he had been making for over a decade: "Scarcely had I set foot on my native soil, ere I learnt that the same malignant spirit which had before influenced you to ruin my reputation was still at work, and you were ungenerously traducing my character whenever an occasion occurred which suited your views. . . . I am also informed that you have tauntingly and boastingly observed, that you would cheerfully meet me in the field and hoped that I would act like a man."[16]

Three interminable letters, two from Decatur sandwiching one from Barron, of five, nine, and three printed pages respectively, passed between them from late October to December. It is profitless to replow their sterile terrain, marked by Barron's glowering sense of injury that neared paranoia and Decatur's sneering contempt that kept it aflame. It should be enough to say that charges and countercharges flew back and forth about their early association, Barron's surrender of *Chesapeake*, his alleged unpatriotic remarks in Brazil, his sailing under a wartime British permit, and his failure to come home before 1818.[17] Yet for some reason, probably pride, Barron never made it clear to his opponent that poverty alone had been responsible for his long absence abroad—at least until he did that while both were lying prone in Bladensburg. In earlier exchanges they had made pertinent comments about dueling. Decatur said: "I do not think that fighting duels, under any circumstances, can raise the reputation of any man[,] . . . but, in my opinion, the man who makes arms his profession, is not at liberty to decline an invitation from any person, who is not so far degraded, as to be beneath his notice. Having incautiously said that I would meet you, I will not now consider this to be the case, although many think so, and if I had not pledged myself, I might reconsider the case."[18]

If Decatur had said nothing more, that gratuitous observation in his last sentence, according to contemporary mores, would have compelled Barron to challenge, but instead, Barron addressed the same issue. He also considered dueling "a barbarous practice that ought to be exploded from civilized society; but, sir, there may be cases of such extraordinary and aggravated insult and injury, received by an individual, as to render an appeal to arms, on his part, absolutely necessary; mine I conceive to be a case of that description."[19] During January they decided to resort to that activity they deemed so savage, so useless, and so essential. Barron, with an eager Elliott delighted to play his second, issued and Decatur accepted an invitation to the field. The latter's choice of his second would have been inconceivable only a few months before—William Bainbridge.

The most enigmatic question for a Bainbridge biographer to answer is: did he merely swim along in an irreversible current set in motion by Elliott, or did he actively plot with that latter-day Iago to manipulate Barron into killing Decatur? There is evidence both ways, although a conclusion tends to arrive at a verdict of guilty rather than innocent.

To support the thesis that Bainbridge was no more than a current rider, prior to 1815 his relations with Decatur could not have been more amiable. Bainbridge had a most sizable debt of gratitude to repay, and he could never have forgotten it. Midshipman Joseph Bainbridge, William's younger brother, and Decatur were shipmates when they stopped at Malta in 1803. Ashore, Joseph was first insulted and then jostled by James Cochran, a British civilian, although he has been incorrectly described as the "private secretary of Sir Alexander Ball, British governor of that island."[20] The American knocked him to the floor. Cochran, called in some unauthenticated accounts "a sure shot at ten paces, challenged and Decatur acted as Joseph's second." Aware that his principal was unversed in small arms, Decatur insisted that the distance be set at a murderous four paces—twelve feet! Unbelievably, both missed on the first exchange, Joseph's shot piercing the Briton's hat. Decatur then offered the sensible advice, "Aim lower, if you wish to live." On the second fire Cochran was killed instantly by a bullet through his forehead.[21] Perhaps partly in gratitude for the above, and partly by the recollection that Decatur had sat on the court of inquiry that cleared him of blame for *Philadelphia*'s loss, Bainbridge's pre-1815 letters have frequent comments such as "the gallant Decatur" or similar descriptions. As Susan Decatur emphasized, Bainbridge had "frequently been our guest for weeks at a time! and declaring that he loved my husband as much as he did his own wife and children."[22]

To the contrary, the theory of Bainbridge as an active plotter against his colleague is backed by the fact that he had hated Decatur from 1815 until at least late in 1819 and with ample cause. Hardly was the conflict with Great Britain over than Congress declared war against Algiers (with Tunis and Tripoli possibly to be added later) for continued depredations against American commerce and for unneutral, pro-British activities during the War of 1812. Here was Bainbridge's golden opportunity to repay these Barbary powers for earlier humiliations that they had heaped on him. In 1801 the dey of Algiers had compelled him to pull down the American flag and run up the Algerian flag on the thirty-two-gun ship *George Washington* in order to carry a tributary mission, complete with gifts (including an entire menagerie) to the Turkish sultan in Constantinople. Worst of all, Bainbridge had stranded the thirty-six-gun *Philadelphia* in Tripoli Harbor during 1803 and been forced to endure nineteen months of captivity at the hands of the bashaw Yusuf Karamanli.

In 1815 Bainbridge commanded the seventy-four-gun *Independence*, America's first ship of the line, and officially requested permission to lead a squadron to write finis to the Barbary menace once and for all. He could anticipate that his previous embarrassments in North Africa, his seniority, and his brilliant victory in the forty-four-gun *Constitution* over the forty-four-gun *Java* off Brazil late in 1812 would ensure the granting of his request. But he failed to foresee how Decatur, with the utmost selfishness, would elbow him aside and seize for himself the distinction of ending the Barbary wars for the United States.

Decatur had long been at the naval pinnacle of national acclaim, both officially and publicly. He could not have been more attractive personally—handsome, affable, intelligent, and merciful, beloved by his sailors above all other officers for he had an ability to enforce discipline with little resort to the lash. Professionally, he had demonstrated sterling courage in hand-to-hand gunboat strife off Tripoli, daring skill in incinerating *Philadelphia* in front of the bashaw's castle, and calculated efficiency in overwhelming and bringing in as a prize the thirty-eight-gun HMS *Macedonian* in 1812.

But then his career soured. During 1813 his squadron had been trapped by the enemy in Long Island Sound, and the frigates *United States* and erstwhile *Macedonian* had to be laid up in New London for the duration of the war. Decatur's crowning blow happened during January 13–15, 1815, when he had surrendered the forty-four-gun frigate *President* to a superior British force because some thought that his decision to give up had been premature. On his return home he resolved that he must clear his name of this taint. He wrote an anonymous naval colleague that "I have lost a noble ship, but I hope it will be considered that there has been no loss of honor." He reread that sentence and crossed out "I hope it will be considered" to substitute "I shall satisfy the world."[23]

He met with author Washington Irving, who urged him not to "lose the opportunity of emerging from the cloud which has come over his celebrity by the loss of the *President*; that here was a chance for a brilliant dash; and that he should precede Bainbridge, who was fitting out at Boston, and . . . 'whip the cream off the enterprise.'"[24]

Secretary of the Navy Crowninshield was even more helpful in enabling Decatur to bring about Bainbridge's abasement. Mary Crowninshield wrote her husband during mid-March 1815 that she hoped that he would not give the Mediterranean assignment to Bainbridge, "as some think Decatur is the most fit for it—this is what I pick up here and there."[25] For whatever reason, the secretary caved in completely, writing Decatur: "In short, my dear sir, your wishes are to be consulted; any service or station that is at the disposal of this department, rely on it, you may command."[26] In response to Decatur's request for the Mediterranean, Crowninshield gave him the new forty-four-gun *Guerriere* as his flagship, command of another squadron to be outfitted in New York, and ordered him to depart "without delay."[27] The Navy Department then sped ships, supplies, and men to Decatur at the expense of Bainbridge and other commanders.

Rumors about the rapid buildup in New York must have reached Bainbridge in Boston, but clearly, he could not bring himself to believe that his double cross would be so total. Even as late as March 19, he could still refer in a private letter to "the noble conduct of the gallant Decatur."[28] But by the first week in April finally he began to comprehend what was being done to him, writing a close personal friend: "I do not think the Secretary has acted [well] toward me in keeping in utter *Ignorance*, as the *feelings* of an *Officer* justified."[29] When he received official confirmation that Decatur would precede him to North Africa, he charged that Decatur had been anything but "courteous" to him and that he had become "disgusted" with our *Premier*, and the "neglectful manner I have been treated."[30] It is easy to appreciate the consummate indignation with which Bainbridge must have received the news that Decatur had sailed on May 20. It was further exacerbating to his pride when he was ordered to follow with a second squadron to the Mediterranean, mourning that "I am totally indifferent to going out."[31] But, of course, he had no choice but compliance, sailing from Boston on July 2 and coming into Gibraltar on the thirty-first.

Suffering from an acute attack of measles, Bainbridge was further prostrated by the tidings there that Decatur had captured already two Algerian warships before dashing on the enemy's capital where he had slapped together a makeshift peace, dictated, as he complacently put it, "at the cannon's mouth." He next raced on to Tunis and Tripoli, forcing both countries to pay sizable damages. The US consul at Gibraltar perceptively noted the reason for "the haste in which he brought matters to a conclusion," commenting that Decatur would "*sacrifice* his *friend* to *aggrandize* his own fame [emphasis added]—had Bainbridge not been close at his heels, be assured that reasons for continuing the war would not have been found wanting."[32]

Meanwhile his aggrieved rival could only follow his instructions and show his fleet at all the Barbary capitals, complaining that: "Peace having been made prior to my arrival[,] . . . I have been deprived of the opportunity of either Fighting or Negotiating."[33] Bainbridge sped past Algiers, Tunis, and Tripoli before putting into Gibraltar on September 29. Both squadrons had assembled there with Decatur's flagship the only missing vessel. Just as Bainbridge was setting out for home on October 7, *Guerriere* swung into the harbor, sailing past the cheering sailors. But his simmering opponent kept *Independence* full speed ahead, forcing Decatur to chase and overhaul him in a boat.

What happened when the two met on board is conjectural, but at least, their time together was short and gelid. Bainbridge's only reference to the occasion is a single curt sentence in his official report to the department: "As I was standing out of the Bay of Gibraltar, the *Guerriere*, Com. Decatur, was going into that port for a supply of provisions."[34] Many years later Susan Decatur recalled what her husband had told her about it. Bainbridge had "received him as a total stranger!—never asked him a single question relative to our affairs! and never offered him the slightest hospitality! This is the person who had frequently been our guest for weeks at a time!" She claimed that from that moment, "until a *very short* time before the awful sacrifice of my beloved husband's life in 1820, they never recognized each other when they met!"[35] Naturally in no way could she understand that their former house guest had been most cruelly exploited by her "beloved husband."

On that same day Bainbridge led most of the ships of both squadrons out of Gibraltar. A few hours later, Decatur in *Guerriere* also slipped away, won the transatlantic race, arriving at New York on November 12, three days before Bainbridge came into Newport, Rhode Island. There was yet another stab of agony in store for Bainbridge—how the Mediterranean exploits of each were judged by the press, for Decatur indeed had followed Irving's advice about "whipping the cream off the enterprise." Two comments in the same Philadelphia paper sum up admirably the stark difference in evaluations. In one article, Decatur was said to have given the Barbary powers "an electric shock as it was never before discharged from a Christian battery. . . . This is a glory which never encircled the brow of a Roman Pontiff; nor blazed from an imperial diadem."[36] The other read in toto: "We are happy to announce the arrival at Newport on Monday of the U.S. Squadron under the command of Com. BAINBRIDGE."[37]

A modern work pinpoints why Bainbridge had every right to hate Decatur: "Looking back, there is a ruthlessness about Stephen Decatur's audacity at this period which clearly stems from his determination to 'satisfy the world' of his untarnished renown. To his self-vow may be traced the manipulation of a pliant Secretary, the brazen confiscation of personnel and equipment ordered for other commands, the calculated indifference to fellow-officers, and the embarrassing confusion thus brought upon a senior Commodore."[38]

This crushing disappointment for Bainbridge was only the beginning; his purgatory continued for the next few years. Contrary though it may seem to normal psychological patterns, his correspondence appears to show that the generally warm, affectionate, considerate, and usually optimistic man turned into a churlish, unhappy misanthrope. He met with one frustration after another from his twin bêtes noires, Secretary Crowninshield and Decatur, the latter having joined Commodores John Rodgers and David Porter on the newly established Board of Navy Commissioners. Bainbridge was checked in several efforts to oust Captain Isaac Hull from command of the Boston Navy Yard so that he could replace him, castigated for making a temporary naval appointment, and criticized for ordering minor alterations on *Independence*'s gun carriages. As his relationship with Decatur had been severed, he poured out his wrath on Rodgers, with whom he had never been close, and Porter, formerly his chief naval friend, thereby starting a rift that would eventually become unbridgeable. Not until 1819 was he able to awaken from his nightmare with his appointment to command the seventy-four-gun *Columbus*, to be outfitted for a Mediterranean cruise.

By that time an amazing transformation had taken place in the erstwhile Bainbridge-Decatur relationship. Susan Decatur remembered that during late 1819 her husband was strolling along a Washington, DC, street when a carriage suddenly stopped and Bainbridge leaped out, running over to clasp the other's hand, while exclaiming, "Decatur, I behaved like a great fool, but I hope you will forgive me; but you always contrive to reap laurels from my misfortunes." Somewhat nonplused, Decatur replied, "I have never done anything but what I believed to be my duty, and if you are convinced of that, go home with me and take a glass of wine." Bainbridge pleaded another appointment "but would return to Washington and would then come and take up his *abode* with him as usual." She continued: "I said to my husband that it seemed to me an act of great assurance to invite himself to be our guest after allowing five years to elapse without speaking or writing to him when there had been no cause for offense[,] . . . and I was afraid that he had some other motive than that of repentance. But I had no idea that he would come—he, however, did come, probably just after Christmas [1819] and remained with us two or three weeks."[39]

Soon Decatur accepted Barron's challenge. The latter immediately selected Elliott as his second, who doubtless anticipated with relish a potential retribution for whatever wrongs he believed had been done to him by the Perry--Decatur clique. Decatur had no such facile solution, for he was turned down for the same capacity by Commodores Charles Morris, Rodgers, and Porter, all of whom argued heatedly that he above all had no need to prove his valor. Finally, Decatur asked his houseguest to stand up with him, and Bainbridge accepted with alacrity. Early in February, Decatur told his second to proceed with the necessary arrangements for the duel, leaving him "entirely the choice of weapons and distance, as also the time."[40]

On March 8 Bainbridge and Elliott met on *Columbus* and agreed that the duel would take place at nine o'clock in the morning on the twenty-second of that month at Bladensburg, Maryland, just outside the District of Columbia, "and the weapons shall be pistols; the distance eight paces, or yards; that, previous to the firing, the parties shall be directed to present [aim], and shall not fire before the word one is given, or after the word three; that the words one, two, three, shall be given by Commodore Bainbridge."[41] These arrangements may furrow brows on two counts: they made very likely a fatal conclusion and worked much to Barron's advantage.

First, at least ten paces usually separated the duelists, and any curtailment of that already short span from thirty to twenty-four feet considerably increased the possibility of death or serious injury. In the typical hostile encounter under the code duello, the principals stood at attention, sideways to one another, either with arm cocked and the pistol pointing upward at head level, or else with the arm relaxed and the weapon hanging by the side. At the signal each would have to present and aim before firing, ensuring that misses would be frequent. But the Bainbridge-Elliott conditions had them aiming already so that each was drawing a bead on the other and at the word had only to press the trigger.[42]

Second, the terms also helped Barron, for Decatur was far more experienced in private war, having fought one duel, having been talked out of another, and having seconded three times. Barron, prior to 1820, had never participated in an engagement. Furthermore, he was notoriously nearsighted, and the shorter the distance from his opponent, the better for him. Under these conditions it is understandable why Elliott would try to even the odds in this particular, but how was Bainbridge aiding his man by acceding to them? He made the self-incriminating admission to Decatur that "Captain Elliott dealt much on Barron's defective sight, but [it] had no influence on my mind, for I had resolved a month since . . . that the distance should be eight paces." [43] Why? How does a closer range help the superior marksman with quicker reflexes? In fact, this provision impelled Decatur to alter his entire strategy for the encounter. Earlier he had told friends that at ten paces he planned deliberately to miss his antagonist, but at eight, he dared not and decided that he must at least wound him. Susan Decatur knew for sure why the reasons so contrary to her husband's interests had been set: "The whole affair was gotten up through the malice and cowardice of one of the seconds, Captain Elliott, and accomplished through the envy and jealousy of the other, Commodore William Bainbridge."[44]

With one pertinent exception, the tragic details of what transpired at Bladensburg on March 22, 1820 are well enough known to need little recounting here. Suffice it to say that at the word "fire," both Barron and Decatur slammed home their bullets into the other's hip at approximately the same spot near the socket, but Decatur's struck just to the outside of Barron's ileum, ricocheting down into his thigh, inflicting a severe, painful, but not mortal wound. Barron's hit a hair's breadth to the inside of Decatur's socket, and glanced off into the groin, severing arteries. As both toppled to the ground, Decatur gasped softly, "Oh Lord, I am a dead man," dying after hours of protracted agony at ten o'clock that night.[45] Admiral David Dixon Porter in his filiopietistic life of his father provided convincing details about Elliott's prompt and panic-stricken flight from the field, proving that he knew about the duel and was hovering nearby to learn the outcome. The elder Porter, arriving with Rodgers moments after the exchange, observed that the fallen Decatur was being well attended to but that Barron lay prostrate, shivering from cold and shock, alone save for one of the doctors. Porter gently raised him to a sitting position and was told, "My second, Captain Elliott, has gone off with the carriage, and it will be hours before I can be moved." Incredulous at such a betrayal, Porter leaped on his horse and raced after Elliott, finding him within a mile. Elliott opened the carriage door, got out, "asking in a trembling voice, 'how things fared on the ground.'" Porter shouted, "they fare so badly sir, that you left your friend weltering in his blood upon the bare earth; go back and do what you can to lessen the mischief you have aided in committing; go back and do your duty to your wounded friend."[46]

He rode back to Barron's side, but the minutes ticked off with no sign of Elliott. Finally Porter intercepted a passing carriage, commandeered it, and helped in Barron, who had "bled profusely and was very weak." They set off for Washington, DC, soon meeting the absconder, heading as slowly as possible in the other direction toward Bladensburg. Once again, Porter pulled and pushed Elliott to join Barron, who finally reached the capital to begin his lengthy and pain-wracked convalescence.[47] Having experienced such signal disloyalty, probably the only reason that Barron did not cut off all relations with Elliott was their long-standing dependence upon the other.

En route to Washington, DC, Elliott told Porter how unfortunate it was that Bainbridge had not stopped the proceedings after the Barron-Decatur conversation, but "Porter did not reply, feeling too much contempt for the man whom he saw as already trimming his sails to meet the coming storm. . . . The fact was, Elliott thought both parties had been killed, and appalled at the consequences of the duel, and fearing arrest as an accessory [or possibly becoming the victim of a lynching] he took flight." In a letter to Perry's close friend, Navy Purser Samuel Hambleton, Porter summarized his conclusions: "he fled from the field, taking with him the only means of conveyance for his wounded friend; that he left him for one hour in a helpless state on the wet ground, and that Barron was at length beholden to strangers for the means of getting from the place. Self, self, was Elliott's only consideration."[48]

This magnanimous postduel service of Porter was all the more laudable in that he had long viewed Barron with disdain, supporting Decatur in all the controversies involving the two since the *Chesapeake-Leopard* affair and ensuing court-martial, 1807–8. Except for such inevitable altercations between such volatile egoists, Porter and Decatur remained mutual admirers. A significant omission, however, in some otherwise excellent accounts of this meeting is that Barron suddenly violated the "code of honor," which held that once a challenge had been given and accepted, no communication should pass between the principals except in the form of bullets. Just after the deadly exchange, while lying side by side on the grass, Barron called, "Now, Decatur, if we meet in another world, let us hope that we shall be better friends." He later explained that his infraction of dueling etiquette was "to give Commodore Decatur a chance to acquit himself of an act from which he had no earthly provocation." This is precisely what happened when Decatur answered: "I never have been your personal enemy, sir."[49] Here is the moment when seconds Bainbridge and Elliott could have halted the entire proceedings in order to explain to their principals that if someone challenged as an enemy specifically denied that allegation and had, in effect, apologized for a misunderstanding, the very reason for the duel had been erased. But Bainbridge kept silent, and Elliott, probably terrified that his chosen means of retaliation against Decatur might be lost, shouted, "Gentlemen, back to your places!" thus speeding along his opportunity for vengeance.[50]

In correspondence with Henry Clay, Susan explained why she had become a social recluse, refusing to attend public events, lest she meet with any of the three she held responsible for her husband's death. She considered Barron the least culpable, for he had acted openly and honorably. But Bainbridge had "proposed such terms as render'd destruction to one or both inevitable. . . . He placed them close together, and made them take deliberate aim at each other." And after the duelists' proposed reconciliation, "Captain Elliott order'd silence! and Commodore Bainbridge order'd them to take aim now[.] If this was not cold blooded murder, I know not what it is: Associate with such Monsters? No—Never! I would rather take my position in a State prison, and live in fellowship with avow'd cutthroats and robbers, for I believe them to be the better men! These are dreadful charges, but I have documents to prove them."[51]

One cannot perceive accurately Bainbridge's true emotions in regard to the fatal event and his responsibility for he referred to it seldom indeed. From the multitude of his letters examined, only two short mentions of the occurrence have been spotted. A week after the meeting, he asked Porter to excuse the brevity of his note, as he felt so deeply "the death of my lamented friend Decatur."[52] Three days later, he informed another correspondent that, "I have been much affected in the death of my friend Decatur," adding stoically, "however, the vicissitudes of my life has fortified my mind for trying events."[53]

At this juncture Elliott must step aside to allow concentration on Bainbridge's motivations, but it interrupts not at all the flow of this narrative, for their partnership remained a nexus.[54]

It is possible to defend Bainbridge against Susan Decatur's implacable certainty that he had worked in tandem with Elliott to destroy her husband. In addition to the aforementioned events in which Decatur had earned Bainbridge's undying gratitude, it is comprehensible that the sullen rage caused by his rival's outright theft of his opportunity for retaliation and lasting acclaim against Barbary would burn itself out within five years. Hence, his spur of the moment reunion with Decatur late in 1819 could have emanated from no more than an honest desire to renew a valued friendship. Nor does he seem to add up as one to engage in underhanded and malevolent conduct ascribed to him by Decatur's widow. As shown by his many clashes with naval superiors during and after 1815, when Bainbridge thought that he had been wronged, his response was anything but muted for he carped and complained at the top of his voice. It would have been much more in character for him to have baited and taunted Decatur, even at the risk of a hostile encounter, rather than to nurture a silent hatred for years, prior to joining Elliott in sub-rosa maneuverings to kill him through the agency of a third party.

Yet there is abundant evidence the other way—that Susan Decatur's suspicions were justified.[55] There can be no mistaking the anguish that Bainbridge suffered when it finally sank in that Decatur had used Secretary Crowninshield as his instrument in order to slake an unquenchable thirst for glory. And Bainbridge would surely have held his new enemy at least partially responsible for his steady succession of personal frustrations by the department and the Board of Navy Commissioners from 1815 into 1819. If a sudden reconciliation, even with one who had double-crossed him, is likely for one with Bainbridge's generally affectionate nature, its timing could hardly have been more suspicious. By late 1819 most high-ranking officers knew that the acrimonious communications that went back and forth between Barron and Decatur had made a duel practically certain. Coincidence is raised to improbability when Bainbridge darts from a carriage to accost Decatur, invites himself to be his houseguest, and becomes the second of a man who he believed had stolen from him an almost guaranteed place in history as the single-handed terminator of North African abasements of his country for three decades. Bainbridge had, with an Elliott whose culpability seems beyond doubt, set the terms for the duel so as to make a lethal consequence for Decatur highly probable. The interchange between the combatants moments before they fired presented the best of reasons for sidetracking the proceedings, but Bainbridge said nothing, permitting Elliott to hasten matters along to their implacable conclusion. Furthermore, if furtive moves against an adversary are uncharacteristic of the pre-1820 commodore, later Bainbridge used as his tools a couple of junior officers in efforts to seize for himself command of the Boston Navy Yard.[56]

A final item is even more damaging to Bainbridge's reputation. In the archives of the New York Historical Society lies a special unpublished edition of James Fenimore Cooper's *History of the Navy of the United States.* Not only does it contain many holograph letters of famous American naval officers but it is beautifully illustrated by John S. Barnes, Bainbridge's grandson by marriage. One volume contains Barnes's handwritten insertion, explaining that an invoice that he had found was one of the few papers saved from the "holocaust" of Bainbridge's personal correspondence. He goes on to state that after the death of his widow, Susan Heyliger Bainbridge, in 1857, the commodore's daughters decided to burn his "most valuable letters."[57]

Barnes gives no reason for their action, so the question remains, why would they have done this unless his letters contained material damaging to his historical reputation? It is barely conceivable, from the point of American Victorian mores, that evidence of some delinquencies, criminal or amatory, might have led to the destruction, although his biographers have found nothing in the vast mass of Bainbridge material to suggest such a necessity. Otherwise, with the possible exception of the commodore's efforts to push Hull out of Boston, anything else in his life that would have required such protective action seems nonexistent. Therefore, his daughters' conflagration gives credence to the belief that his private files may have held damning evidence about Bainbridge's complicity in Decatur's death. Obviously, this conclusion cannot be stated categorically; perhaps the most useful verdict might be that pronounced in some trials in Scotland—"not proven."

SEVEN

Cruising and Diplomacy in Lower South America

AFTER WINNING HIS seven-year campaign for an independent command, Elliott prepared the frigate *Cyane* for her cruise to Brazil, Argentina, and modern Uruguay. There he would work as a single-ship predecessor to what would become shortly the Brazil Squadron under Commodore James Biddle. Elliott was supposed to protect neutral American trade, for although the Brazilian-Argentine War had been declared already, no one in the United States was as yet aware of its outbreak.

Just before departure, the captain opted to pat himself on the back a couple of times. He told the secretary that "I would be glad to have a regularly ordained clergyman on board." Jarvis further writes: "This request is one proof among many others that might be cited, of the attention uniformly paid by Captain Elliott to the morals and deportment of those under his command." In addition, the secretary sent some twenty "young midshipmen" to accompany him on his voyage: "The confiding of him of a trust so extremely delicate and responsible as this shows the high estimation in which he was held by the President and the Secretary of the Navy, not only as an energetic and skillful commander, but as a discreet and worthy man." He set up a school for the middies, and a professor from West Point conducted mathematics classes in particular. Soon Elliott informed the department that the students were doing so well that "each one will be enabled to appreciate fully your motive in assigning to me the task of their instruction."[1] No one well informed about the early navy will judge these religious and educational accomplishments worthy of such undue emphasis. Almost all of the larger vessels and some of the sloops provided the same services without their commanders extolling such as if they were unique.

Cyane left New York City on December 26, 1825 for Brazil, touching first at Pernambuco and on February 24 landed at Salvador (Bahia), salutes being exchanged at both ports. At Salvador on March 5, 1826, a "very unpleasant" incident occurred. *Tentadora*, a slave trade schooner, "luffed athwart her [*Cyane*'s] bow, caught her forward boom, carried away most of them, fell on board and hooked her main yard," during which an American sailor was killed, falling from a mast to the deck. Suspecting that the act was premeditated, Elliott protested most forcibly to Salvador's governor, who not only arrested and imprisoned the slaver's captain but also sentenced her owners to make full restitution for the outrage. According to Elliott, for there is no confirmatory evidence, he "remitted the claim to damages," although her owners offered him a bribe of $5,000 if he would drop "all proceedings against them, which, as may be readily supposed, was indignantly rejected."[2]

Why had Elliott turned down collecting the cost of *Cyane*'s repairs, which meant that his own government would have to pay for them? He explained: "The energy and decision of Captain Elliott in this case had an ulterior object." British exporters were permitted to speed their goods through Brazilian customs by posting "sureties" for each other, but Americans had to pay 2.5 percent to brokers for that service. Elliott's appeal reached Emperor Dom Pedro I, who agreed with him and removed the "needless or unreasonable vexations" to permit US parity with the British.[3]

Once Elliott had reached Brazil he recognized that hostilities had erupted already with Argentina, making his original instructions from the department passé, for now he confronted the far more troublesome issue of safeguarding his country's interests during a foreign war. The area of operations involved the mouth of the vast Río de la Plata with Brazil on its southwestern shore, Argentina on the northeastern coast, and just below, the territory claimed by both combatants, Banda Oriental (Eastern Bank)—modern Uruguay. American trade with Brazil and Argentina was well worth protecting, amounting in 1825 to some $3 million and $2.5 million in imports and exports respectively. But late that year, the outbreak of war over Banda Oriental between Brazil (free from Portugal in 1822) and Argentina (independent from Spain in 1810) potentially could wipe out such a lucrative trade.[4]

The course of the conflict was desultory, but at its beginning, Brazil seized dominance at sea and pronounced a blockade forbidding all neutral carriers from approaching Buenos Aires. Well before, the US government had made public its position on blockades.

1. They could be imposed only by a recognized nation at war that maintained control of its realm; insurgents had no such privilege until they had toppled the former government to assume and hold power themselves.

2. Sufficient advanced notice of these restrictions must be given to American skippers and shippers so that they would know that any violations were at their own risk.
3. To be legal and binding a blockade must be effective, that is, any stretch of shoreline and its ports must have enough warships on hand to seal it off. In that case Washington, DC, would notify its merchantmen that it should be honored, and if this warning were ignored, they could expect no backing from their country.

Elliott accentuated splendidly the above precis in a strong letter to Vice Admiral Don José R. E. Lobo, commanding Brazilian forces in the area:

> The United States will not acknowledge a blockade as valid against its civil marine, unless confined to particular ports, each one having *stationed before* it a force sufficiently great to prevent the entry of all vessels carrying materials to succor the besieged: and no vessel shall be seized, even in attempting to enter the port so blockaded, till she has been previously warned off. . . . The undersigned will also avail himself of this occasion to express his regret that the representative of his imperial majesty [Admiral Lobo] should have found it necessary to adopt a course, in relation to the United States, so well calculated to disturb the harmony and good feelings which exist between the two governments. . . . He will also insure him that indemnity will be claimed for, and, if necessary, the undersigned will feel himself called upon to bring into operation that arm of the nation's naval force placed subject to his control, in repelling all improper encroachments on American vessels, and on her maritime and neutral rights.[5]

American policy in this situation was designed to negate the detested "paper blockades" in which a nonbelligerent merchantman might visit several times unmolested a so-called blockaded port, only to see a hostile man-of--war appear suddenly to confiscate the ship and her cargo. Early in the Latin American revolts against it, Spain illustrated how unreasonable was this procedure by declaring over 1,500 miles of South American coast blockaded when it could come up with only *three* warships to enforce it! Upholding his government's stand on this issue would be Elliott's primary accountability while in the South Atlantic.

It is advisable here to stress a truism. No diplomat, however adroit, knowledgeable, and outwardly accommodating though he may be, can achieve success when his goals run directly counter to what his foreign equivalents consider the fundamental interests or national honor of their country. A case in point: the insistence of US diplomats from 1793 to 1815 that the British must renounce their impressment of American sailors into the Royal Navy. London could be more flexible on other issues—boundary disputes, for instance—but never on impressment, which they deemed absolutely vital to victory over Napoleonic France. On that, they stonewalled even such famous statesmen as John Jay in the 1790s and John Quincy Adams and Henry Clay in the 1820s.

This chapter and chapter 8 should show that Elliott possessed a flair for diplomatic bargaining with his foreign counterparts, so different from his tenacious pursuit of his enemies at home. In Latin America, 1825–27 and 1829–32, stalemated or rapidly changing conditions enabled him to gain important concessions from Spaniards, Brazilians, Argentines, Mexicans, and Haitians, much to his native land's advantages.

An Elliott biographer comes to a quandary about handling the controversy between the American, dedicated to enforcing his country's disapprobation of illegal blockades, and the Brazilian Lobo, striving to uphold his emperor's edicts severing neutral trade into and out from Argentina.

Should it be necessary to haul the unsuspecting reader through the wordy, dull, and repetitious eight letters that passed between the two until victimized by torpor? No, let it be sufficient to report that Elliott pounded away on the theme that Lobo's December 1825 blockade announcement must be restricted to the immediate neighborhood of Buenos Aires. Lobo insisted that he must enforce it throughout the Rio de la Plata's huge estuary from Cape Antonio, Argentina, all the way to Montevideo (later, in Uruguay). Less pain and more comprehension will come if the Elliott-Lobo correspondence is reduced to their most pertinent exchanges (see below).

While this dragged on, Elliott found himself in a more menacing situation. When the captain first encountered the thirty-five-ship Brazilian fleet off Cape Antonio on May 4, 1826, he had determined already that never would he submit himself or his county to a subordinate status, and he would fight to prevent it. When the oncoming *Cyane* was spotted, a heavy frigate, a "corvette" (between a frigate and a sloop); and three sloops headed her off, demanding that a boat be sent to explain the ship's presence. Elliott wrote the secretary that this order was "*peremptorily refused*," although he would accept a boat coming over to him; he maintained this stance throughout his tour. When, as expected, the frigate's captain denied him permission to proceed toward the Argentine capital, Elliott replied that he had witnessed both British and French corvettes sail unimpeded through the blockaders and that he would do the same, which he did, adding that he had a message for Admiral Lobo. Elliott gave the Brazilians a thirty-minute ultimatum, at the end of which: "I should proceed, prepared to resist all consequences[,] . . . and I should defend the ship to the last moment." Opposition collapsed, enabling

Cyane to reach Buenos Aires where Elliott, before heading out for Montevideo, exchanged compliments with Admiral Guillermo Brown, an Irish sea dog who had been hired to direct the Argentine Navy.[6]

Elliott had performed most capably in this instance, but typically, he had to pause to regard his own true grit with the greatest admiration: "On being informed that he could not be permitted to proceed, he replied that he would fight his way. This was bold language to be cast in defiance from a little Corvette of 34 guns, against a Frigate, a Corvette, and three brigs! A *coward*, or even a commander who would fight well on equal terms, or with odds somewhat against him . . . would have turned away from the blockaded coast, and represented the affair to his government. But Captain Elliott is 'made of sterner stuff' than to yield a point of national right or honor to what he deems unjust pretensions, by whatever force such pretensions may be asserted."[7]

As a military professional, Elliott took the keenest interest in the strategies, tactics, weaponry, and zeal of the combatants. Even before he had reached Rio, he had formed a low opinion of Brazilian abilities: "His Majesty's army is constituted almost entirely of disaffected men sent there with discon[ten]ted feelings in irons from the Northern Provinces."[8]

This martial absorption, however, remained secondary to Elliott's main task—to reach an accord with Lobo in the form of an acceptable compromise. The American argued that the Brazilian blockade could apply only to the closest sea approaches to Buenos Aires and its cross-river town of Colonia. His opponent maintained that it must be enforced throughout the Plata's broad estuary. Late in April, off Montevideo, the two finally met for the first time, having to work though interpreters, as neither spoke the other's language. Elliott thought that his efforts had succeeded in toto. He wrote exultantly to his rival: "The very frank and free conversation which I had with your excellency this morning, has greatly relieved my mind" about the effect of "your blockade on the commerce of the United States." In return, his nation would be sure to obey the curtailed interdiction of Buenos Aires's environs.[9]

He was totally wrong; Lobo moved not an inch, avowing that the extended blockade of the Plata was still extant. The Brazilian followed it up a few days later by attributing the American's confusion to simple misunderstanding, "and if you have understood in any other manner, I am not culpable for it" because of "the mistakes which interpreters sometimes make." He concluded, "You are aware that His Imperial Majesty approved my [blockade] manifesto; it is not in my power to destroy what has been published."[10]

Elliott then turned to intellectual prowess to inundate his opponent, although what he hoped to gain by it is uncertain. He hurled at Lobo an impressive number of treatises on international law, all supporting his own position on the legality of blockades, at first restricting himself to British works, then roaming far afield in his second letter, hitting him with such names as Crotius, Vattel, Chitty (*On Belligerent Powers and Neutral Rights*), von Moltke, and Sir William Scott (the preeminent English authority railing against paper blockades), replete with obscure footnotes. Perhaps stunned, Lobo made no reply, and possibly Elliott's only victory was in the form of the migraines that may have been inflicted on the admiral's hapless Portuguese interpreters.[11]

Throughout this service Elliott had been on the alert to help American merchantmen apprehended for blockade violations but for months to no avail because the disposition of these seizures would have to await final decisions by the Brazilian admiralty courts.

Meanwhile, in view of his inability to counter the Argentine Brown's naval pyrotechnics, Lobo had been replaced by Admiral Pinto Guedes. Shortly prior to his homecoming, Elliott found that three American vessels had been taken by Guedes's squadron but released on the questionable ground that they had not been told properly about the interdiction. Cognizant that this provided him with an opportunity to guard against such future incidents, Elliott "very adroitly waived all discussion of neutral and belligerent rights." He then "applied for the release of these [and other like] vessels as 'an *executive officer*' [i.e., as a personal favor]." He did this in expectation that the Brazilians would accommodate Americans in order to ensure their neutrality. "Thus by firmness and energy, did he . . . protect the commerce of the United States against unfounded pre tensions."[12]

After skirmishes with Brazilians to support his country's rights against foreign usurpations, Elliott added Frenchmen and Austrians to his list. His "biography" related that he displayed the same "firmness and energy" when several sailors deserted from a French frigate at Rio on June 1, 1826. French commodore Du Plantys demanded permission to board *Cyane* and search for them: "Captain Elliott replied that under no circumstances would he allow it; that he trusted the French commander had too great a sense of propriety to urge the measure and that should he do so, the attempt would be forcibly resisted. He immediately made every preparation for resistance, and the French commander, seeing his determination, abandoned the point."[13]

A spat between Americans and Austrians ended in effusive expressions of mutual esteem. An Austrian soldier, serving with the Brazilians, deserted and was supposed to have sneaked aboard *Cyane*. Major Chevalier d'Ewald, acting Austrian in charge, asked Elliott if that were true, and when Elliott said it was not, he was told that his ship could not leave the harbor until questions had been answered, but *Cyane* ignored the detention. A short time out, however, the absconder was found hidden below. Elliott realized that if given to the Austrians without conditions, he would undoubtedly be executed and requested that his life be spared, which was granted: "Monsieur le Commandant: Still more convinced of the nobleness of your sentiments, from the honorable manner in which you have just acted, it is with the greatest satisfaction I give you the assurance that from personal respect to you, the soldier . . . shall not be punished."[14]

Elliott was not one to permit Europeans to outdo an American in cordiality and affection: "The generous manner with which you met my intercession in behalf of the man who had, *unknown* to me, secreted himself in my ship, tends greatly to enhance the already just high opinion I had entertained. . . . The promptness with which your heart has been opened in extending the hand of both *charity* and *forgiveness* to a *poor soldier*, must leave you in possession of a feeling more easily imagined than described."[15]

During his many months in the Plata region, Elliott's doings were not only relayed to the Navy Department but also to Henry Clay, secretary of state in the John Quincy Adams administration from 1825 to 1829. Dispatches from US Charges d'Affaires Condy Raguet in Rio and John Forbes in Buenos Aires, as well as by José Silvestre Rebello, Brazilian minister to Washington, DC, kept Clay up to date about the captain. Most of these letters are pro forma, requiring no additional comment here.[16] Two, however, merit some discussion.

Forbes told Clay with approval that Elliott's defiance of Lobo's squadron on May 4, 1826, meant that, "the doctrine of the right to exclude neutral ships of war from a blockaded port, will be abandoned in this hemisphere," as indeed it was eventually.[17]

Brazilian minister Rebello had some harsh remarks to make about what he saw as Elliott's patently pro-Argentine bias and against the interests of his own country: "These manifestations of gratuitous hostility . . . have, in addition to the individual character which they have previously possessed, become in some measure national, by the act of the American Naval Commander [Elliott], who, with an air of menace, demanded the surrender of property belonging to citizens of Buenos Ayres which had been lawfully captured by the cruizers of H. M., the emperor of Brazil, on the mere allegation that its being covered by the American flag, which act for the American newspapers is a great subject of boast."[18]

Rebello's assault on Elliott concerned in part the American merchantman *Ontario*, which had looted some Brazilian vessels, but except to demonstrate how the commodore used the case for self-promotion, the details are unimportant. Considering his minute coverage of his Brazilian tour (twenty--seven printed pages), it leads to a suspicion that Elliott may have omitted the

Ontario situation deliberately, for it differed so remarkably from an otherwise unimpeded stream of congratulations from his foreign negotiators, Rebello excepted.

Niles Weekly Register, a foremost American newspaper, made universally flattering references to Elliott during 1826–27. This implies that he must have carried on his own regular correspondence with big city US editors, creating a well-oiled publicity machine to make sure that his feats abroad would be widely circulated at home. Editor Hezekiah Niles spread across five entire pages the account of his confrontations with Lobo, concluding that "though Captain Elliott is probably uninstructed as a diplomatist, it was believed that he had admirably performed the part of one, out of his own good stock of materials"; and "the gallant captain has acquitted himself excellently well."[19]

The *Niles Weekly Register* also reproduced the letters that passed between Elliott and the French and Austrians concerning the case of deserters from their respective warships; and much delayed, the "highly creditable" story of how he had handled the incident when the slaver *Tentadora* had rammed *Cyane* at Salvador, Brazil, on March, 5, 1826.[20]

In a final brandish Elliott used again his "biography" to demonstrate his absolute devotion to the United States. None other than Emperor Dom Pedro I had "offered him an Admiral's commission, with the highest salary that any officer could receive in the naval service of the Empire." Elliott responded that his father had died defending his country, and since Elliott "had attained the highest rank and honors that could be given [by] the American Navy; he would not give one timber head of that navy for all the other navies in the world."[21]

Elliott's naval and diplomatic career in lower South America was over, and in both fields, he merits a "well done." He had defended his nation's honor by never sending boats to other warships when ordered to do that. He had skillfully handled the occasion at Salvador when the slaver crashed into *Cyane* and, according to himself at least, refusing a bribe thereby achieving parity with Britain in speeding American exports through Brazilian customs. In his first encounter with blockade-enforcing Brazilians he had brazened it out against a far superior force, aiding in the establishment of the right of nonbelligerent warships to sail wherever they pleased. He saved some American merchantmen by his subterfuge of persuading Guedes that as "a personal favor" to commanders, he established a fruitful precedent. He stared down the French from searching *Cyane* even in the face of an ultimatum and manipulated most graciously the instance of the Austrian deserter. Yet some inner urge compelled him to present them as if such contributions were unique, although his colleagues would be expected to react much the same in similar circumstances or be likely to receive departmental castigation.

During August 1827, a little before *Cyane* would have to depart, the accomplished James Biddle arrived as commodore of the Brazil Squadron.[22] At once Elliott's problems became Biddle's, and Biddle carried on the same campaign for limited as opposed to paper blockades but with the same negative result for a time. It should be recognized that throughout the war the United States had no better than third ranking among the foreign navies plying the western Atlantic. If America had some trade worth protecting there, the British and the French had semistrangleholds on South American commerce, for it was to Europe that most Latin Americans looked for their economic and cultural models. Considering this grim naval situation, Elliott's accomplishments may well be dubbed "meritorious."

By the time that Biddle had shown up, the war had stalemated. Even though Brazil's naval prowess was lacking miserably in proficiency, it still had so many warships and guns that even Brown could not gain maritime control for Argentina. Ashore, neither country had the manpower, finances, or willingness to forge a decisive victory. Continuing foreign insistence that the conflict must cease roiling global economic patterns led to the Treaty of Rio de Janeiro, August 28, 1828. Banda Oriental's independence was approved by its huge neighbors, as both Brazil and Argentina accepted gladly a free Uruguay rather than having it go to strengthen the other.[23]

His "biography" erroneously reported that Elliott reached his home at Carlisle, Pennsylvania, in June 1827, but he was still exchanging letters with an Austrian officer on July 12, so it had to be later that summer. There "he remained until 1828, engaged in agricultural pursuits; for at *home*, Captain Elliott is a Pennsylvania farmer . . . fighting the battles of freedom, by cultivating the soil of her enlightened and high-spirited yeomanry."[24]

EIGHT

Naval Recruiting in Pennsylvania, Cruising and Diplomacy in the Gulf of Mexico and the Caribbean, and the South Carolina Nullification Crisis

TOWARD THE END of Elliott's dabbling in agricultural pursuits at Carlisle and before his next cruise, he chose to participate in an unusual jog along the path of his naval career—inland recruiting for the service. This short interlude is the subject of a learned and informative article by my friend Dr. Harold D. Langley, naval historian at the Smithsonian Institution. His "The Grass Roots Harvest of 1828" goes into this subject at considerably greater length than is possible in a biography of the commodore, and those needing more should refer to him.[1]

While returning home from a visit to Washington, DC, Elliott mentioned to the secretary of the navy that he had passed along the mountainous route "from Philadelphia to the Potomac." He observed that there were many "young and ablebodyed men," neither farmers nor factory employed. He thought that if active naval recruitment could be carried on in that region, it "would not only prove beneficial to themselves but equally to both the civil and military marine." If the department approved, it should set up "a chain of rendezvous in the important towns of the Valley of Virginia, Maryland, and Pennsylvania." Since the government had no "other service for me, I would with pleasure become the superintendent."[2] The response from Samuel L. Southard was mixed: "A change in the present plan [of naval recruitment] is not at this moment indispensable; should it become so, your views will be reconsidered and *probably* adopted."[3] Southard was already worried about manpower requirements, having mentioned that topic in his *Annual Report for 1825* and resurrected it only for seaport rendezvous in 1827.

Elliott's suggestion struck so responsive a chord that the experiment commenced in April 1828 with the commodore in charge. Assisted by lower--ranking officers, recruits began to be enlisted at Pennsylvania's Carlisle, Chambersburg, and Harrisburg (all later centered at Baltimore). Two classes were to be chosen, presumably for the normal naval three years' service: boys from fifteen to seventeen (later lowered to fourteen) and men from eighteen to twenty-five (later extended to twenty-none). Although implied rather than spelled out, both Southard and Elliott expected that hale, native-born Americans should become better sailors than some of the riff-raff prowling port city alleys, many foreign born, some of whom were drunkards or other delinquents.[4]

Langley concluded his article with: "By his appreciation of local needs and sentiments, and by his use of newspaper advertisements, local assistance, martial music and distinctive uniforms, Captain Elliott showed that he had a good sense of public relations. He and his little band of inland recruiters were the advance guard of an organization which, in the 20th century, would reach into virtually every city and village in America to build the Navy and the future."[5]

Here Langley's summary concentrates admirably on the lasting heritage of the "harvest" experiment, not for aiding Jacksonian democracy but for spotlighting its true posterity. Following his inland experiences in trying to persuade farmers and laborers to don the garb of "tars" (sailors) in the blue water navy, Elliott's widely admired (at least by the department) accomplishments provided enough momentum for him to be granted another major naval and diplomatic assignment. Early in September 1829, the secretary sent him orders to "command the Naval Forces of the U. States in the West Indies and the Gulf of Mexico." From his flagship *Peacock*, based at the Pensacola naval establishment, he would oversee four other sloops and two schooners, a squadron considered by the department "amply sufficient" to protect the "lawful commerce" of his fellow citizens. He should circulate frequently among the islands and the coast of Mexico to sniff out and frustrate any illegal interferences with American shipping. He must cooperate with Treasury Department revenue cutters to help them enforce "the Revenue Laws." He should be especially prudent in keeping the strictest neutrality between the Spaniards and their rebellious former colonists.[6]

A little later he received further instructions, somewhat out of the ordinary for normal naval duties. He must use his sloops and schooners to experiment with cotton sails. For too long the country's marine had been dependent on abundant Russian and Scandinavian sources, in particular from

Sweden and Norway-Denmark, to provide hempen and linen canvas sailcloth for warships and merchantmen alike. But this was subject to interruption by any war in northern Europe. So the US government lent an eager ear to southern senators and representatives to substitute cotton for foreign imports, as domestic production of it was bountiful.[7] After several months of testing, Elliott passed along to the secretary with his endorsement of his subordinate officer's report that cotton sails "will stand every test. We found as little difficulty in managing them in heavy wet weather as the other sails, and that they hold wind better, nobody will deny."[8]

Once settled in as commandant of the Boston Navy Yard Elliott, during mid-1833, "in a letter of recent date," summarized the cotton-sail experiment: "I am now using the cotton manufacture freely at this establishment . . . both for ships and crews, and hope soon to see all our ships and seamen clothed with it, which I have no doubt will ultimately contribute largely to supplant the Russian duck from use." Another reason for his enthusiasm was domestic: "One objection of Southern politicians against a protective tariff, is the alleged diminution of a foreign demand for cotton. Commodore Elliott saw that by this substitution of cotton for hempen canvass, this objection would be obviated, and much progress made in allaying the spirit of discontent."[9] Here is another example of Elliott's growing partiality for the South, soon to become permanent after Bostonians reacted with such fury to his affixing a wooden effigy of President Jackson on the bow of "Old Ironsides" herself in 1834.[10]

On September 25, 1829, Elliott's squadron left New York for Pensacola. This was a voyage long enough to enable him to formulate instructions to the officers of his warships several times lengthier than those of the secretary to him. They added up to some four thousand words in twelve closely printed pages and may have left his lieutenants befuddled by the amount of information they were supposed to ingest and retain. He admonished them to recognize the distinctions between licit and illicit blockades, maintain noninvolvement in Spanish-Mexican hostilities, carry out the laws against the slave trade, keep on the lookout for pirates, and perform dutifully the requirements of an officer. Most commendably he urged them to avoid "gross abuse" of the sailors, when their transgressions were "a minor fault, an accidental mistake, or an unintentional omission." While grousing about how much they had to memorize, some of his underlings may have decided that their commander had demonstrated erudition, intelligence, and concern for them.[11]

By and large the Mexico toward which Elliott was heading was collapsing into anarchy. Divisions had widened between Spanish-born and native-born whites and mestizos, so-called liberals versus conservatives and clericals against anticlericals, over the ever present influence of the Catholic hierarchy. In effect, however, these were no more than military blocs vying for power. Almost no one was working to bridge the seemingly impassable gulf between the white upper classes and the great mass of impoverished, landless, and apolitical Amerindians. This chaos was reflected in governmental instability to the nth degree. From 1822 to 1860 there were thirty-six Mexican presidents averaging a little less than eight months in office before being toppled by another general with his own meaningless " plan" for the country's unity and resurrection.

Nor was its foreign situation much better. Mexico had declared its independence in 1821, but Spain refused to recognize it until 1836, and the possibility of a vengeful reconquest was seldom absent from the country's psyche. Indeed, Madrid retained it for four years before losing the mighty San Juan d' Ulúa fortress right in Vera Cruz Harbor. In 1829 Mexican hysteria was generated by a temporary Spanish seizure of the port of Tampico, resulting in the ill-considered deportation of its Spanish-born inhabitants, their comparatively best educated and prosperous class (see below). With remarkable obtuseness, they were allowed to migrate with all their wealth, plunging the nation into a lasting economic depression.

Elliott arrived at Pensacola late the same year, passing his tenure at the leading port of Vera Cruz, from which he would often delve into the political and economic maelstrom that was Mexico. His first confrontation broke out late in 1829 over the kidnapping of sailor John Lewis from an American merchantman. Lewis was treated most callously and slapped into chains after surviving a thirty-six-stroke lashing. Elliott argued about the case with Francisco De P. Lopez, naval commander of Vera Cruz, on the basis of international law, stressing the illegality of the abduction and asking him to admit it and release Lewis. Lopez responded on the same lofty plane of responsibilities in nation-to-nation relations but refused to heed either. Back and forth they went once more, but nowhere in their seven-page correspondence is there any indication of Lewis's fate. When Elliott left Vera Cruz early in January 1830, the matter was still in limbo.[12] Nevertheless, my research on this same case for my magnum opus *Gold Braid and Foreign Relations* proves that eventually Lewis was released.[13]

Almost simultaneously the news came in that two Mexican gunboats had fired into the American ship *Ajax* at Sisal in Yucatan, far to the southeast. According to Elliott's "biography," he sent *Erie* under a "Captain Cowper" (actually under Commander David Conner) to attend to it, and he did so, extracting from Mexican authorities there an apologetic admittance that it had been no more than a case of mistaken identity.[14]

Early in February 1830, most of the squadron gathered to investigate the circumstances at Matanzas, Cuba, to the east of Havana, where the slave ship *Manzanares* had robbed a Boston vessel of her lucrative cargo. Elliott wrote about it to Don Francisco Dionosio Vives, captain general of the island, who tried to track down *Manzanares*, but Elliott felt that his own more drastic action was necessary. Departing from his usual veneration of international law, he proceeded to Matanzas and began a minute search of every slaver in the harbor. He pledged that he would continue this until those responsible had been brought to justice but ceased this dubious legal procedure after receiving confirmation that *Manzanares* had been sunk off West Africa by a British antislave trade patrol.[15]

As indicated before, Elliott felt compelled to include frequent testimonials about his own outstanding qualities as a man and a naval officer. It cannot be ascertained why he would choose to place the insertion of his second letter regarding *Manzanares*. The alert reader will see that such was completely inconclusive: "They are offered as another instance of that energy and decision which characterize all his movements when engaged in the service of the public, and which have been successfully exerted for the protection of his fellow citizens."[16] The facts about exactly what occurred to the American brig *Elizabeth* also at Matanzas could hardly be more opaque, for Elliott saw fit to send only one letter of his, again to the captain general of Cuba, and provided no background material whatever. Evidently that merchantman had violated a local ordinance that departing vessels must go out during daylight hours to avoid piratical onsets during the dark. All that his letter says is that "*Elizabeth* was rigorously dealt with."[17]

In the midst of his chief responsibility of upholding American interest in the Gulf and Caribbean, Elliott had a sad duty to execute. The sloop *Hornet* was long overdue in port. Under Commander James Lawrence, she had been widely hailed for sending to the bottom the British brig *Peacock* off British Guiana in 1813.[18] During August 1829 Commander Otho Norris took her along the Mexican coast during the hurricane season, compelling Elliott to write to the secretary from Pensacola: "Respecting the *HORNET* . . . , it becomes my painful duty to convey information [from one of his officers]. On the 10th, a gale unusually severe, came on[,] . . . and she foundered, and all onboard sunk into an untimely and lamented end."[19] The same journal gave irrefutable proof of her finale, quoting a Mobile paper that at Tampico "a number of hats . . . with the word "*Hornet*" on them, had drifted ashore on that coast."[20]

It is uphill work to figure out the almost impenetrable story of the American merchantman *Kremlin* on her way past Hispaniola to New Orleans during the late spring of 1830. As she neared Havana, she had been tailed for hours by the Spanish-registered slaver *Fenix*, carrying eighty-two Africans for sale in Cuba. She was approaching *Kremlin* with apparent hostile designs but was thwarted by the timely presence of the schooner *Grampus* under Lieutenant James P. Wilson, one of Elliott's officers. Wilson seized the slaver, her people, and human cargo, sailing them to Pensacola where he was rewarded by Elliott's "warmest approbation" prior to going on with them to New Orleans.

The presence of these enslaved persons taken from a Spanish vessel and brought upon American soil turned the case into a diplomatic and domestic basketball, bouncing off the rim among Wilson, Elliott, and the secretary of the navy; the US marshal, the US district attorney, and the Spanish consul, all in New Orleans; a Louisiana "special court"; and the attorney general in Washington, DC.

What should be done with the enslaved individuals? If *Fenix* had stormed *Kremlin*, they could be freed, but she had not, thereby avoiding any charge of piracy. Deliver them to their Spanish owners? But that would be impossible until Spanish and American courts agreed as to the legality of Wilson's seizure. Liberate them in the United States? Under existing state laws that could not be done. Come to some sort of compromise? The decision among the legal parties was to keep the enslaved in custody until they could be returned to Africa, but whether the funds for that purpose were made available was problematical. At this juncture the documentation stops. As it applies to Elliott minimally and is not even mentioned in his long "biography," specific identification of the eleven letters circulated, some of them lengthy, about *Fenix* from June 4, 1830, to January 5, 1831, would require an inordinate amount of space; it shall be dropped forthwith.[21]

Another diversion from Elliott's normal responsibilities in maritime and diplomatic routines took place in 1831. He was spending that summer at Norfolk when he and other white people in Virginia and elsewhere in the South were appalled by what had transpired in Southampton County near the North Carolina line. Nat Turner, an apocalyptically oriented itinerant preacher to his fellow enslaved persons, despaired over his inability to follow his vocation while locked into his lowly status as a field hand. During August he gathered around him initially a tiny group of enslaved persons that grew to no more than forty. They pounced on the outlying plantations of the area, killing fifty-five white men, women, and children. Retaliation was swift and merciless; Turner was eventually caught and executed, along with some two hundred others of Black origins living in Virginia and North Carolina. This was the foremost enslaved person insurrection in American history, and as Dixie's terror of such an uprising was never far below the surface, it shocked slaveholders as never before or since. Henceforth most southerners literally feared for their lives; moderates on the slavery issue there were dealt a crippling blow.[22]

According to himself, Elliott responded to this crisis "with his usual alacrity." He halted one of his sloops on the verge of sailing to Brazil, boarded her with some of his sailors and marines, dispatched others on an overland march, and sailed up the James River to the heart of the violence. After its suppression he returned to Norfolk.[23] Actually the navy had little to do with its sanguinary ending for that had been accomplished by available units of the US Army, state militia detachments, and volunteers. This fact Elliott skipped over in order to include congratulations to him from a militia general, the governor of Virginia, and—most gratifying—the president of the United States, Andrew Jackson, "who has desired me to state to you that the promptitude with which aid was rendered, and the cheerful and humane feelings exhibited in the execution of the duty, are highly creditable to yourself and the officers and men under your command." In short, you have his "cordial and entire approbation."[24]

This terminated Elliott's first cruise in the Gulf and Caribbean. That he had been successful was affirmed by an editorial reprinted in Baltimore. He was extolled for binding together naval-civilian relations in that area; although his name was not mentioned, it clearly referred to him: "It is always a grateful duty for us to notice such manifestations of respect, as we have generally observed, (and we say with national pride) that the urbanity of manners, the firmness of character, and the correct deportment of most of our naval officers, will make them popular (and we think deservedly so) wherever they are, and we trust that they will continue loved and respected by our friends, and feared by our enemies."[25]

Elliott was on leave from the early summer through the late fall of 1831, and his second tenure in and out of Pensacola would last until the fall of 1833 when he left for South Carolina during the nullification emergency of that year (see below). As far as the sources reveal, his next cruise was the only time that he took with him his son Washington Lafayette Elliott, aged eight. This has to be mentioned for it is one of Elliott's extremely rare commentaries on his closest relatives. According to the father, the boy was "rather a refractory spirit (as he himself was at that age)," breaking his mother's household rules "with almost impunity." He resolved "on giving him a quarter deck set, for the purpose of bringing him into proper obedience. . . ." On a visit to Black-ruled independent Haiti, the Commodore invited some of its leaders to dine aboard his ship. This upset Washington, and he snapped at his father, 'Well as soon as I get home if I don't tell ma, you have been sitting down at table and eating and drinking with a parcel of black ________!'" Owner of at least one enslaved individual, Elliott did not rebuke him, but at a later shipboard dinner, he saw with amusement that his son was "regaling himself in company with Gen. Inginac's sable daughters." His father claimed that

Washington "soon yielded to the ship's discipline," but one may be skeptical about that. The boy spurned the navy, joined the army, and ended as a general in the Union forces during the Civil War.[26]

During this voyage Elliott had not devoted all of his energies to paternal responsibilities. In conversations with Americans trading there he was informed that Haiti was taxing their exports "on a less favorable footing than the English, French, and other nations," namely an additional duty of 10 percent. The same General Inginac who had entertained him and his son agreed that the assessment was unreasonable, promising to recommend its abolishment to the president of the republic. It is unclear whether this was done, but its likelihood is probable. As a French squadron cruised offshore, Haitians worried about an attempted reconquest by their former colonizers and were most desirous of American friendship.[27]

Back to his regular assignments in July 1832, Elliott met a delayed eventuation arising from the Mexican ousting of its Spanish born population in 1829. Temporarily in *Fairfield* at Tampico, he was accosted by three Spanish businessmen who had managed to avoid expatriation, swearing that they had become US citizens in Florida a few years before. For support they pointed to the recent Mexican-American Treaty of 1831, which proclaimed that neither government could interfere with the basic rights of residents of the other engaging in legal occupations. Elliott agreed with them and took up their cause with General Estaban Moctezuma, in charge at Tampico, sending him a copy of the treaty. Moctezuma professed that he had received no official knowledge that it had ever been ratified, and stood firm in his refusal to permit the Spaniards to remain. Here Elliott had by far the better legal case, but since circumstances of their US citizenship claims were so amorphous, he merits kudos for banking his aggressive fires and dropping the matter. At least he was able to transport the three homeless Spaniards back to the United States in one of his schooners.[28]

Elliott saluted his own "intrepidity" once more when *Fairfield*, outward bound from Vera Cruz, was battered by a "violent gale and in danger of being lost on the shoals." To save his own and the lives of his two hundred men, "he was obliged to jeopardize his own. He went aloft, and amid showers of rain and tremendous gales, directed the course of the ship for three hours, and steered her clear of the shoals." His "biography" says that he had accomplished this feat even though he was seriously ill from "endemic fever." A common medical practice of the time was to treat many ailments with a compound that led to mercury poisoning, and this might have brought about a "collapse" that sent Elliott into convalescence for a few months.[29]

Elliott's personal relationships, so often stormy, are always a matter of interest to his biographers. During his two separate cruises, 1829–32, he seems to have been amiable with his subordinate lieutenants, even the mercurial John Percival. Indeed, "Mad Jack" received commendation from Elliott as to how he had handled the case of the American ship *Corsica*. She had piled up on an insignificant key called Anegada claimed by the British but outside of any agency of their Virgin Islands government and notorious for the supposed "lawless character" of its Black inhabitants. "Fearing for their lives and property," *Corsica*'s people hurriedly left the islet to find Percival's *Porpoise*. Since international law was precise that abandonment of property for rescue was legal, salvage rights clearly belonged to Americans alone. But a Royal Navy spokesman asserted that a British claims court must decide how to divide the profits. His argument was obliterated by Mad Jack's praiseworthy insistence to the contrary. Elliott summed up the case by noting that Percival's "conduct in the matter has been judicious, and such I would expect from an Officer zealous in the discharge of his duties."[30] This warmth vanished, however, when both were stationed at the Boston Navy Yard a little later.

The situation between Elliott and Captain Alexander J. Dallas was a bit different. Dallas was a seasoned officer, entering the navy in 1805, moving steadily up the promotional ladder, and achieving his captaincy in 1828.[31] Whether there had been any previous unpleasantness between them is impossible to say, but surely in such a small and tightly knit coterie as the officers' corps, each would have known about the other's character and reputation.

In April 1830 Dallas was appointed "commandant of the Pensacola Navy Yard," superseding Elliott who had to vacate the premises, taking *Peacock* to Norfolk where he remained for some time.[32] Trouble arose from Dallas's awareness that Elliott had come into Pensacola earlier that year, "with a sickly crew," and thought it advisable "to erect for their temporary accommodation . . . on lands belonging to himself [with] some slight sheds. . . . Accordingly, requisitions were made for lumber and timber for that purpose, to about fifty to sixty dollars in amount, and the buildings were erected."[33] To Dallas this appeared damning evidence that Elliott was personally corrupt, and he demanded a departmental investigation of the matter. In reality Dallas had no case at all, for the secretary found to his satisfaction that Elliott "had no private interests " at stake, "as he has neither used the buildings for private purposes, nor sold them, but on the contrary, has allowed the Government the use of his own land where the buildings stood, and has made no claim whatever for compensation for that use."[34]

Thus vindicated, Elliott might well have dropped the issue, but he turned ugly once he had unearthed the degree to which Dallas had gone to incriminate him. Examining his financial records and spreading unflattering stories about him among both employees at the navy yard and the personnel of all the squadron's ships were bad enough. Much worse, "he has even descended so low as to catechize officers belonging to my command, to know if they were informed of any act of mine which could be made the subject of a charge." He publicly accused Dallas of spreading "falsehood."[35]

It is a subject of some surprise why Navy Secretary Levi Woodbury took so keen an interest in this quarrel, devoting almost ten pages to it in three letters: "I cannot but regret the state of the feelings . . . which has arisen between yourself and Capn Dallas, and we have observed with pain its progress to the point at which it now arrived [illegible]." Woodbury went on: "The respectability of the parties concerned, in impairing the dignity of the Naval Service, and interfering with the [illegible] of the high trust reposed by the government in both." Despite Elliott's wounded feelings he had erred in the "employment of the harsh phrase you have used. . . . Your cause would have been better sustained by eschewing this."[36] The secretary insisted that Dallas and Elliott must reach some sort of mutual accommodation with the other to defuse the crisis, but there is nothing in the correspondence to show that either man edged even slightly toward apologizing.

By this time each officer had filed charges denigrating his foe, and both demanded a court of inquiry or a court-martial to settle the case in his favor. But Woodbury would have nothing further to do with it: "Entertaining these views . . . on all the facts before the Department, I hereby, with the approval of the President, notify you both, that it is not deemed advisable, for the public interests, to take any further step in the premises."[37]

The navy had had its fill with the feuds, assaults in the press, courts of inquiry, courts-martial, and duels during the 1820s, all well publicized, which had decidedly lessened the service's image before the people. Many held that unless its reform was thorough, the damage to its reputation might be irreparable, and a few malcontents even called to its elimination. A Roman holiday of judicial inquiries played before reporters jotting down every word about each allegation that the combatants could dredge up would only operate to the navy's discredit. So both were sent on their separate ways, and there appears to be no proof that they ever again came in contact, hostile or otherwise.[38]

Soon after the department's abrupt dismissal of his tiresome controversy with Dallas, Elliott was notified that General Antonio López de Santa Anna, Mexico's premier political jack-in-the-box, had seized temporary control of Vera Cruz and was fitting out a privateer, perhaps to harry even neutral commerce. Once at sea, she would be a clear threat to American trade in the Gulf. Very likely the secretary's allusion to Santa Anna's raider was to *Montezuma*, dispatched in the summer of 1832 to blockade the mouth of the Rio Grande.[39] Elliott chose Lieutenant Josiah Tattnall in *Grampus* to go to Matamoros on the Texan frontier to investigate the situation there. That officer reacted impressively. Learning that *Montezuma* had just looted one American merchant vessel and was detaining another with $200,000 in specie aboard, he struck hard and fast. Sailing into that harbor, he liberated both ships, even though a Mexican man-of-war was nearby, boarded and put a prize crew on *Montezuma*, escorted all three ships to open sea without resistance, and sent her officers and crew off to Pensacola for possible trial and punishment. It had been done handsomely.[40]

This made Elliott curious enough to accept an invitation to dine with Santa Anna at his hacienda near Vera Cruz. On arrival he found a party of about fifty at a large table playing monte (a Spanish card game in which the players bet against a banker), and the American was informed that he could "bet as *high* as I *pleased*." But "I answered that I was rather too old a soldier to engage in a game I knew nothing about." Elliott asked Santa Anna to visit with him in *Fairfield*, but Santa Anna refused, explaining that "he would feel his head insecure in that town," so the commodore had to be content with "dining pleasantly" with his host sometime later.[41]

Perhaps his sensible reluctance to play monte had caused Elliott to recall an exchange of letters about a year before concerning gambling in his West India [Indies] Squadron. The secretary had sent him copies of recent edicts cracking down on this practice. Midshipmen, many young, callow, and away from home for the first time, were the usual victims of the easy credit available everywhere to US military and naval officers. But when Elliott investigated the subject from his flagship *Natchez*, somewhat to his dismay he discovered that his higher as well as lower rankers had been pilfered of large sums in gaming dens and had to be bailed out by "relatives and friends." He urged the department to issue a "General Order" forbidding gambling in the navy as "not only destructive to the prospects of the individuals concerned, but also calculated in no small degree to impair the respectability of the service."[42]

Had their squadron commodore been cleaned out by Santa Anna's cronies, it could have been ruinous to his supereminent position among his officers and men, once the story inevitably was circulated. Of course, dire threats of punishment against gambling proved to be about as ineffective as those against drunkenness.

In another instance of concern about the welfare of his squadron's people, Elliott and all others were terrified by any manifestation of yellow fever, recalling the lethal cruise of Commodore Biddle in *Macedonian* in 1822 with its 50 percent mortality. When a number of *Natchez*'s crew fell ill, he outlined in a long letter how thoroughly he had investigated the outbreak. He informed the department that he was sure that it was no more than " bilious fever [liver bile]," much to everyone's relief. That his medical diagnosis was undoubtedly wrong is not important; "yellow jack" remained absent.[43]

The commodore paid no less attention to the condition of his ships, keeping the government aware of the need for repairing their deficiencies, a loose copper bottom in *Natchez*, for example. His requirement that his men-of--war must be kept immaculate incited a new dispute with Commander John G. Clack, about whom Elliott had already formed a negative opinion, referring to him as "notorious." He found that Clack's vessel had to be "freed from the insects and vermin which multiply exceedingly in warm climates . . . ; she must be more thoroughly purified and cleansed."[44]

After nearly three years in the enervating weather in the Gulf and Caribbean, Elliott had tired of his unrelenting and unpredictable responsibilities and felt that he was still convalescing from his attack of "endemic fever." He asked for and was granted leave in Boston before assuming command of the navy yard there, an assignment that he coveted originally because of its more forecastable duties but soon most ardently regretted.[45]

Prior to taking over that post, Elliott passed an interlude in connection with the South Carolina nullification issue (see below). Once in Boston, he would be head over heels in torrid controversies amid the furor about his putting Jackson's wooden statue on the frigate *Constitution*.

All of chapter 7 and the last portion of chapter 8 have been explored in considerable depth compared to some other aspects of Elliott's naval and personal life. They concentrate on him at the commencement of his diplomatic career, an area in which he shone and which was duly recognized by the department. This is demonstrated by his succession of major commands abroad, despite his proclivity for feuding with so many of his service peers, which made him one of the most unpopular officers of his time. To the contrary, his personal relations with his foreign negotiators tended to be amicable and, on the few occasions when they were not, always conducted in scrupulously polite language. This was no flash in the pan characteristic. Elliott did the same in his brief visit to France with Edward Livingston, US minister to France, in the spoliations crisis with that country during 1834–35. In his last command at sea, August 1835–July 1838, with *Constitution* he toured around the Mediterranean and the western Middle East corresponding and exchanging visits with rulers and diplomats of numerous political entities. His intercourse with them appeared almost infallibly affable and sometimes productive.

Already Jackson had selected his officers to command the armed forces. He made the obvious choice of General Winfield Scott to head the army, while Elliott would lead the navy as "Commandant Charleston, S.C. Station." To be teamed with so famous a soldier and diplomat as Scott was a signal honor for him.[46] The president had written the secretary of the navy that "I am becoming more and more convinced of the propriety of our having Captain Elliott a float at the Norfolk Station that he may be ready to take command of the squadron it may be necessary to employ."[47] As Elliott put it, he "was selected by the President for this difficult and responsible command and very reluctantly left . . . to engage in the civil broils of his own countrymen." He went on to praise Scott in such a manner as to make sure that he himself was included in it: "Firmness and address [used in my dictionary's subheading of "skill and tact in handling situations"] were necessary. In selecting these officers, the President *knew* his men. Their valor, constancy, and sagacity had been thoroughly tested on former occasions."[48]

Elliott's squadron at Norfolk totaled only two: his flagship *Natchez* and the little schooner *Experiment*. As commodore he ordered the movements of both ships, the former under Commander John P. Zantzinger and the latter under Lieutenant William Mervine, both responsible for operations even when their superior was aboard. At both Norfolk and Charleston, Elliott was often ashore busy with paperwork and other duties; when he cruised it was in *Natchez*, the more spacious vessel. From the correspondence, *Experiment* left Norfolk on January 5, 1833 but not arriving at Charleston until the seventeenth. It had been an unforgettable voyage. Elliott said the day after that "on the 10th we parted company with *Experiment* at the commencement of a gale of wind which in its velocity accompanied by a height of sea probably as violent as any other happening on this coast for a few years past." There must have been some heart-stopping moments for Elliott and his shipmates when *Experiment* struck three times on its sandbar while approaching Charleston.[49]

These naval activities coincided with the height of the crisis during the first weeks of 1833. On January 16 Jackson sent his Force Bill to Congress where it was eventually passed. On the twenty-third a "giant public meeting" gathered in Charleston. "A systematic military organization for the city" was set up, and former governor James J. Hamilton urged unsuccessfully that if the Force Bill should be adopted, he would "recommend secession." Simultaneously the Nationalists sounded a strong conciliatory note: "All occasions for conflict . . . should be sedulously avoided" while Congress was debating the tariff issue. Speaking for Jackson, Secretary of War Lewis Cass informed Scott on the twenty-sixth that "it is the earnest wish of the President that the unhappy difficulties in South Carolina should be terminated without any forcible collision," and if such does occur, "it should not be justly imputable to the United States."[50]

How was the country lining up in regard to these developments? It is not easy to decide. Reasonably accurate public opinion polls would not appear for another century, and in the 1830s, what the populace thought about disputatious topics had to rely on newspaper editorials, testimonials from prominent citizens, and later election results, all subject to oversimplification or misinterpretation. But it seems that most in the North and West stood with Jackson. However, when South Carolinians called for support from other states supporting slavery they received a slap across the mouth instead. Their supposed allies appear to have concluded that nullification was neither the issue nor the time to challenge so popular a president. That of course was in the strongest contradistinction to 1860–61 when a heavy majority of Dixie's states supporting slavery sided with Charleston's secessionists.[51]

Behind the scenes Henry Clay—"the Great Compromiser"—was busy. When on February 12, he persuaded Calhoun to join him, the problem was on the verge of solution. Clay then introduced his "Compromise Tariff of 1832," and both houses approved it by March 1. Protectionists had to swallow hard while permitting duties of over 20 percent being reduced to that figure over the next ten years. Although Jackson signed the Force Bill the next day, South Carolina repealed its nullification ordinance on the eleventh, demonstrating that its resistance had been worthwhile.[52]

As the crisis was ebbing, a letter from one US Army lieutenant to another must have echoed a common chord throughout the nation: "But the scene has been appalling, and God grant that it may never be our lot to witness another domestic strife of such fearful and bloody promise at any future period in our lives. Both parties were braced up for the battle, had buckled on their armour and flung away the scabbard, awaiting the signal for the conflict. At this critical juncture the olive branch was thrown down at their feet as the pledge of returning peace; full many a Mother and daughter of Carolina has cause to bless the name of Henry Clay. . . . He is winning daily golden opinions from the people, and as the cloud of war which hung over the land passeth away I doubt [not] he will be hailed as the political saviour of our country."[53]

While US naval officers had gone about their responsibilities before the stalemate had been broken, they made contact with South Carolinians of all persuasions. Several of them expressed their surprised delight that even though they might soon be shooting at one another, even the "fire-eaters" of Charleston had been remarkably courteous to them. This cordiality was cemented when a dangerous conflagration swept the city on February 17. Elliott and Scott at once sent detachments to battle the flames. Lieutenant David Farragut in *Natchez*, later to be the navy's first admiral, reported that this aid "made a very favorable impression on the citizens," and soon "the chief occupation of the officers was attending parties and dances given by the Charlestonians."[54] Elliott commented to the department, lauding the work of both services in quenching the fire and attesting to "the most harmonious feeling" between himself and Scott. Woodbury responded that he received this information with "much gratification." The secretary continued, ordering the commodore to report to him after accompanying both of his ships to Norfolk.[55]

Late in March Elliott notified the department that "I consider the Nullification problem nearly at an end in South Carolina" and mentioned his sending his ships out of Charleston, and, because of his "delicate health," he asked for and received a long leave. [56] Years later, the commodore summarized his experiences in Charleston: "Of all the public services which Commodore Elliott has been engaged, this was the most delicate, the most embarrassing, which most required prudence, sagacity, and resolution. The excitement among the nullifiers of South Carolina was extreme, and the slightest manifestation of rashness or irresolution on the part of either Commodore Elliott or General Scott, might have led to events of which the bare contemplation is horrible."[57]

During late January and February 1833, circumstances far apart from nullification enabled Elliott once more to affix his star to the diplomatic firmament, providing more details than necessary about it, as was his wont. The French consul in Charleston wrote him that the captain of the French merchantman *l'Aigle* (to Elliott, *Eagle*) feared for the safety of her "valuable cargo" and begged the commodore to dispatch one of his warships to convoy her well out of port. Elliott doubted that she was in any real danger until the consul assured him that a small schooner, heavily armed, had sailed from the harbor on the day that *l'Aigle* was supposed to depart. She might be lying in wait well away from Charleston to make a "piratical attack." While Elliott was in the process of adopting a more positive attitude, the threatened French ship hoisted anchor on her own. Soon intercepted by Mervine in *Experiment*, on the lookout for her, he escorted her well out to sea. Elliott was delighted that his small squadron had assisted "the agent of a nation," France, known as "an early friend and ally." He warmly told the consul, "I beg you, my dear Sir, to feel assured . . . of my readiness at all times to be at your service." Secretary Woodbury was "much gratified" at how the commodore had handled the matter.[58]

On March 26 *Natchez* set sail out of Charleston Harbor. "Commodore Elliott's broad pendant was lowered. . . . A salute was fired in his honor and three cheers were given him by the crew," and one can nod understandingly when Farragut adds in an aside, "at his order."[59] Scott was picked up as a passenger, and the sloop left for Norfolk on April 4.[60]

One final directive remained for Elliott to execute in South Carolina. The department asked him to conduct an inquiry about the desirability of Charleston as a permanent US naval establishment.[61] He happily replied in the affirmative, explaining that he would "serve to convince the disaffected people of Charleston that . . . he was not unmindful of their interests as part of that Union." Peering through his prosouthern prism, he saw that the city was "exceeding eligible as a naval station."[62]

From his base at Norfolk and during frequent visits to Charleston, Elliott, employing his typical promptness in getting at his work, began a stream of letters to presumed experts in that state for applicable information about South Carolina and its major port. As a naval establishment would be sure to jump-start the local economy, he received enthusiastic replies during late 1833 and 1834. A pro-Charleston consensus was reached: its harbor was easy of access for smaller vessels to cross over its sandbar, immense quantities of stone and wood were available nearby, skilled and unskilled cheaply priced labor was abundant, and, close to the West Indies, it could well protect the country's interests in that sphere.

Elliott and his South Carolinian accomplices foresaw that the basic objection to a Charleston base would concern health; almost everyone could recall its awful yellow fever epidemic in 1794. But his respondents counterattacked, arguing that only the area within two miles of the city center was dangerous and then only during midsummer. One of them played their trump—recent mortality studies of the leading seaports along the Atlantic proved that only Boston enjoyed a demonstrable superiority to Charleston as a salubrious habitat.[63]

Elliott's noticeable and growing affiliation with those below the Mason-Dixon Line presumably would be placed on hold when he departed for Boston on May 12, 1833. He considered that he had every likelihood of expecting at least as friendly a reception there as he had received from Charlestonians where the slightest miscalculation might have precipitated a fraternal war. In part because of his own mistakes, he was to be bitterly disappointed.

NINE

Commandant of the Boston (Charlestown) Navy Yard

AS A NAVAL ADMINISTRATOR

WHEN ELLIOTT APPEARED in Boston during that May, his mettle as a navy yard commandant would be tested primarily in two areas: to highlight the degree of his mastery over materials and men and how he would cope with the tempest bearing down upon him after he had affixed a wooden statue of the president on USS *Constitution* herself. To complicate matters, chronologically between the two, severe mob violence against Catholics erupted in neighboring Charlestown, the site of the yard. Circumstances dictated that Elliott had to be a somewhat detached observer, but he was in charge of, by far, the strongest armed force in the area, and that fact cannot be ignored. How and where to describe these riots have caused much time and effort, to such an extent that momentarily I considered treating them in a separate chapter, but as a mere four manuscript pages are devoted to them, it would have made it the shortest segment of the book. Instead, they shall be handled as one of several events highlighting Elliott's tenure at Charlestown.

It must be strongly accentuated that these upheavals in Charlestown composed an aberration, bearing little or no relationship to earlier and later portions of this work, except as part of the continuing analysis of Elliott's character, personality, and career. James Fenimore Cooper's best-selling *History of the Navy of the United States of America* summarized the Navy Department's evaluation of Elliott and his colleagues occupying the same highest level in the service. He apparently enjoyed the government's favor under all Administrations and had commanded the *Ontario* in Decatur's squadron in the war against Algiers and was successively on the Brazil station and in command of the West Indies and of the Mediterranean Squadrons. No officer of his rank, indeed, had filled so many important stations afloat as Elliott since the peace of 1815.[1]

Even so, Cooper forgot to mention some of Elliott's other high-level appointments, such as his diplomatic sojourn in the Gulf of Mexico; Charleston, during the crisis of Nullification; commanding navy yards at Boston, 1833–35, and in the last year of his life, at Philadelphia, which contributed as well to Cooper's favorable and distinctive assessment of his naval career.

Some words of substance about the Board of Navy Commissioners (BNC), for that organization is essential to understand much of the following. It had been created in 1815 to ease some of the crushing burden of paperwork that had swamped the navy secretaries and their clerks during the War of 1812. It consisted of three (later five) senior naval officers, bringing some professionalism into what had been almost completely civilian dominated. Elliott in Boston became one of the most necessary conduits between the Navy Department and the BNC, vis-à-vis himself and his fellow officers.

Piled atop other mandates, the BNC was to bring about the founding of a naval academy (not accomplished until 1845); and the creation of ranks higher than that of post captain (inoperative until the grade of rear admiral during the Civil War).[2] At this time commodore was an unofficial title bestowed on an officer commanding simultaneously more than one USN vessel.

Focus here must restrict itself to Elliott's management of the Boston yard and how well he followed his orders to direct the repairing, maintenance, and outfitting of men-of-war, *Constitution* especially. This had to be coupled with his responsibility to devote similar attention to the yard's buildings, supplies, docks, machinery, and security, along with other less essential duties. In these areas Elliott's accomplishments were highly commendable, in the main, rivaled only by his pronounced aptitude in diplomacy (see chapters 7, 8, 10, and 11).

It should be reemphasized that this is a life of Elliott, not a biography of *Constitution*, nor a treatise on early nineteenth-century navy yards, nor a work on the intricacies of wood and canvas ship construction. Those absorbed in such topics should refer to the astonishingly detailed output of compiler Edwin C. Bearss, *The Charlestown [Boston] Navy Yard, 1800–1842*. It is gargantuan: 1,444 pages buttressed by a mind-confusing 3,581 endnotes! As a personal aside, Bearss thanks only two historians for their assistance, the first essential to him, the second marginal at best: "Commander Tyrone G. Martin, former skipper and later biographer of *Constitution*; and Professor David F. Long of the History Department at the University of New Hampshire, both read the manuscript and shared their encyclopedic knowledge of *Constitution*, Commodore William Bainbridge, and naval lore." I am gratified for this testimonial, but it is most unfair to Martin. Except for my life of Bainbridge and what "naval lore" I have amassed, my contributions, compared to the commander's have been infinitesimal.[3]

When Congress had granted "ministerial duties" to the board, its wording had been imprecise. "Everyone admitted that the Commissioners could oversee the procurement of supplies and all pertaining to the construction, repair, and maintenance of warships." But were they also responsible for the placement and movement of navy vessels and personnel? Absolutely not, ruled President Madison, for these requirements must remain in civilian hands, and that decision was final.[4]

An Elliott biographer must scan the many hundreds of letters in Bearss's ponderous volume 2, exchanged between Elliott and the BNC, searching for evidence as to how well he was meeting his responsibilities. Reviewing the board's correspondence, it becomes evident that in general its members restricted themselves to men-of-war and the operations of the yard, deeming none of their business the personal behavior of officers—that was left to civilian authorities for adjudication.

In the two years that Elliott was commandant at Boston, only three men--of-war required major overhauls, the sloop *Erie* and frigates *Potomac* and *Constitution*. Others that needed comparatively simple repairs or replenishing of supplies were in and out of the yard after Elliott's supervision of their restorations or provisionings. "Old Ironsides" was the greatest challenge, as well as having the closest affiliation with him. So much attention has to be directed at her, necessitating some glances at the marine technology of the "Old Navy."

A most curtailed summary of that noted warship will bring the story up to Elliott's advent at Boston: following her brilliant services in the Quasi-War against France, 1798–1800; the Barbary Wars, 1801–5; and the War of 1812, she spent most of the 1820s in the Mediterranean, often interrupted by essential layovers in Boston and at Mahon in Spain's Balearic Islands, the navy's European station at that time. On her arrival home in 1828 there was some consideration in American naval and political circles that she should be taken out of service. Many still think that she was spared from such an ignominious end by Oliver Wendell Holmes Sr.'s poem, "Old Ironsides," but that is not true. Granting that it did enlist considerable public support for her retention, no one in the new Andrew Jackson administration dared consider seriously "a proceeding so repugnant to the best feelings of all the people, as to have her retired permanently."[5]

From 1830 to 1833 Commandant Bainbridge had recognized that the aged frigate was in such sorry condition after more than thirty years of duty that the most far-reaching repairs and reconditioning would be mandatory to make her seaworthy once more. By Elliott's term, two of her most serious deficiencies were being rectified: she was decidedly "out of line" but "straightened" over many months, as well as "badly hogged," a situation corrected by arching very gradually her keel to elevate her previously drooping forward and aft sections to form a more correct line from stem to stern.[6]

The ailing Bainbridge began to surmount a major obstacle to the department's primary objective. Boston's public dry dock, the only site where a sizable man-of-war could be taken apart and reassembled, was not yet ready for *Constitution*, even though her ballast had been removed and her gun placements had been determined. On June 24, however, that ship finally could move into the dry dock. Within a month Bainbridge was dead, having already been superseded in command of the yard.[7]

Elliott took over on May 12, 1833, to commence a tenure that would last until March 6, 1835. He threw himself into hectic exertions to make "Old Ironsides" fit, while at the same time working to improve the yard's operations.

In the first, all of *Constitution*'s planking was removed and pieces of her timber and metal castings sent to prominent individuals—President Jackson was delighted to have enough of her wood to have a "phaeton" (a light, four--wheeled carriage) made for him. Starting from below, her three main decks were replaced, commencing from the berth (where the crew was housed) to the gun (carrying her main batteries) and to the spar (open and running the vessel's full length); a "poop deck" was erected over the extreme stern, sometimes acting as the roof of the captain's cabin. The pumps were retained, partitions erected, interior woods chosen, and work on the ceilings started. The outer hull was completed and then recoppered, while caulking and exterior and interior paint was applied. In October and November *Constitution*'s "channels were [put] in place" (channels are metal ledges along the ship's sides that secure rigging and keep ropes free of the "gunwales" (raised sides). December and January witnessed sails and masts going in, rigging and canvas tested, provisions and water stowed aboard, and anchors selected.[8]

Typically, the process went something like this: be it the use of cotton sails or the renovation of a warehouse, the board would issue an order to Elliott to which he could accede or offer alternative suggestions. He was free to come up with his own recommendations, but in all cases, the commissioners made the final judgments unless directed otherwise by the navy secretary or the president.

What had been hoped would be a shaft of enlightenment about Elliott turned out to be a disappointment. To aid in evaluating him as a naval officer and a man, one must look to the navy secretary's letters and an assortment of other sources.

Nor could the files of the department, although abetted by Bearss and several other works, give us much more about Elliott's status as executive director of the yard, intermingled as they were with missives from the BNC. We had expected Boston newspaper commentary to fill this gap, but by late 1834 and early 1835, its press was focusing solely on Elliott's role in placing Jackson's effigy on *Constitution* and brushing off alternative matters as inconsequential.[9]

It is time now to train a spotlight on Elliott's interpersonal connections with his officers and men, amid a few other matters. When Elliott took over at Boston in May 1833, at once he let all under him realize that it was *his yard*, and he would run it as he wished. Those recalcitrant would be overridden or, if persistent, be ousted by one means or another. Frequently Elliott would act impulsively, and being quite unable to admit a mistake, he held onto them tenaciously, sometimes for years. When disagreements occurred between him and some of his senior officers with egos as pronounced as his own, discord was practically guaranteed.

Yet the new commandant was able to start with a success. He and almost all of his colleagues had an abiding interest in educating the midshipmen. This was the vital testing period for these teenagers. To gain their lieutenancy within a reasonable time was the high wall to be scaled for that promotion was given only to those deemed worthy of lifetime employment in the service. In addition to seamanship and all the other nonacademic knowledge that they must garner, proficiency in mathematics was crucial; the recommended level of study of French and Spanish secondary. Elliott hammered home these arguments so effectively to Levi Woodbury, secretary of the navy, that he was provided with a capable mathematician as a teacher. He recommended further that every midshipman not otherwise employed must report either to Boston or two naval stations in the South for training in that subject. Within a few months Woodbury made Elliott's suggestions official departmental policy.[10]

Trouble quickly loomed however. Those on duty at the yard were required to attend Sunday religious services there, and Elliott ordered his officers to be present as personal representatives of moral enlightenment for their underlings. It was not, the commandant insisted, to promote any doctrinal position, although he undercut himself by appointing an Episcopalian as pastor. Officers, already burdened with heavy weekday schedules, either wanted to have more time with their families or expressed outrage about this violation of their religious rights under the First Amendment. To make it worse, three of Elliott's senior officers led the opposition: Commander Joseph Smith and Lieutenants Thomas W. Wyman and Edward B. Babbit, the latter demonstrating almost open contempt for his superior.[11] The navy commissioners adopted a hands-off attitude in this instance, permitting the officers to show up on the Sabbath or not, as they wished.

Insofar as documentation can attest, Elliott was able to expel only one officer, and that was by mutual consent. Commander John "Mad Jack" Percival, already a legend in his own lifetime by his flamboyant eccentricities, affection for and from his sailors, and masterful seamanship, detested Elliott, later calling him "a liar." After an unimportant tiff Percival was compelled to apologize most reluctantly. He was delighted to escape from the yard to command the sloop *Erie* for a cruise to lower South America.[12]

When Elliott issued orders to lower ranking petty or warrant officers (clerks, highly rated craftsmen, etc.), he could work his will on them more effectively. To be sure, he lost his case when a yard storekeeper managed to stay on the job after Elliott had demanded his ouster regarding how much he had paid his clerk. A master blockmaker was fired following a disagreement over his wages. Elliott did well with a clerk of the yard, accused by the commandant of publicly expressing anti–Democratic Party opinions and taking frequent unauthorized absences from duty. After some months he was discharged.[13]

Elliott was ever conscious of governmental expenses, a commendable quality, and his letters to the secretary and navy commissioners often stressed opportunities to economize, some of which were adopted, much to the public benefit. But at Boston he took advantage of the weak bargaining position of the yard employees, forbidding any to reside outside its limits, which many had been doing. Then for a time he imposed an irksome "pass system" in which the laborer had to get clearance from his boss before being permitted to vacate the premises.[14]

Elliott next concentrated on lowering his workers' payroll, galloping roughshod over any resistance. In the fall of 1833 his requisition repair moneys were slashed from $16,000 to $12,000, but he compensated for it by twice trimming "the pay of his mechanics." The next spring carpenters struck because they were paid a dollar a day less at the yard than their counterparts in Boston. Elliott "declined boosting their pay one cent," and they returned to the job the next day. He congratulated himself as a "strike-breaker." In January 1835 he made his final antilabor flourish, firing the caulkers en masse and hiring scabs, but two days later, he took the former back at the same wages.[15]

Calling notice to another phase of Elliott in regard to his sailors and marines, Bearss has disappointed us. Studying his index, we could find not a word about how the commodore enforced discipline in cases in which punishment by the lash was applied. To be sure, he has seven listings under "Discipline," but every one of them is before Elliott's tenure, 1833–35, and all concerned the marines alone. This is unfortunate; how a high-level officer treats his enlisted men is helpful in analyzing his career.

As Elliott's energetic performance of his duties is traced through the pages of Bearss, a couple of emergencies earned his attention. During a routine inspection of the ship of the line *Independence*, stationed at the yard, he discovered that when he came aboard she had "four feet of water in her hold," caused by some "rogue" who had broken off a valve below the waterline. "But for Elliott's vigilance 'she must have sunk during the afternoon or night in a depth of 50 feet of water.'"[16]

During December 1834, the commandant considered so grave the possibility of mob action against seven Spanish-speaking pirates who had robbed and tried to murder the people of a Salem merchantman that he and his officers attended their trial, heavily armed but dressed in civilian attire, and left after death sentences had been imposed.[17] Nonetheless, his activities there were evidence of Washington's assessment of him as an able, industrious, and economical officer, which, added to his efficacy in diplomacy, earned him repeatedly high-level appointments to warships and yards.[18]

Elliott also had to contend with the opinions of the US Marine Corps stations at the yard. Relations between the regular navy and its land as well as its sea arm had been disturbed frequently by jurisdictional disputes, for marines were regularly assigned to combat vessels and naval establishments ashore. Their officers were convinced that their naval equivalents in rank thought them inferior. Actually, the two branches got along quite well under Elliott, despite a few unimportant disagreements, as intimated by his note to the department praising Lieutenant Colonel W. H. Freeman, the corps's commander. Indeed, Elliott was grateful for their presence when disgraceful rioting convulsed Charlestown in 1834.

THE ANTI-CATHOLIC RIOTS AT CHARLESTOWN, AUGUST 1834

Anti-Catholicism was a form of hateful intolerance among many in pre-Civil War America and, unfortunately, later. The Congregational Church, the state church in Massachusetts and supported by public taxation of all, was still in power into the 1830s. Practitioners of that Calvinist-oriented sect were terrified that Irish Roman Catholics would wrest control from them. Many Protestant ministers fueled anti-Irish discrimination and detestation with the most incendiary sermons. Some back hack writers churned out trumped-up best sellers featuring their most lurid anecdotes: "In these books appeared tales of secret passageways connecting nunneries with the homes of the clergy . . . and of confessors who abused both their trust and the young ladies whom they confessed."[19]

Charlestown was a community particularly receptive to such inflammation. Between November 28 and December 1, 1833, a number of skirmishes broke out involving Irish railroadmen and teamsters against Protestant crowds that were incensed further after a townsman had been beaten to death. The next evening some five hundred gathered to exact vengeance, leading to hints that the navy yard itself would be stormed the next day. Elliott assembled his full complement, heavily armed, around the rim of the yard, after which cooler heads among the rabble abandoned their plot. He claimed that he was on top of the situation, ordering "double vigilance" should a new crisis emerge there.[20]

About this time the US Marine Corps was enlarged at Boston and put on standby, ready to move against the Charlestown rioters, although no such enhanced action was ever necessary. Late the following summer, the Ursuline Convent atop Benedict Hill in Charlestown was earmarked for destruction. This order of nuns, dating from the Catholic Counter-Reformation of the 1550s and very much alive today, specialized in education. Some dozen or so sisters and sixty pupils had set up a thriving school. On August 11 a mob appeared, the mood of which may be summarized by a placard waved by one of them: "To Arms! To Arms!! Ye brave and free the Avenging Sword unshield!! Leave not one stone upon another in that curst Nunnery that prostitutes female virtue and liberty under the garb of holy Religion!"[21]

At a prearranged signal about eleven at night, tar barrels were ignited: "Led by the same forty or fifty organized men who had been active from the first, they burst open the doors and entered the convent building as the . . . sisters present hurried the . . . pupils through a rear door and into a nearby place of refuge. A little after midnight the torch was applied to both the school and a neighboring farmhouse belonging to the Ursulines. A large crowd stood by until each building had been consumed by flames."[22]

The governor of Massachusetts had called out the militia, abetted by local private military organizations, but they were unable to cope with the emergency, and the disorder continued. On August 12 "men and boys" scaled "Mount Benedict" and destroyed anything that the original rioters had missed, but militiamen thwarted the sacking of a nearby Catholic church.[23]

On August 27 the sheriff of Middlesex County harkened to reports that his jail, holding thirteen of the arrested leaders of the August 11 arson, might be attacked to liberate the prisoners. He asked Elliott to be prepared should his sudden aid be required. The usual seventy marines and two hundred sailors were put on alert, but the night passed without incident. Under instructions from Navy Secretary Mahlon Dickerson, Elliott asked for reinforcements of 125 men from Commandant Charles G. Ridgely at the New York yard, who quickly dispatched them to Boston, but the crisis was ending by mid-September, and they were sent back to Ridgely.

Some Protestants reacted with disbelief and horror that an event could occur at a nineteenth-century American town in which some seventy women and children could have been murdered, but the evidence suggests that many others had been so deeply imbued with the "No Popery" crusade that they applauded the assault. Every one of the riot leaders arrested were acquitted without the jury leaving the box. The Ursulines filed a stream of lawsuits to compensate for their heavy losses but never received a penny.[24]

In an address at Hagerstown, Maryland, almost a decade later, Elliott provided further details about the mob action and its incendiarism. He swore that personally he had arranged for nearby quarters to house the sisters and their flock. More than that, he even enrolled his daughter Catherine in the school. The lady superior of the order wrote him that the girl was still in attendance some two months after the rioting, but then, the records become silent about any further schooling for her. A little later the Ursulines left Charlestown for more cordial surroundings in Catholic Montreal, but whether Catherine went with them cannot be ascertained. Elliott devoted some understandably emotional prose to his daughter's final destiny: "That beloved child has since gone to a better abode, where sorrows cannot come. Once she was all life and joy; but the persecution that was heaped under her father [in reaction against his affixing Jackson's image to *Constitution*] took root upon her young spirit—a sadness settled on her fair brow—she gave up the world—devoted her efforts . . . to religion and charity, and finally died—a martyr!"[25]

It must be admitted that Elliott had done little to quash the riots, but two mitigating factors stand out: he and his well-disciplined and heavily armed contingent might at any time have intervened to clear the mob-filled streets with muskets, pistols, and bayonets. Moreover, the Navy Department always feared that its forces at home and abroad might become political footballs among contending groups, and its advice to its commanders was to exercise restraint until competent political authorities had begged for their assistance.[26]

BACKGROUND OF AND REACTIONS TO HIS AFFIXING ANDREW JACKSON'S EFFIGY ON "OLD IRONSIDES," JULY 1834–MARCH 1835

All of his adult life, Elliott was an avid and compulsive reader of the press, national as well as the local papers wherever he resided. As an ultra-Jacksonian Democrat, he remained in touch with the *Washington Globe* and kept tabs on the opposition's leading journals, *Daily National Intelligencer*, and Baltimore's *Niles Weekly Register* especially. In Boston, while commanding the navy yard, his favorite newspaper and ideological soulmate was the strongly Democratic *Boston Morning Post*, which "soon became the undisputed leader of the party's press in Massachusetts, if not throughout New England."[27] This absorption served him well in describing the president's triumphant sojourn in the Bay State and New Hampshire when Jackson was hailed with the most perfervid acclaim of almost all of his hosts.

In no way, however, did this prepare Elliott to cope with either the fallout of the president's victorious fight in 1833 with the Second Bank of the United States or, in a result unexpected by him, with the frantic Boston opposition the next year to his adorning "Old Ironsides" with a wooden image of "Old Hickory" (see below). These drew upon him not the eulogies that he forecast but a convulsion of abuse that at first bewildered and then embittered him irrevocably. Hence, some probing in depth of newspaper coverage appears essential.

How could Elliott have concluded other than that the Yankees loved their president when he read in the *Post* that he "will be received and entertained here in the most splendid, cordial, and gratifying manner? The name of Andrew Jackson is spoken of in a different tone now, from what it was some twelve months ago [during the election of 1832]." Again, "the people, whether political friends or foes of the President, will enter upon the ceremonies of his reception with a magnanimous and honorable feeling of gratitude... They respect him as a brave and patriotic General, whose glory is the glory of the country. . . . They are not insensible to the great benefits he has conferred upon our common country [by promoting unionism over nullification in 1832]." And again, "Jackson rode around Boston saluting the people, and was received with reiterated and tremendous shouts of approval." Boston was not alone in its reaction to Old Hickory's visit; Concord, New Hampshire, emulated the same spirit of its larger neighbor. Even Harvard College, the bastion of the nation's classical, scientific, and religious lore, awarded him an honorary degree.[28]

The staid *Boston Evening Transcript*, cited as "modest, conservative, non-partisan, and in good taste," was no Jackson supporter. Nonetheless, it joined in the chorus: "He will be greeted, with enthusiasm, in the stronghold of the opposition and will receive on all hands and from all classes every mark of respect which his elevated station, his venerable age, his undoubted patriotism, his military service, and his love of the Union, demand and require of the whole people." Shortly after, "long before his arrival the Hall [Faneuil] was filled. . . . As he passed by, he was cheered by an immense multitude assembled, eager to be presented to him."[29]

On June 25 a shadow was cast over the city by a headline: "SERIOUS INDISPOSITION OF THE PRESIDENT . . . arising from fatigue, over-excitement, and change of the habits of life," which might compel him to break off his tour. Within two days, however, although still "exhausted," he was able to go to Lynn, Marblehead, and Salem before concluding his trip to New Hampshire on July 1. Elliott must have read but ignored as inconsequential the *Transcript*'s warning that things might be different in the future. "The President . . . [has found] himself among a peculiar people . . . of whom not a fifth part will be his . . . friends."[30] Elliott was a naval officer not a political practitioner. Had he been, the changing political tides about to occur might not have so dumbfounded him. But as he perused the evidence of this almost indomitable unanimity of opinion, how could Elliott have avoided the conclusion that he was moving from crisis ridden South Carolina to a far more hospitable climate in the Bay State and its capital? Nor had he misread the Bostonian pulse at that time. Not being a clairvoyant, in no manner could he have foretold that within a few months Massachusetts, Jacksonian adulator, would become a Jacksonian abhorrer, a switch that would reinforce his already strong Democratic bias against the president's Whiggish opposition into a lifelong obsession.

"When Elliott arrived at his new post in Boston on May 12, 1833, he knew all about the unrestrained enthusiasm with which Bostonians had hailed the president for compelling the nullificationists to rescind their proclamation about state sovereignty. This enabled the commandant to start his job with a favorable impression of its people. . . . 'Where was his reception apparently more cordial . . . ? They were all Jackson men! . . . Universities with their honorary degrees, and crowds with their hands to be shaken, jostling each other for an opportunity to be civil.' Elliott asserted that Jackson had to depart with no more than 'a glimpse of New England, for fear of being killed with kindness.'"[31]

All of Elliott's happy anticipations were swept away by an alpha to omega shift in Boston's public opinion. He explained nothing about why this had occurred other than to quote two short sentences only the latter his own: "But soon there will come a frost" and "the deposits were removed!"—and that is every word that he has to offer about it, requiring further elaboration.[32]

The reason for Boston's rapidly altered opinion of Jackson came from his behavior on the matter of rechartering the Second Bank of the United States. This had been based upon Alexander Hamilton's First Bank, 1791–1811. The main features of both were one-fifth public and four-fifths private ownership and acting as a depository of governmental funds, rather than a separate treasury for that purpose. By the early 1830s it had become a financial semimonopoly, lauded by conservatives in the Northeast and the maritime areas as a check on easy credit and a way to maintain a stable currency. For the same reasons, it was disliked increasingly in the South and West, avid for an expansion based upon low interest loans. A head-on confrontation broke out between Jackson and Nicholas Biddle, longtime president of the Second Bank, during which Biddle gambled recklessly and lost. Although the bank's charter still had four years to run, he tried to get it renewed in 1832, only to have the president veto it. Nonetheless, most Bostonians remained calm, enabling its citizens to greet him enthusiastically the next spring.[33]

Jackson's decision in September to remove federal funds from the bank was the key factor in driving the city's economic, political, and social upper strata into an almost frantic backlash against him. Rumors had abounded for some time that the president might strike such a blow, but the country was still taken by surprise by the announcement. The enthusiastic *Post* reacted simply and swiftly by repeating verbatim the *Washington Globe*'s recital of the facts sprawled across its own front page's six columns. Then its editors wheeled into place their big guns to accentuate their support: "In this country the monopolists want the Bank, as it is, and the control of it. They want the Government Deposits. They want high [tariff] duties, to increase the deposits, and appropriations for internal improvements, to make high duties perpetual. The use of money will necessarily be theirs—and to secure this they want one of their own body to *preside* over the United States—the rest of the offices would follow."[34]

Under the banner headline, "THE PEOPLE AROUSED!" the enemies of the Second Bank, at a meeting in Boston, adopted no fewer than twenty-eight separate resolutions, of which the third one set the tenor for the rest: Their opposition wanted "to assume that of a partizan organization, exercising a wanton tyranny over the funds and credit of the commercial classes, and waging a general warfare of intimidation and corruption, upon the press, the people, and their government."[35]

The "Bank War" proved to be the crucible melding the disparate anti-Jackson elements versus Jacksonians.[36] Jackson versus Biddle's bank also served as the catalyst for Elliott's placing the president's effigy on the hallowed *Constitution*. Until they broke over him, he had no reason to be aware of the thunderheads bearing down on him. He expected that the pro-Jacksonian spasm would endure, without comprehending that it had the tensile strength of tissue paper when met by harsh economic and political realities. Knowing that Jackson would return to Boston, he "cordially joined in all the preparations to greet him. Elliott concluded that he "could not perform an act more gratifying to the people of Boston, than by placing upon the bow of what they called their favorite ship, the image of the very man before whose living image they were almost bowing down to worship."[37]

As stories about what Elliott was up to circulated through the city, Jackson was being transformed from Boston's idol into "a roaring lion, an Arab chief, a tyrant, a bully, an ignoramus." His advocate Elliott was pilloried so unmercifully that he exclaimed: "Then are hoisted the flood gates of editorial vituperation, and down pours the foul torrent upon the devoted head of a brave and honorable officer, whose crime was an attempt to please his defamers!"[38]

Such was the uproar that Elliott paused to consider alternatives for the effigy of the president. During his tenure at the yard, *Constitution* had no more on her bow than a "billet head" (an ornament other than a figurehead), and Elliott decided to respond to the pleadings of a few Bostonians by substituting Jackson's statue instead. There may well have been another reason for the change, although we have no specific documentation to prove it.

The inland areas were much more attached to the army—manned in part by local militiamen and the tiny governmental force and in the West, essential for curbing the threat of the Native American tribes—than the coastal districts. To place a military man with no nautical experience whatever on the bow of the nation's most popular warship might enhance recognition and support for the navy. In toto, it could show that the defender of the Union at the recently concluded nullification crisis was at the same time the champion of all Americans, Amerindians, some minorities, and of course, enslaved persons excluded.

Without notification to his naval superiors in Washington, DC, Elliott hired Laban S. Beecher, probably the best-known Boston woodcarver, to begin the Jackson likeness for a stipend of $300. The craftsman proceeded well, eventually producing a life-sized Jackson, grim-faced, wrapped in a dark cloak, with a copy of the US Constitution in one hand and a tall hat in the other.[39]

Beecher provided Elliott with other adornments for the famed frigate, this time on her stern, with small busts of Commodores Hull, Bainbridge, and Stewart, her commanders during her three War of 1812 victories over her British opponents. There is some confusion as to how long they remained there. Commander Tyrone G. Martin is not sure: "It is said that they outlived the original figurehead and remained on board for almost 40 years."[40] Marion S. Brewington, an astute commentator on maritime affairs, depicts photographs of the complete effigy, and the partial reconstruction of the cranium after it had been mutilated by Samuel W. Dewey (see below).[41] But then Brewington goes on to make a statement that defies understanding: "These carvings were never placed on the stern" and shows a photo of it, in which the three busts are clearly visible.[42]

Elliott was at his best disingenuous as to how he persuaded the Board of Navy Commissioners to endorse his representation of the president about the frigate, asserting that its members had bestowed their permission for it.[43] Since 1815 the policy as to ship decorations ordered by commanders on their own was precise: only ships of the line (those of sixty-guns or more) could be so embellished; sloops and frigates must have no more than "slightly carved work of the scroll or wreath character . . . on their bows." Rumors that Beecher was well underway with his project were confirmed when Elliott wrote the commissioners that the figure bore "a strong resemblance" to Jackson. Evidently because the effigy was almost completed and would have to be paid for in any case, Elliott got away with his defiance of naval regulations.[44]

These other matters never interfered with Elliott's main concern—the venom splashed on him by most Bostonians. He responded to his tormentors with unslaked fury aimed at the Whig press, other publications, handbills, and anonymous letters. His enemies, aware that the Jackson likeness would go on the ship, insisted that it be removed: "The editor of the leading national Whig paper was importuned to ply his editorial guns with more vigor than ever. He was told that the image must '*come off*' that Captain Elliott, having thus far sustained himself in this assault, a reaction would ensue in his favor, unless vanquished!" The press charged him with a "deliberate, studied, and flagrant insult to the Boston Community for refusing to do it."[45] But after the appearance of the inflammatory handbill below, Elliott was justified in complaining that the city's journals "opposed to the Federal Administration, contain no rebuke to this threatened violence—no caution against this meditated infringement of the laws! None! None!! None!!!"[46]

This handbill has been used so often in discussions of the Jackson figurehead that its omission here was considered, but as it does summarize so well the passions of the day, it should still be included.

> FREEMEN AWAKE! OR THE CONSTITUTION WILL SINK
> It is a fact that the old "Glory President," has issued his special orders for a Colossean [*sic*] Figure of his *Royal Self* in Roman Costume, to be placed as a figurehead on Old *Ironsides!!!* Where is the spirit of '76?—Where the brave Tars who fought and conquered in this glorious ship, where the mechanics, and the Bostonians who have rejoiced in her achievements? Will they see the Figure of a Land Lubber at her bow? No, let the cry be "all hands on deck" and save the ship by a timely remonstrance expressing our indignation on a voice of thunder!
>
> > Let us assemble in the "Cradle of Liberty," all hands up for the *Constitution*—let the figure head (if mortal man be worthy) be that of the brave HULL, the immortal DECATUR, or the valiant PORTER, and not that of a tyrant. Let us not give up the ship . . . !
> >
> > North-enders! Shall this Boston built ship be thus disgraced without remonstrance? Let this *Wooden God*, this Old Roman,

> building at the expense of 300 dollars of the people's money, be preserved to the *Office Holders* who glorify in such worship. But for God's sake,
>
> SAVE THE SHIP from this foul disgrace!
> [Signed]
> A NORTHENDER[47]

This incessant salvo of abuse, culminating in a death threat, was so repugnant to Elliott that understandably he developed a lasting antipathy toward Bostonians. Although we lack documentation to prove it, he must have harkened back frequently to Charleston during the nullification crisis to make the sharpest differentiation between the behavior and character of South Carolinians and those of Massachusetts. Elliott, commanding the naval forces, and General Scott, commanding the military, had been required to circulate freely among the southern "fire-eaters," both sides heavily armed. A miscalculation by either bloc could have sparked the conflagration. But invariably the unionists were treated with gentlemanly politeness, in recognition that they were only carrying out their orders.

On the other hand, the people of Massachusetts, disregarding Elliott's obligations to his government, heaped ugly invective and warnings of physical harm upon an officer who, according to his own lights, had been doing no more than endeavoring to please Bostonians, heretofore Jacksonian deifiers. The disparity between the two sections he thought so fundamental as to be irreversible. Elliott's prosouthern axis, noticeable earlier, became fixed for the rest of his life.

"The commandant warmed to his task. Being a Pennsylvanian, he was imperfectly acquainted with Boston: he knew not the spirit of its politics. He did not know that its ruling party, claiming all its 'respectability,' considered all expedients lawful to gain a political end, and felt no compunctions in shooting with poisoned arrows or stabbing with poisoned knives. . . . No quarter was to be given to a political adversary. . . . He was to be hunted both abroad and at home, at his business or his fireside; that in the veritable spirit of a bull of excommunication. . . . They *cursed him in all parts and interdicted him from every thing.*[48]

More to the point, Elliott labored to retaliate by inflicting real political and economic hardship on Boston, urging the secretary to offer his "helping hand" to put deserving Democrats into positions of power there and elsewhere. Moreover, no additional warships should be constructed at the Boston yard. Instead, award such contracts to other cities, "where we have *made friends*, and I cannot see the justice or propriety," in using a place where "there is so much deadly hostility toward the Administration."[49] Despite this enthusiastically partisan appeal, Elliott was unsuccessful on both counts. "Worthy Democrats" were swept out of office automatically when the Whigs took over, and Boston continued to be a major site for the building and repairs of US men-of-war.

The handbill had been aggravating enough, but one lone pamphlet was even worse for Elliott, as it impugned his courage. Matthew Calbraith Perry, of later Japanese fame, was the leading defender of his elder brother Oliver Hazard Perry and his reputation. He accentuated Elliott's strange behavior at the Battle of Lake Erie in 1813, dubbing him either as a coward or a conniver, trying to snatch the victory for himself.[50] Others dug up his recent controversies with Captain Percival and Lieutenant Babbit while both served under him at the yard to label him as a brutal and overbearing officer.

Anonymous and scurrilous accusations and threats, a few addressed to his own house, and others from different sources were almost impossible for Elliott to tolerate dispassionately. For instance during the American Revolution, "when the minions of despotic power dared to insult and outrage the people," they received "A COAT OF TAR AND FEATHERS as a suitable emblem and adornment for such contemptible fools." Another sounded the same trumpet—Elliott should "wear a tar and feather proof coat" the next time he appeared in Boston. And then the life-threatening ultimatum: "Take Jackson's name off the dock. Or in 48 hours you breathe no more."[51]

While still caught in the maelstrom of hatred that enveloped him, Elliott was told by woodcarver Beecher that he had been approached by "three respectable citizens" who offered him $1,500 for the image, adding that as much as $20,000 might be raised in the city to get it. As Beecher could not guarantee its safety in his shop, Elliott sent a detachment to pick up the effigy and had it brought to the yard's "machinery house," which was made available for the work's continuation. On April 28 it was attached to the frigate's bow. Sometime over the next few weeks *Constitution* was moved a short distance from the dock and moored between two laid-up ships of the line, *Columbus* to her portside and *Independence* to her starboard.[52] Elliott worried about efforts to kidnap the image and thought the most likely danger was from Bostonians employed at the yard. Extra men were placed on *Columbus*, with "a sentry stationed where he could see the figurehead, while a second was on a nearby wharf, and a third patrolled the frigate's forecastle. From one of *Columbus*' open ports, a beam of light outlined the graven features."[53]

On the night of July 2 the city shook under a tremendous thunderstorm with lightning continuously flashing amid a drenching downpour. A single oarsman in a rowboat (Samuel W. Dewey) put out from the Boston shore, crossed the harbor, crept around *Independence*, sculled to *Constitution*'s side, climbed up dangling ropes to the effigy, and began cutting below the lips. But when his saw hit metal the screech aroused the sentry who peered intently in his direction until the storm drove him to a shelter. A few more cuts and the head was severed just above the chin,[54] after which he returned to the city and hid it.

Elliott had every right to be apprehensive about protecting *Constitution.* Only three days after this first assault on her, a second attempted to eradicate what remained on the frigate's bow, but Elliott's extra lookouts spotted two men approaching in a boat. One escaped over the yard's wall, but the other evidently drowned.[55]

It was soon common knowledge, among the Whigs, that Dewey, a merchant marine skipper, was the successful prankster. Having just returned from the Caribbean, he dropped in at the office of his employers, who brought him up to date about the interplay between Elliott and the city. Dewey remarked casually that for whatever pittance he was offered, he would attend to the matter ($100 was paid to him later by his advocates).[56] The Whigs and Democrats reacted to the exploit as might be expected, "with wit and laughter" by the former and "wrath and indignation by the latter." One passé history of the noted frigate claimed that among the Whigs, "a club was formed and various gentlemen assembled at a dinner in which the head formed the centerpiece. When the members met in the street they were in the habit of drawing their hands across their chins by way of indicating their enjoyment of Dewey's cut."[57]

This information seems to have driven Elliott to the verge of apoplexy, although his long-delayed letter to the department about it was quite restrained. In his "biography," however, published within a few months, he threw away any trace of moderation: "The head of the image was sawed off!! Yes! The premises of the nation were clandestinely invaded, a national ship was mutilated and defaced, and the constituted authorities of the nation insulted . . . ! The press was replete with approving, with exulting paragraphs. . . . Yes! The citizens of Boston were exulting over a crime! A violation of the laws! A lawless moblike act!"[58]

If the above may be called overly hysterical, it paled in comparison to the commodore's reaction to how some Whigs celebrated Dewey's accomplishment. He learned shortly thereafter of a banquet held at a Boston "coffee--house" to honor Biddle, president of the Second Bank of the United States, with forty-four prominent Whigs as guests: "After the cloth was removed, the servants were sent from the room, the doors locked, and,—Bostonians! blush while the revolting story is told! THE HEAD OF THE IMAGE WAS

BROUGHT IN, LAID UPON THE TABLE, AND BACCHANALIAN ORGIES WERE HELD OVER IT!!! And this is the chivalry of Boston . . . ? They assembled at a Pandemonian banquet, and celebrate with licentious orgies a violation of the laws, an indignity to the chief magistrate of their country! the representative of its executive authority! Shame! Shame!"[59]

Almost immediately the navy commissioners and the secretary showed up on an already scheduled visit to the yard. Dickerson "ordered the covering of canvas [by Elliott] to be continued on it, saying that no repairs or alterations of it should be made while the ship remained in Boston."[60]

As for Dewey, his identity remained undisclosed—to Elliott at least—until he named himself as the culprit six months later. He had carried the head to Washington, DC, planning to present it to Jackson, but the president was ailing and unavailable. Undaunted, Dewey went to the Navy Department, demanded to see the secretary, and told him about his exploit. Dickerson was "aghast" and started to have him arrested, only to hear the discouraging answer, "You cannot inflict any punishment," as he could be charged with no more than "trespass, and if a Middlesex [County] jury don't give me damages, my name's not Dewey." Recalling that there was then no law "against defacing warships," Dickerson recognized his defeat. "You are right, sir. Now tell me all about the affair."[61]

On March 2, 1835, the renovated *Constitution* sailed for New York City on the first leg of two successive cruises to Europe. On her way out of the harbor the Whigs were alleged to have made their last exertion to prevent what remained of the Jackson statue from leaving with the ship. According to Elliott, he had been informed that cannon would be placed on small islands at the end of the channel and fire upon her. One has to concur with Elliott that "it is impossible to believe that they were serious in threatening this insane scheme[,] . . . [but] it shows by what expedients they are willing to accomplish their desires." As the frigate swept toward the open sea, in a final gesture of contempt for his enemies in Boston, Elliott had cloaked his figurehead with a five-striped flag representing the five New England states, Massachusetts in particular, which had opposed many administrative measures to prosecute the War of 1812, even flirting with the idea of secession from the Union.[62]

To wrap up the history of the Jackson image: at Boston in 1848 the final and best reproduction of it was carved by J. D. and W. S. Fowle; today it is at the US Naval Academy in Annapolis.[63] One out-of-date historian recounts an anecdote that our research cannot authenticate: When Dewey's story "reached President Jackson, he was highly amused and reported to have said, "I never did like that image! Give the man a postmaster's job!"[64]

Shortly before he died in 1845, Elliott published his *Memoir*. In it he reminisced about his own accomplishments, some true, some whitewashed, and some false, while venting his fury at those who had crossed swords with him.[65]

IN THE COURT-MARTIAL OF LIEUTENANT EDWARD B. BABBIT, 1834–1835

As if Elliott, by placing the Jackson figurehead on "Old Ironsides," had not implicated himself in enough turmoil to satisfy the most intransigent individual, he was plunging simultaneously into another head-on controversy by doing his utmost to ruin Lieutenant Edward B. Babbit professionally and personally. Elliott exhibited a malevolence even beyond his usual level and therefore deserves a somewhat extensive treatment.

To suggest that Elliott had sufficient reasons to view the Babbit family at least in part as a hostile clan, the story must revert to 1805 when Elliott and Fitz Hugh, brother of Dr. William D. and Lieutenant Edward B. Babbit, were fellow midshipmen in USS *Vixen* and again in 1807 when the two officers served together in USS *Argus*. Since Elliott became convinced that the other was a "perjured villain," he fought without success to block Fitz Hugh's promotion to lieutenant (see chapter 1).[66]

This account must now leap forward to May 1826 to establish the connection between Elliott and Dr. William D. Babbit, his senior surgeon, while the commodore was commanding *Cyane* on the Brazil Station. Although there is no reason to doubt that their association was amiable, the circumstances of the doctor's death turned into a matter of grave consequence in the joust between his brother Edward and Elliott, culminating in the former's trial in 1834.

While *Cyane* was at Montevideo, Uruguay, Dr. Babbit requested and was given permission by Elliott to go ashore. There he met "Dr. Bond," the city's US consul, who told him that one of his patients, who was also "a personal friend from Philadelphia," had been smitten with smallpox and asked for his assistance. Babbit at first declined to attend, as he had serious doubts about whether his own vaccination against that sometimes lethal disease was still effective. Since the vaccine's injection, he had been "salivated" several times to treat liver complaints and fever, perhaps making him susceptible to reinfection. Nevertheless, he decided to risk a visit to Bond's friend.[67]

Frankly, we were baffled as to how the presence of saliva could apply to fighting smallpox, until we noted that the *Oxford English Dictionary* carried a subheading under "salivate" that meant "to treat with mercury," but we still needed more. Three of our colleagues at the University of New Hampshire provided us with further information. Mercury is a poison, and some of its compounds are deadly. Even if applied in less virulent forms, its repeated use could first weaken and then kill a patient. They speculated that the medical knowledge of that time could not assess accurately the toxic effect of the doses, and that Babbit may have been already dying, and his last smallpox attack merely hastened the inevitable.[68]

On his return to the ship Babbit revealed his apprehension that inadvertently he might spread the disease among his shipmates. Although no symptoms had yet appeared, the doctor was removed from the crowded gun deck where the lieutenants resided to the airier and more commodious "cockpit"; the midshipmen there were ordered to the gun deck. No attempted cures mattered, however, for Babbit's fears were soon confirmed. While *Cyane* was en route to Rio de Janeiro, the doctor fell gravely ill and his assistant surgeon knew that it was smallpox. According to Elliott: "Every attention and kindness which could be extended by his messmates, was shown to him on our passage. . . . I think he expired one or two days before our arrival, which was after a passage of fourteen days. The body, however, was kept, although a putrid mass; and, with my officers, in the presence of some of the crew, I saw him interred in the Episcopal cemetery at Rio de Janiero—placing, with my own hands, the last shovel full of earth upon his grave."[69]

This would seem to show that Elliott, even though despising Fitz Hugh, regarded Dr. Babbit with affection and esteem. But when the commodore took command at Boston in May 1833, brother Edward B. was stationed there already. The two clashed almost at once when that lieutenant, with ill-disguised contempt, refused to obey Elliott's order about mandatory officer attendance at Sabbath services.[70] In such situations Elliott tended to react simply by having the offender reassigned elsewhere, but here, he determined to rid himself of Babbit by making accusations against him damaging enough to compel his court-martial.[71]

Babbit, through the medium of his defense attorney, and eight years after the fact, in essence accused Elliott of being responsible for his brother's death in 1826. Political overtones were clear. Charles G. Loring, his counsel, was a leading member of the Massachusetts bar, and a prominent advocate of the soon-to-be-named Whig Party, dedicated to seizing power from the Democrats and their president. Elliott, to the contrary, was nationally recognized as a loud public supporter of the Democrats and Jackson, their champion. So Loring, by supplying fuel to the already incendiary Jackson figurehead affair, was delighted to promote his own political cause by denigrating that of the commodore.

Loring's stagecraft in his opening statement and the content of it infuriated Elliott, and he quoted Babbit's paragraph so offensive to him: "I might appeal to the facts, as I alone of the three sons of a widowed mother, who entered the Naval service of the United States, survive to maintain her. That one of them [Fitz Hugh], holding the rank I now stand [lieutenant] fell honorably at his post in battle, during the last war, and I might point to the grave of the other [William] in a foreign land, who received his death blow while executing an order given the *prosecutor* [emphasis added] under circumstances which it is believed he will never forget, leaving a widow and children who look to me as their protector and guide."[72]

Elliott wrote acidly that: "The counsel read this paragraph with what was intended for a thrilling emphasis, with a glance directed at Commodore Elliott, the object of which seemed to be his annihilation. . . . Commodore Elliott heard this with astonishment and scorn; astonishment that he should be the object of an imputation so heinous as the murder of the late Dr. Babbit, for such was the obvious meaning of the counsel's words; and scorn of its baseness, whosoever it was, that could invent such a slander."[73]

Before commencing his counterattack, Elliott determined to enter clearly into the records that he was deeply committed to promoting the welfare of the surgeon's widow and her two young children. He wrote Edward Everett, Massachusetts congressman and famed orator, that the laws did not permit the Navy Department to furnish any money to them, so congressional action was necessary. Everett responded that he was introducing a bill for such a purpose, and that the commodore should call also for assistance from the chairman of the House Committee on Naval Affairs, but all to no avail.[74]

This, however, was distinctly secondary to Elliott's main task—to force Loring and his client to admit publicly in their malign and irresponsible intimation that he had been directly responsible for the doctor's death by compelling him to attend Bond's patient. With his typical meticulous attention to detail, Elliott began corralling supporting letters from as many officers as possible to prove that Dr. Babbit had made his own ill-fated decision to go ashore. No fewer than eight of his colleagues responded that either they knew that the commodore had given no such instructions or had no reason to infer that he had.[75]

In this instance Elliott was unquestionably the victor; he had proved that he never compelled the doctor to treat the man felled by smallpox. Yet further correspondence was required before Loring and Lieutenant Babbit would admit the same. The commodore started his barrage with a long letter to Loring, demanding that in fairness he must know the identity of who had decided to include the false allegation—Loring? Babbit? Or both?[76] Loring replied by objecting to "the tone of your letter," and since he had had no further word from him, "I do not acknowledge any accountability to you upon the subject."[77]

One assumes that there must have been some acrimonious conversations between Loring and Babbit about the lawyer's insistence to include that paragraph in his opening presentation against the lieutenant's initial objections. At least Babbit thought it wise to send an apology of sorts to his persecutor, commenting about "the passage in my defense that you complain of as erroneous and objectionable. Had you applied to me on the subject . . . you would have received that explanation which would have prevented your looking elsewhere for the responsibility of that paragraph. . . . I, therefore, am alone responsible for any statement or remark made in my defense." He concluded: "I am as solicitous to do justice to you as I was to obtain it for myself, and if I have made an erroneous statement, it will give me the greatest satisfaction to correct it as publicly as it was made, and to express my deep regret, that I should have unintentionally done you this injustice; and if you will furnish me with the documents relative to this matter, they shall be made as public as is or may be, the defense."[78]

The most inflexible antagonist might have been assuaged by this, for what Elliott had wanted had been conceded—Babbit was the man responsible for it. But no, ignoring the lieutenant, he replied to Loring alone: "I cannot admit a right in you to interpose an irresponsible person [!] between us. . . . I must and still do insist in my right, to hold an individual responsible for his errors until a correction is properly made. It therefore rests with yourself to decide whether to close this whole matter, or compel me to remain for subsequent action."[79] Political considerations are the only explanation we can provide for Elliott's strange behavior. If he could force Loring to accept accountability, he might score points against that anti-Jackson adherent and for the president.

Elliott wanted no trial by newspapers in the matter that might allow the public to come to its own conclusions about the rival assertions of Babbit and himself. Rather, he would destroy the lieutenant's reputation and perhaps his naval career by hauling him before court-martial judges on four separate charges.

Before expounding on the above four accusations, a short explanation of how the naval judicial system operated during this era would seem advisable. Naval courts usually emulated those of the civil system. Such charges as those leveled by Elliott against Babbit would usually come first before a naval court of inquiry, the equivalent of a grand jury, to decide whether there were grounds for an indictment. If there were, the case would then be tried by the court-martial judges, the equivalent of a petty jury (of one's peers), and if the accused were found guilty, punishment would be inflicted by agreement between the president and his secretary of the navy.

In this instance, the commodore had enough influence with the Navy Department to bypass any inquiry and proceed directly to Babbit's court-martial. To be sure, Elliott disclaimed any personal responsibility for this move, avowing that the decision had been that of Dickerson alone, describing him as "a gentleman no less distinguished for his correctness of transacting public business than for the purity of his principles and his nice sense of honor." That the secretary of the navy was the one who "thought that the passage in Lieutenant Babbit's defense which had reflected so unjustly upon Commodore Elliott could not be overlooked by the Department." He insisted that the accused must make further explanations as Babbit was under consideration for promotion to commander.[80]

Evidently Babbit on his own had anticipated the need for an abject apology. He may well have been terrified that if he did not he might lose a commander's extra pay, which would help him to support more adequately his brother's widow and children. He caved in completely, writing Dickerson that: "The paragraph alluded to, was inserted under an impression of my own, that such was the fact, and I now cheerfully state that my present conviction is that there was nothing improper in the conduct of Com'd Elliott, in the unfortunate circumstances that led to my late brother's death."[81]

Poor Babbit might have spared himself further mortification from his implacable foe. Elliott had received a copy of the above letter from the department and continued to castigate his subordinate, commenting that "had your deportment in this Yard before your trial been such as it was after it, I should have been spared the necessity of preferring charges against you, and you from the trouble of answering them." Here, for the first and only time in this clash, Elliott added a merciful note: "I . . . remove so far as I am concerned any barrier that does, or may exist between you and your promotion; that you may still continue to be a protector and guide to the widow and children of your late brother. . . . You are at liberty to file a copy of this communication in the Navy Department, and reap any advantage that may arise from its candid tenor."[82] Whether the above had any beneficial consequences to Babbit cannot be proven. But the lieutenant was promoted to commander on March 3, 1835.[83]

Possibly the court judges may have noted with approval Elliott's removal of himself as an impediment to Babbit's advancement. If so, Elliott might have thrown it away by interjecting a long letter to former secretary of the navy Levi Woodbury utterly extraneous to the issues at hand. He used it to demonstrate "how uniformly attentive is Captain Elliott to the morals and deportment of the men under his command at the Boston Navy Yard." Naturally he said nothing about a few of his officers there who openly defied his order that they must attend Sunday church services at the yard. No matter how much he may have considered himself a paragon of the Christian gospel and a shining personal example to the moral improvement of his people, the judges may have spotted how completely these admirable activities contrasted to the almost endless hostility with which he was hounding Babbit.[84]

Babbit's court-martial commenced on October 16, 1834, and continued until the twenty-ninth. It was under the presidency of Captain William M. Crane and composed of Judge Advocate Charles W. Cutler, acting as the prosecuting attorney; Babbit, the accused, who in effect became his own counsel; and thirteen judges. All were veterans in the service and had already or would eventually tally a distinguished naval record.[85]

If this book were a case study in how the naval judicial system operated, possibly meticulous engrossment should be devoted to the testimonies offered. But for a life of Elliott it would seem an exercise in needless tedium to bore into the attestations of the scores of witnesses called by both sides and their responses to incessant cross-examinations. Nor were the paginal delineations much help. For instance, just as the question of Babbit's use of "warping chocks" appeared to be reaching a critical junction, one side or the other would interject the matter of the lieutenant's presence on the deck when *Potomac* was being docked or why the bowsprit had not been taken ashore or how Babbit estimated the amount of ballast in that frigate's hold, only to go back to the "warping chocks."

Attention must also be directed at the organizational inconsistency of the charges. Since Elliott's motivations for, and the content of, his hate-filled assault upon his subordinate, must be the core of this chapter, perhaps the most productive way for this to be done is to pay little notice of the numerical listing of the charges, and except in passing largely ignore one, three, and four—all connected with Babbit's behavior in the sloop *Erie* and the frigate *Potomac*. This will permit special emphasis on charge two, "Un-officer-like Conduct," by far the most damaging to the defendant and the one that aroused his greatest resentment (for amplification, see below).

To be sure, Elliott had spread his net wide enough in these three charges to mark Babbit as an arrogant usurper of powers denied to him under naval law by illicit alterations in *Erie*, "without the knowledge or consent of the Commandant of the Navy Yard, his commanding officer."[86] "Neglect of Duty" (charge three) and "Disobedience of Orders" (charge four), concerned the lieutenant and *Potomac*. Moreover, both the charges themselves and their three specifications were word for word. One or more of the judges might have cocked an eyebrow or shaken a head about this similarity. Why had not "Neglect" and "Disobedience" been combined? They both pertained to exactly the same circumstances; perhaps some of them concluded that the only explanation was Elliott's effort to pad an already weak case.

At this point it is obligatory to fill out more fully our reasons for delaying charge two—"Un-officer-like Conduct"—until after these brief comments on charges one, three, and four. The latter three pertained on the whole to shipboard alterations that in no way interfered with the operations of *Erie* and *Potomac*. But when Elliott struck hard at everything that Babbit was supposed to exemplify, not only to demolish his service reputation but his status in contemporary American society, for in both, "officer" and "gentleman" meant the same.

Those of us who concentrate on early US naval history and biography have come across the words "officer-like" and "gentlemanly" scores of times, but we had never read anything that would permit us to describe them accurately, until a new book appeared at just the right time for us. Christopher McKee, professor of history and librarian at Grinnell College in Iowa, published his magnus opus titled, *A Gentlemanly and Honorable Profession.* He emphasizes that although these terms were used incessantly in naval correspondence, no one had defined them with any precision whatever. So McKee himself has done so: "Behavior of [an officer and] a *gentleman* was a broad umbrella embracing ethical conduct, internalized discipline, avoidance of indulgence or self-destructive excess, courteous and harmonious relationships with one's peers, manners, personal cleanliness, neatness in one's belongings and surroundings, refined personal interests, and the habit of associating with and emulating one's social equals or—better yet—those of superior social standing. . . . It was an amorphous and internalized code of conduct, acquired as much by observation as by admonition or by reading and study. Much of its force derived from the officer's perception of the social stratum to which he thought he belonged or that which he aspired to achieve."[87]

The crux of charge two concerned Elliott's testimony that Babbit, knowing that he himself had been responsible for the alterations in *Erie* and aware that it might mean the carpenter's dismissal from the service, nonetheless tried to foist off on him the blame. By denying these facts "willfully and maliciously," Babbit had committed perjury (although that word was not used). "By . . . thus endeavoring to screen himself from reproof by denying an order which he had given, in a manner derogatory to his rank as an officer of the Navy, he was totally subversive to all military rule and discipline."[88] If Elliott could accomplish his purpose, Babbit, would stand before the world not only as a liar but a perjurer, quite unfit to be an officer and by extrapolation no gentleman as well.

Obviously the events of June 27 prompted Elliott to take the most drastic action against his enemy. *Potomac* was undergoing repairs at the yard with Babbit in charge of operations. According to his commander, he had disobeyed orders to remove some masts and ascertain accurately the amount of ballast in her hold, removing it if carrying too much. Worse still, he had been told by Elliott to be at the dry dock at three in the morning and had not appeared on time to oversee bringing the ship to the side of the wharf. Actually, the testimonies of Babbit and others had thoroughly refuted each allegation, but the inflexible Elliott charged ahead.[89]

With ardent eloquence Babbit described the aftermath: "And for this [the events of June 27] was I abruptly, and without a moment's opportunity for explanation, suspended from duty—ordered to my quarters, and there confined for the space of twenty-six days, and after a lapse of almost four months, am now exposed to the mortification and anxiety of being arraigned as a criminal before this honorable court."[90]

He went on: "And I confess I am scarcely able to repress the feelings with which I contemplate this accusation and the evidence upon which it is founded. . . . It is with an indignation almost unutterable, that I look upon such a blow, stricken by such a hand, at the honor of the naval service—a blow which, if successfully give, should drive every honorable man from its ranks. . . . The accusation is of wilful and malicious falsehood; an offense in all ranks and stations allied with infamy; the imputation of which, in civil life, is among the deadliest of insults [leading to a duel]; and which in naval and military service, is justly considered a crime deserving exemplary and disgraceful punishment."[91]

Next, he backtracked a little with a somewhat diffused attack upon his tormentor: "I will not demean myself nor degrade the service by intimating that one of its officers, high in rank, and filling so high a post would be betrayed into a base attempt to destroy the reputation and prospects of another, by a wilful and deliberate falsehood: no—I will attribute it to inaccuracy of recollection—distraction of thought—agitation of mind, or the involuntary workings of perverted passions, benumbing the memory—to any thing rather than the disgraceful crime with which he has charged me, upon this record." A page later, however, Babbit let fly his real belief as to why his ordeal had been mandated. It was no more than "the gratification of [Elliott's] deadly hostility to the accused."[92]

The outcome of Babbit's court-martial depended upon the combatants and their supporters as to which had been the more creditable. Few could have attended the sessions or read the documentation without concluding that Babbit had routed Elliott. Yet the American judicial system, naval as well as civil, is replete with examples in which juries return verdicts that fly in the face of the evidence. Babbit had ample time to reflect on what might happen to him if convicted on all four—or even any one—of the charges. Dismissal from the navy was unlikely, for testimony throughout had been controversial. But surely Babbit faced suspension from active duty without pay for months or even years, attended by personal disgrace and possible financial ruin, at least temporarily.

The lieutenant might have saved himself apprehension; he was vindicated triumphantly when the court delivered its verdict on October 29, 1834:

> The court having maturely and deliberately weighed and considered the foregoing charges and specifications, and the evidence in support of the same, and the allegations, and evidence adduced in behalf of the accused,

are of opinion that none of the specifications under the several charges are proved; and do adjudge that the same Edward B. Babbit is not guilty of any of the said charges, and do hereby acquit him of the same.
[signed]
W. M. Crane, President of the Court
Charles W. Cutler, Judge-Advocate.[93]

It was a most humiliating debacle for Elliott. His failure to have Babbit convicted as un-officer-like and ungentlemanly had redounded on himself to demonstrate that he himself could hardly be deemed either.

For reasons unexplained in the sources, the court's findings were withheld from the public for an indeterminate time, a decision most assuredly unfair to Babbit. Over the next few weeks, however, one of the most prominent national newspapers reported that Bostonians, ever mindful of Jackson's effigy "disgracing their beloved frigate [*Constitution*]" were flocking to support the accused: "It is said that a purse of five hundred dollars has been made up and will be tendered to Lieutenant Babbit to defray the expenses incident to the investigation."[94]

The commodore's reaction to this crushing setback was remarkably uncommon, both generally and specifically. Most in his uncomfortable condition would have spent much effort accentuating the unfairness of the verdict and in every way trying to reestablish his tarnished reputation. The fact that Elliott did not is puzzling, for he was a grudge carrier of the first rank, as proven by his replenishing of the feud with Towson for twenty-two years after Black Rock and with Perry following the Battle of Lake Erie in 1813, long past his rival's death in 1819, and which continued beyond his own twenty--six years later.

Elliott behaved for the rest of his life as if no verdict acquitting Babbit had ever been rendered. Rather, in letter after letter, as well as in his de facto autobiography, he never referred to Babbit's acquittal. The only aspect of their confrontation was on the single issue of Babbit's apology to him for his offensive paragraph with its intimation that Elliott had been responsible for his brother's death in Uruguay in 1826.

This chapter is of the highest importance to one attempting to analyze Elliott's character and personality, as well as his stature in early American naval history. During his command of the Boston Naval Yard, 1833–35, it appears that Elliott's discretionary judgment—his realization of how far he should go in pursuing private vendettas—was eroding. This led beyond the pummeling he received from Bostonians for the Jackson figurehead to the numerous pitfalls into which he would stumble while commanding the Mediterranean Squadron from 1835 to 1838.

Babbit's case would be a direct forerunner of another arraignment even more damaging to Elliott's career when the latter earned the undying enmity of *Constitution*'s Passed Midshipman Charles C. Barton, an officer ranking even lower than Babbit. Their mutual rancor reached such a pitch that the Navy Department had no option but to accede to each of their demands. Barton's trial preceded Elliott's, and he vanquished the commodore when he was victoriously acquitted of all charges.

Note, however, that Babbit's success did no more than embarrass Elliott personally, as proven when his adversary was appointed to head the Mediterranean Squadron, a position ardently coveted by scores of other high-level officers. On the other hand, as the next chapter will demonstrate, Barton's achievement prompted in large part Elliott's court-martial panel to bring about the commodore's conviction and suspension from the service from 1840 to 1843, splashing an irremediable stain on his naval record (see. chapter 12).

Before his tenure at the Boston yard was over, on the political front Elliott had jolted the complacency of pro–Bank of the United States and Whiggish elements locally and nationally by his extremely pro-Jackson stance. Moreover, he had roiled the naval establishment by his dogged persecution of Babbit. Once in command of *Constitution*, while cruising in the Mediterranean early in 1835, he also mishandled the case of Barton under somewhat the same circumstances (see chapter 12). Both are deemed so pertinent to evaluate the repellent aspects of Elliott's makeup as to deserve special emphases in this chapter and the next. They have necessitated this brief hiatus before returning to the chronological sequence about his short diplomatic errands to Europe, prior to his taking over the Mediterranean Squadron.

Ten

Diplomacy in Europe and as Commodore of the Mediterranean Squadron

In early drafts of this work, we tried to combine all of Elliott's cruises to Europe during the 1830s but, on further reflection, divided them into chapters 10 and 11. The reason for this reconsideration was that the second segment, commanding the Mediterranean Squadron, August 1835–July 1838, needed several times as much coverage as the first.

Although this initial 1835 cruise has been labeled correctly as "diplomatic," Elliott's position was quite unlike those during his previous tenures abroad in lower South America, Mexico, and the Caribbean, as narrated in chapters 7 and 8. In them he operated as a squadron commander and as such enjoyed great liberty to do what he wished, subject only to later evaluations by the Navy and State Departments.

Yet, when he was instructed by Jackson to accompany Edward Livingston, former US secretary of state and current minister to France, and his family, the job was to carry Livingston aboard the *USS Constitution* to conduct delicate negotiations with the French government. Should these fail, every likelihood existed that a Franco-American war would be forthcoming. Of course the captain and the diplomat would converse at length about the crisis. Elliott's laudable accomplishments in foreign relations would ensure that his opinions would be considered carefully. All the same, Livingston was the man responsible and to him would go the eulogies or castigation for whatever ensued.

The Washington-Paris contention was long-standing, dating back to the Napoleonic Wars, after which Americans became increasingly resentful about Paris's delays in repayment for illegal French seizures of their merchantmen and cargoes. The confrontation ostensibly was settled in 1831 when France pledged to disgorge 25 million francs in six annual installments, starting in

1833. But then its Chamber of Deputies balked at providing the stipulated amount, partly because of political infighting and partly because of monarchical dislike of upstart republicans. In December 1833 the announcement was made that nothing would be paid.

Jackson, in his annual message to Congress, was so incensed that he retaliated. He recommended that if the French did not meet their obligations in their next legislative session, he wanted Congress to authorize him to expropriate enough of their property in the United States to equal in value the amount owed. Although the deputies did vote the required sum, they so resented Jackson's harsh words that they attached a string: nothing would be forthcoming until the president had apologized for his insulting request. This, he loudly avowed, he would never do. Late in 1835, however, he offered an "explanation" of his recommendation. The French announced that they were satisfied with this interpretation, but, Jackson could and did deny that he had ever apologized. All along foreigners had been urging both parties to curb any aggressive tendencies, lest worldwide economic patterns be disrupted, and this helped matters to a successful conclusion. By May 1836 the French had paid in full the installments still outstanding.[1]

But the above was all in the future when Livingston and Elliott departed for Europe. Indeed, the crisis was at its apex, for both nations had called home their envoys from the other, in effect severing diplomatic relations. Several US naval officers, Biddle among them, asked the department for combat commands, sure that their services would be required.[2]

Livingston and Elliott arrived at Le Havre on April 10 after a twenty-five--day passage and dashed off for Paris, bearing with them the president's inflammatory request to Congress the previous December for retaliatory measures against the French. This, as we have seen, was rejected brusquely, and both men returned to the frigate, expecting that war would be declared before they reached home. Had that calamitous event transpired, it might have been presaged, just out of New York, by one of the worst tempests that Elliott had ever encountered in his many years at sea: "A monstrous wave was sighted rushing out of the darkness at them with the force of a careening freight train. With a sickening lurch *Constitution* rolled into a trough ahead of the wave and then was hit by the towering wall of water. A thunderous roar blotted out all sound as it cascaded across and into the ship. . . . [Even worse, a twenty-four-pound gun] had leaped from its carriage and propelled through its port side by the heavy water. It was dangling outside the ship . . . its more than two tons of cast iron threatening to beat in the bow [but an ax succeeded in cutting it loose and into the sea]."[3]

Heading from Le Havre to New York on May 16, the ship stopped at Plymouth, England, for five days before racing down the channel for the Bay of

Biscay, but atrocious weather was not yet over. A gale was raging in the bay, and *Constitution* was heading straight for the Scilly Islands, a shipping graveyard just off Land's End, the southwesternmost point of England. "The high winds drove her leeward so far that she was in danger of being wrecked[.] Elliott daringly ordered all possible sail set in an attempt to drive her westward of the land before the winds could drive her onto it to leeward. It was a chancy thing." That it was indeed.[4] In this instance Elliott had demonstrated either consummate audacity or the utmost recklessness, but luck was with him. The strain of the shrouds was so extreme that the chain bolts "actually were being drawn out, as a claw hammer pulls a nail. It was touch and go; the race in doubt. Rocks covered with spray were seen all around as the ship continued to careen through the sea at nine knots and better."[5]

"At length the light bore upon our quarter, and the bold Atlantic rolled its whitecaps before us. During this time all was silent, each officer and man was at his post, and the bearing and countenance of Captain Elliott seemed to give encouragement to every person on board. . . . He relied on his nautical skill and courage, and saved the *Constitution*! with the lives of five hundred men to weather Scilly on that terrifying night."[6]

Perhaps Elliott realized later that he had been gambling for stakes too high when he had not put into port overnight for the storm abated the next day. He writes not a word about his courageous/rash acceleration of *Constitution* down the channel in the several hundred pages of his "biography," other than to say: "In this voyage, my ship encountered one of those severe trials, to which vessels are sometimes subject, and we came near being wrecked."[7] But Elliott saves the full story of the event in note 1, of his *Speech*, allowing readers to view the near disaster with the words written by an "eye-witness" (Jesse Erskine Dow) on board "Old Ironsides," whose portrayal of Elliott strikes the highest notes of accolade: "With but a bare possibility of saving the ship and all on board, he [Elliott] placed his reliance on his nautical skill and courage, and by carrying the mainsail when in any other situation it would have been considered a suicidal act, he weathered the lee shore and saved the Constitution."[8]

Now let us revert to the diplomatic aspects of this cruise: By the time *Constitution* had docked at New York City, Livingston had determined to downplay his fear of imminent hostilities with France to deliver an upbeat message to his fellow citizens. A large crowd had welcomed him at City Hall where the press covered well his speech: "We are glad to learn from the conversation of Mr. Livingston that his return to the United States is not to be taken as an evil omen. . . . He has not perceived among the people or in the government of France, any hostile disposition towards us. On the whole we find nothing to shake our often expressed confidence that our affairs with France will be brought to a satisfactory and friendly issue."[9]

Elliott's first cruise during 1835–38 concluded with an orgy of "Reciprocal Compliments" between the naval officer and the diplomat. Livingston presented Elliott with "a superb gold box . . . beautifully chased [grooved], with the Commodore's initials on the outer lid, and bearing the inscription within 'A Souvenir of the *Constitution* to Commodore Elliott, from his friend Edward Livingston.'" It was accompanied by a letter on June22: "Dear Sir: I pray you to accept a trifling memento" of the "kind attention" that he and his family had received. "With it, I pray you, sir, to receive the assurance of my highest esteem."[10]

There is no evidence that Elliott ever matched the golden box, but at least, he could equal his companion in epistolary mastery: "Dear Sir, permit me to acknowledge your very flattering note, accompanying the beautiful gold box . . . which will be cherished in my family. . . . [After praising Livingston for his excellent diplomacy in Paris], I shall esteem myself more than fortunate, if in the discharge of my duty, I have rendered myself worthy of the compliment which you have thus bestowed upon me. Be pleased to present my affectionate regards to your amiable lady and daughter, whose fortitude looked above the privations incident to a protracted and boisterous passage across the Atlantic"[11]

When Elliott returned to assume command of the Mediterranean Squadron, his letters to the department, September 1835–February 1, 1836, composed a mosaic suggesting that he considered the emergency still operating. It is not readily apparent why he chose to append what has to be called an anticlimax. Possibly it was because of his differing between his two voyages. In the first, Livingston, not he, bore the brunt of responsibility for determining a peaceful outcome of the crisis. But in the second, should France declare war while his scattered squadron was still in the Mediterranean, facing the unhappy prospect of doing battle with a stronger navy, Elliott would have to adapt to constantly changing situations. This was what probably led him to take a pessimistic outlook.

Even before he had departed from New York, he told the secretary, "The attitude of our affairs with France will doubtless soon compel the nation to don its armor."[12] Livingston then sent a most timely warning to Elliott about his precarious site: "The state of our affairs with France are becoming so extremely critical that I should be much relieved when I hear that your little squadron has passed the Straights [of Gibraltar]. Should a rupture take place depend upon [it] you will never be met but by an overwhelming force."[13] Already Elliott had been preparing for this exigency by sending into the Atlantic the frigate *Potomac* and the sloop *John Adams* under orders to rendezvous at Gibraltar by April 1, observing once more "a war with France is inevitable."[14]

10.1. "Old Iron Sides on a Lee Shore: The U.S. Frigate Constitution Captn. Elliott, Weathering Scilly, on Her return from France, with the Hon. Edward Livingston on Board on the Night of the [Eleventh] of May 1835," drawn on stone by A. Hoffy, from a painting by J. Evans; P. S. Duval, Lith. Philad., Library of Congress, Prints and Photographs Division.

After reading Jackson's December 1835 address to Congress—which Elliott thought "displayed moderation, dignity, and firmness"—he considered sending a part of his squadron "to cruise in the English Channel," retaining the rest at Gibraltar. But now, "if France should declare war, I should accordingly return to the United States with the whole squadron," surely a sensible idea rather than permitting his men-of-war to be picked off individually while trapped in an inland sea.[15]

But Elliott's gloom disappeared in a flash after he had received reports from both Europe and America that the French dispute had been settled amiably. He then pulled down the curtain on his connection with these events and proceeded to his experiences as commodore in the Mediterranean, 1835–38.

Sadly, the bonhomie so obvious in his association with the Livingstons was not to be repeated during Elliott's ensuing command.[16] His makeup changed for reasons that shall be amplified later. The companionable and accommodating man who so charmed the Livingston family turned into one who managed to alienate a sizable portion of his officers aboard. This would result in personal humiliation, incur the wrath of the Navy Department, and mark the end of his seagoing career.

Considering the turbulence attending Elliott's term as commandant of the Boston Navy Yard, pertaining to his Jackson effigy in *Constitution*, it is problematic why he was assigned to the enviable Mediterranean command.

It may be that two factors led to this result: (1) The letters between Elliott and Livingston confirm a longtime intimacy between them, and it is certain that Livingston asked for him in particular to command "Old Ironsides" on two brief diplomatic missions to France and Britain during the spring of 1835 (see beginning of this chapter); and (2) perhaps this was coupled with the partiality shown to Elliott by Navy Secretary Dickerson, who understandably presumed that Elliott knew that frigate and her operations well. This made the commodore's continuation at the top the simplest and most sensible way to solve the command problem.

Probably even greater prerequisites for such appointments were his general propensities for them. Elliott possessed a keen mind, most noticeably when he applied it to the service's need for reforms in administration, operational efficiency, ship innovations, or cost paring. His memory had been sharpened by the files he kept so immaculately of all his correspondence with the secretaries of the navy and other top officials, his mental retention of naval regulations, and his oral and written recollections from his many years at sea. These enabled him to realize what sort of information the department required. Elliott's forte was foreign relations, and his superiors appreciated his insightful analyses of current events abroad to reinforce their plaudits about his topnotch diplomacy in South America (see chapters 7 and 8).

But—a trait that must be mentioned repeatedly in this work—Elliott's native intelligence deserted him time and again. For instance, no one could have been more responsive to his own emotional reactions to negative comments and inimical activities against him, but he almost always maintained a blind spot that others might feel the same under similar circumstances. Furthermore, long before *Constitution* reached Europe, the department, many of his officers, and some of the crew had become attuned to the other side of the Elliott coin—his prickly relations with his peers, juniors, and later in the cruise with Secretary of the Navy James K. Paulding.

Apparently, the commodore foresaw the approaching rollers that might inundate him, so in a few letters at the start of the voyage, he accentuated the fabrication that tranquility accompanied his command. The following is typical of the others: "General health prevails and the utmost harmony exists in the squadron." His apprehension was merited. Within six months he would thrash around in a tumultuous sea of crosscurrents, some of them breaking over his head.[17]

As we go along to review another of Elliott's traits, this biography seems to disclose that, at first probing, he was an officer who guarded his flanks conservatively as one who ruled by the book, a mossback in opposition to the latest naval reforms. But this generalization is false.

During his cruise to and while in the Mediterranean, Elliott harkened to a battle being waged in all the major navies between those for and against a gradual shift from sail to steam propulsion. He had argued without avail "to get President Jackson [during the spoliations crises with France, 1834–35] interested in building a steam fleet," and Barron, among others, agreed with him.[18]

Although by the 1830s well over one thousand steamboats plied America's inland and coastal waterways, no such power moved US men-of-war. Rather, they remained by and large the same as those of 1800–35, "one to three decks, massive wooden walls, smooth bore armaments, and a majestic cloud of canvas." They were slow and dependent on winds, currents, and tides.[19]

There were admirals in the British Navy every bit as conservative as their American counterparts. Yet, by 1836, steam-driven vessels in the British and French navies numbered twenty-one and twenty-three, respectively. Even when fighting steamers were constructed from that time into the 1890s, they carried auxiliary sails for such "exigent circumstances as calms, through ice, and over sandbars."[20] Paulding, whose malignancy toward Elliott was overt, formed a huge block of resistance to the new technology, moaning that "I am *steamed* to death," and he would never consent to "seeing our grand old ships supplanted by these new and ugly sea monsters."[21] Indeed, Paulding's biographers have overlooked his "reputation for mulishness as the last Secretary of the Navy in the age of sail and the least progressive of all who held that office."[22] In comparison, Elliott was a maritime innovator; his foe an obstructionist.

This seems an acceptable place to provide some information about the makeup of the US Navy between the War of 1812 and the Civil War, according to the service's geographical responsibilities to foster new trade opportunities and to show Americans residing abroad that their government had not forgotten them. The fleet was divided into several squadrons according to areas (not in chronological order of establishment): (1) Mediterranean (about which much more below), (2) West India (the shores of the Gulf of Mexico and the Caribbean, eventually incorporated into the Home Squadron, (3) Brazil (for the eastern coast of South America), (4) Pacific (for the western coasts of North and South America), (5) East India (for East and Southeast Asia), (6) African (for everything south of the Mediterranean littoral)—this was the most detested posting because of its murderous diseases, brutal temperatures and humidity, and lack of shore leaves.

During Elliott's term of almost three years directing the Mediterranean Squadron, with him throughout were the mighty *Constitution*, 1,355 tons, probably the most successful frigate in the world, prior to being matched and then superseded by European warships; the small frigate *John Adams*, the second by that name, 700 tons; and the tiny schooner *Shark*, a mere 177 tons. The powerful frigate *Potomac*, 1,457 tons, was part of Elliott's command until mid-1834 when she was replaced by the frigate *United States*, 1,576 tons, the sister ship of "Old Ironsides," and which remained through the end of the cruise.[23]

Between 1812 and 1815 the Royal Navy found to its amazement that the American naval force was a foe to be respected and occasionally feared. Of all the world's fleets only the British and the French were more puissant. The US Navy became an enemy to be dreaded and avoided if possible by the others in the Mediterranean—the Spanish, the Turkish, and the still weak Austrian. As early as 1815–17 the Barbary powers of North Africa had realized their helplessness when confronted by superior American firepower.

The narrative flow of Elliott's Mediterranean cruise, 1835–38, may commence by following *Constitution*'s itinerary, pausing to applaud the invaluable contributions of Elliot Snow and H. Allen Gosnell, *On the Decks of "Old Ironsides."* In their appendix B, chronologically they have itemized her ports of call from the frigate's departure from New York City on April 19, 1835, to her homecoming at Hampton Roads, Virginia, on July 31, 1838, listing "Departure," "Arrival," and "Distance Run," for each of the roughly eighty visits. "The voyage covered exactly 46,635 miles and [she] had been at sea almost precisely one-third of her total of 1,221 days."[24] Furthermore, Snow and Gosnell have arrived at these figures by the mind-numbing labor of examining *Constitution*'s multiple log books. This is by no means as simple as it may appear, for one observer might date the comings and goings by when she reached a harbor, while another counted them when she actually docked. In short, those of us working in the field owe them a gigantic debt of gratitude for saving us from the same toil.

Almost all American naval personnel hailed a posting to the Mediterranean, with its striking scenery; usually amiable climate; a great variety of peoples, among them British and other maritime equivalents; easy credit; an availability of nubile young women; and abundant ancient ruins. Most of us who have studied the Old Navy's officers have been impressed by their erudition, founded mainly on a solid grounding in the Graeco-Roman classics. For these reasons and more, Elliott and his people exulted in receiving the most appetizing overseas assignment offered by the service.

Prior to describing the activities of Elliott and his people during the entire cruise, a point must be made. Snow and Gosnell's invaluable port-by-port itinerary bypasses almost completely when *Constitution* was *not* en route to another destination.[25]

During these interims the commodore, accompanied by small groups, left the frigate—sometimes for extended periods. Midshipman Anderson's lively journal becomes essential during this period, especially on a four-week tour to visit the Christian relics in the Holy Land during August 1838. Readers should be most appreciative of that young midshipman's sense of humor and a graceful, almost conversational literary style, which is assuredly not the case in the majority of US naval prose. Moreover, for us as Elliott's biographers, our gratitude hardly can be exceeded for Anderson's perfectly legible handwriting, so delightful a contrast to Elliott's semidecipherable scribbling.[26]

Tracing Elliott's route to his new overseas posting, it began so perilously that the entire cruise almost terminated as soon as the squadron departed from New York City on April 19, 1835. Having endured the two ferocious tempests in his cross-Atlantic tours with Livingston, Elliott discovered that Neptune lay in wait with a full-blown hurricane. Martin shows his flair for oceanic descriptions formulated by his many years of service in the modern US Navy:

> The sky was obscured completely by dense, black clouds when dawn came dimly, and the waves had grown huge. *Constitution was* in the so-called "dangerous semi-circle" of a hurricane—the worst place to be. In no time at all, the frigate's world had become one of mountainous waves spuming great tendrils of spray ahead of them: of driving, lashing rain; or rolling dark cloud cover alive with Nature's energy. All were called to the spar deck with the ominous call, "All hands to save ship!" . . . There was a sudden silence at seven the next morning. *Constitution* was in the "eye" of the hurricane, an area of seeming calm and silence in the midst of so much turmoil. The sailors knew it would be a short respite. . . . First, the darkness returned, and then the seas, stoving in ports and crushing boats. Finally the winds returned in a terrible blast, threatening to take the masts right out of her. This was the worst the storm had to offer, and having survived the onslaught, *Constitution* and her crew had merely to hang on as the rest of the hurricane swept by.[27]

Martin is able as well to narrate a couple of memorable stories, one initially grisly, the other laughable. "As the frigate entered the Gulf Stream on this same cruise, an unexpected squall washed overboard one of her lieutenants. The night was pitch-black and the ship clipping along at twelve knots. Lowering a boat to search for him would be not only hopeless but endanger those engaged in the effort. A little before midnight the 'Midshipman of the Watch,' and a sailor or two, were checking the log but stopped to cry out in horror when an ashen-faced and drenched head appeared over the stern, soon recognized as the missing officer. Revived by a 'tot of brandy' he gasped out the details of his miraculous escape—as he hit the water he grabbed a line and then a Jacob's Ladder, pulling himself onto the deck with his last burst of energy. It has been indeed a rescue to remember."[28]

In the other Martin story, Elliott inspected the entire ship each Saturday, eyes alert for any infractions. When he peered into the galley he noticed a yellow stain above the stoves. Turning on the midshipman in charge, on the threat of a court-martial for disobedience, he shouted at him that "everything was to be perfectly white—perfectly white, Sir!" A week later the commodore discovered that his order had been executed meticulously by massive whitewashing: "The overhead was white, the caboose was white, the fourteen Black cooks were white, and so was the goat [kept for Elliott's milk]. Elliott was about to explode with his renowned wrath when he realized that his orders had been carried out to the letter. He called off the rest of his inspection and retired to his cabin—hopefully, for a good laugh."[29]

Turning reluctantly from Martin's memorable yarns to peruse the voyage's occurrences in the Mediterranean, there were many stopovers along the way. Two were of considerably greater duration than the others, and we may glance at their similarities and differences. The first was in early 1837 and the second in mid-1838, just before Elliott's homecoming.

Their likenesses are obvious. Both traversed the entire Mediterranean, west to east, round trip, from Gibraltar/Mahon to Turkey, Syria, Egypt, and beyond. During short visits for diplomatic calls and relaxation, each dropped anchor repeatedly on Italian coasts, along Barbary shores in North Africa, and to those ports in what we would now call the Middle East. Lengthier stays interrupted these passages at Gibraltar/Mahon, Lisbon, and British Malta, where the squadron's vessels could be repaired, new supplies of food and water packed away, and extended shore leaves granted to those who deserved such favors.[30]

The main disparity between the two voyages was that in the second considerably longer sojourns were passed in the eastern Mediterranean. There the Elliott-officer vendettas accelerated, while other elements to vex the commodore reached culmination. Throughout the cruise Elliott was determined to jam pack *Constitution*'s gun deck with a host of jackasses, mules, and horses, much to the crew's discomfort and a marked diminution of his frigate's fighting ability. He also collected ancient relics (some of colossal size) that had to be stowed away wherever possible among the squadron's vessels.

Of greater essence, the oncoming coalescence of Elliott's woes was gaining momentum, as specified in the following chapters.

Eleven
Mediterranean Cruising

RELATIONSHIPS WITH SECRETARIES OF THE NAVY, DICKERSON AND PAULDING IN PARTICULAR

Elliott was employed in the service from 1804 until near his death in 1845. During this period almost twenty navy secretaries occupied that lofty position, the heavy majority of whom may be ignored in this biography. But two of them stamped ineradicable marks upon Elliott's career. Mahlon Dickerson, secretary of the navy from 1834 to 1838, was his best friend, encouraging and advancing him. The following is typical of his many letters to his protégé: "I am glad to find your squadron getting on so harmoniously and trust that nothing will occur to give you disturbances."[1]

Trying to find material about the character and personality of James K. Paulding, secretary of the navy from 1838 to 1841, was difficult for almost all references to him apply to his literary output as one of the country's most popular and prolific authors.[2] His letters did give us some insight into why he and Elliott clashed so frequently: Paulding "denied the requests . . . of naval officers for special considerations," and if any one of them craved that treatment, Elliott was the man. Paulding's entry in the *Dictionary of American Biography* mentions that "strife and intemperance in the service he tried to eradicate by rigid discipline." The same article avows that the secretary had a "fine sense of human values," as well as a "love of humor and of life," but one may search in vain for any such characteristics in his treatment of Elliott.[3]

During Elliott's suspension from active duty in the service from 1840 into 1843, it is likely that what he considered Paulding's scurrilous treatment of him seldom left his mind. He wrote with seething resentment: "Since the 22 of June 1840, up to the present moment, I have been under the operation of a sentence of Court-martial as unjust, as unholy and unrighteous as ever has recorded against any officer of our own . . . or any other service; not excepting a Byng, of the British Navy, or a Barron in our own."[4] Numbed already by Paulding's treatment of him, Elliott confirmed that his nemesis was capable of invidious deception as well, referring to their conversations early in January 1840. The secretary hailed him as a friend, denying that he was an enemy and ending, "Say nothing to your friends in Congress, but leave the matter [of his Court-martial] in my hands." When the accused agreed, he erred seriously, for a sizable pro-Elliott bloc in the Senate and House could have ignited a firestorm to confront the prosecution. Rather than being off the hook, Elliott raged, "Judge, however, my surprise when I discovered that the government's prosecutor, J.M. Read, was engaged, and had been for months, in the preparation on which I was to be tried solely. I appraised the Secretary of that information. . . . In answer I received a letter from my *professed* friend, the Secretary, informing me that I must be charged, and J. M. Read would be the Judge Advocate.[5]

A published doctoral dissertation some years ago came up with something of value: "Accustomed as a novelist to have his characters act according to his will, Paulding expected the same unquestioning obedience from his naval subordinates." When Lieutenant Farragut, later admiral, published a signed article contrary to Paulding's instructions, "he received a sharp reprimand from the Secretary, who elsewhere humorously [and perhaps accurately] styled himself 'the most absolute of all despots.'"[6] In mid-1838 Paulding wrote: "I am as you know a pretty obstinate fellow and have my officers know that infractions will no longer be permitted."[7]

A periodical, covering well the armed forces, wrote angrily about Paulding: "Mr. P. may rest assured that until he admits his own responsibilities nothing short of this will restore him to respect and confidence. . . . No officer who has a proper respect for himself or the least esprit du corps should hold any communication with either the Secretary or his office beyond the absolute necessities of duty. A large proportion of officers have already submitted to extraordinary violations of their rank and fairest privileges . . . and should they now quietly suffer themselves to be vilified and abused without any effort to resist it, the inference will undoubtedly be to their discredit."[8] This combination above shows that Paulding had found in Elliott one to illustrate how totally he would try to inflict his will upon his underlings.

A word of explanation, responding to some kind of arcane reasoning, Elliott chose to ignore altogether the prosecution's case against him from 1839 to 1843, opting instead to select what he thought were the most important accusations, ranging downward to the least. The result was an almost impenetrable and confusing maze that, by and large, has to be ignored in this narrative.

BACKGROUND AND DIPLOMATIC ACTIVITIES DURING THE CRUISE ITSELF

Of all the foreign crises between other nations and America, here we may omit the closest approach to war: that with France in the spoliation confrontation, 1834–35. This subject is delineated in chapter 10.

As to other international difficulties, the first tremors of the quarrel with Great Britain over the Maine–New Brunswick boundary did not reach its apex and solution until the early 1840s, well after Elliott's tenure had expired, so we may dispense with it. Other disturbances arose with the sultan of Morocco about the delivery of gifts to that North African state; a thorny struggle concerning Mehmet Ali, involving Egypt, Syria, and Turkey; a tiff with Portugal regarding the final settlement of a trade treaty between them; and late in the cruise, the animosity between Porter, US minister to Turkey, and Elliott, dating back to their participation in the fatal Barron-Decatur duel in 1820 (see chapter 6).

As a Mediterranean commander, Elliott had enough insight to realize that a major part of his business was to flaunt the Stars and Stripes and, by his mere presence even in the most minor ports, to show resident Americans that their government had not forgotten its responsibilities for the protection of their persons and belongings, as well as to probe widely for openings to accrete their trading opportunities.[9]

When Elliott arrived overseas in 1835, rumors abounded that Morocco's sultan was disregarding certain treaty stipulations, much to America's economic disadvantage. Among the commodore's responsibilities was the delivery of costly presents from his government. To do this, he had to pay off varying Moroccan bureaucrats, a process that may be called, bluntly, bribery. American diplomats tended to apologize to the State Department about such withdrawals from departmental funds. They conceded that bribery was ludicrous but essential, since all their European competitors did so and contending the United States could only follow suit.

James A. Field Jr. is my choice for the leading American authority on nineteenth-century US–Middle Eastern relations, and readers might well dip into his *America and the Mediterranean World, 1766–1866*, as well as David H. Finnie's *Pioneers East*.

In transporting his nation's presents to Morocco's sultan, Elliott faced a dilemma. After delivering the cargo to the beaches as had been prearranged, the commodore found that no Moroccan of sufficient status was there to accept them. Reluctant to leave such valuable goods to the first passersby, Elliott ordered them returned to *Constitution* for future delivery, which was accomplished later.

Toward the end of Elliott's first long cruise to the Mediterranean to visit

Mehmet Ali, let us dart a glance at one of the commodore's moments of triumph. Off Jaffa (near modern Tel Aviv) he met with top level Egyptian officials. One of them irked him by loudly boasting about the speed of his frigate to such an extent that the American challenged him to a race. In a strong breeze over a ninety-mile course, *Constitution* not only won but sailed around her rival twice, crossing her bow and stern each time. "It became one of Elliott's favorite stories in later years."[10]

During the course of a commercial renaissance in the Mediterranean, Elliott was accompanied by Secretary of War Lewis Cass who bore with him "the added responsibility of a commercial and political fact-finding tour through Syria, Turkey, Egypt, Greece, and the islands of the Aegean," which in general was accomplished deftly.[11] Egypt-Syria under Muhammed (Mehmet) Ali, 1769–1849, saw Mehmet's successful rebellion against the Turkish sultan Mahmed II, conquering Syria and later becoming the dynastic ruler of Egypt.[12]

While these negotiations were going on, Mehmet presented Elliott with a "cimiter" (scimitar). Cognizant the US military and naval officers could not accept gifts from outside individuals or groups for their own retention, but solely for "transmission to the government," Elliott made certain that his sword was deposited in the Navy Department.[13] Had he not, this act would almost surely have been snapped up by his many enemies and wielded against him in his court-martial of 1840.

Portuguese-American relations were roiled by a five-year delay, 1835–40, during the Jackson–Van Buren presidencies while trying to reach a mutually desired commercial treaty between the two countries. Compared to Elliott's role as an active participant in bargaining with Morocco and Mehmet Ali's Syria/Egypt, in Lisbon's case, he was merely an outside observer, as suggested by his sending no letters to the secretary about it and only one from Elliott himself to Washington, DC, amounting to no more than showing that he understood that a minor crisis with Portugal was continuing.

I am much beholden to my colleague Dr. Douglas Wheeler of the University of New Hampshire's doyen in Iberian/African history, who provided me with essential information about this treaty. But I am astonished that he would imagine that because more than a half century ago I had a few semesters of Latin, and what Columbia University calls most generously, "a reading knowledge of Spanish"—which may be defined as enabling me with some trouble to get the gist of a newspaper column—that I could translate his twenty-page article in Portuguese! But when I pointed this out to him, he provided me with the treaty's most salient features taken from Jose Calvet de Magalhaes.[14] All the following are from either this article or conversations with Wheeler in mid-April 1993.

Wheeler went on to explain that Portugal had been hampered in decision-making by the instability of its government, resulting in frequent ministerial changes that interfered with continuity in policy formulation, coupled with a general bureaucratic inefficiency. Of the much greater import, however, during this time Lisbon concentrated most of its attention to a similar trade pact with Britain, its longtime ally. Finally the Treaty of 1840 was ready to be signed to the satisfaction of both Lisbon and Washington, DC. Freedom of commerce and navigation between them was assured, and especially, Portuguese-American "most-favored nation" status was put into operation, carrying with it reciprocity in which any economic advantages gained by one most-favored nation (lower tariffs, for instance), automatically was applied to all others in that category.[15]

While Elliott was still in the Mediterranean, former US commodore Porter was the US minister to Turkey, living near Constantinople. Elliott asked him for aid to obtain an official pass (firman) to take *Constitution* to the capital but initially was rejected brusquely, although he was able to do that later. Tit for tat, when Porter needed a ship from the squadron to complete a diplomatic errand, Elliott refused until departmental orders compelled his compliance. But their mutual hatred did not abate, and back at home Elliott was "cut dead" whenever the two happened to meet.[16] For an explanation of their hostility, see chapter 6.

When Elliott's diplomatic record in the Mediterranean is evaluated, a composite resulted with an edge going to the positive rather than the negative. He had been effective in declining to abandon on the beach the lavish presents earmarked for the Moroccan emperor, but what other US officer in a like situation would have acted otherwise? The commodore had accomplished all that he could in dealings with Mehmet Ali's Middle Eastern government, and any failure was through no fault of his but rather because of his own nation's change of mind. Circumstances denied him any active part in Portuguese-American negotiations, 1835–38. His spat with Porter added up to nil, thanks to Washington's determination that each must grant the reasonable demands of the other.

Yet all this must be placed in context. Recollections of Elliott's discerning bargaining with South Americans in the 1820s and 1830s were still keen, and his tact and courtesy, combined with a stout stand on his country's rights, were exemplified by the barrage of compliments he received from practically all his fellow negotiators. Elliott's frequent reappearances as he circulated from port to port assured Americans residing there that they were still under Washington's protective umbrella. To be sure, most US commanders emulated him in this respect but not always. Commander Henry Henry in 1844 said, "On his arrival at Constantinople [he] quarreled with the American

Minister and proved himself loud and boisterous in conversation, and rude and inhospitable to the Turks who visited his ship." It is inconceivable why such a character was not promptly replaced, but instead, he was soon promoted to captain.[17]

Diplomacy concerning Morocco, Mehmet Ali, Portugal, Porter, and the double-named Henry aside, Hezekiah Niles, in his weekly issues, championed Elliott, as he would do repeatedly in the 1830s.[18]

DISCIPLINE IN GENERAL

When a study of discipline in the early US Navy is commenced, one can do far worse than to insert a quotation from recognized expert on that topic James E. Valle: "The Old Navy was, like most military organizations of that day, an authoritarian system based on the principle of dominance and domination. It was characterized by organizational rigidity and sought solutions for disciplinary problems through the mechanical application of traditional practices and routine policies. . . . It was noteworthy for . . . veneration for tradition and nostalgia. Its officers were, in conformity with the conventional culture from which they sprang, susceptible to an exaggerated sense of professionalism where concern for the forms and symbols of status outweighed regard for practical results and functional performance."[19] As Elliott appears often in his pages, citations from Valle will recur over this and subsequent chapters.

A word of explanation, for the past few years a walking difficulty has compelled me to conduct my own research in distant locales by mail. For cases involving Elliott I wondered if I would have to visit the US Judge Advocate General's Department (JAG) in Washington, DC, to review "Records of General Courts-martial and Courts of Inquiry of the Navy Department, 1799–1867," cited hundreds of times by Valle. In a long telephone call to him, I asked for his advice. He responded that such would be a ridiculous waste of my time and money, for these files, identified by the JAG and number, were massive and totally disorganized. This forced him to spend many of his long years of research for his book, primarily to systematize them. Rather, I should rely on him for accuracy and completeness, a recommendation that I followed as eminently sensible.

For Elliott, his diplomatic errands with Livingston in *Constitution* from March 2 to June 23, 1835, (see chapter 10) were merely forerunners to by far his greatest career opportunity.[20] He became commodore of the Mediterranean Squadron, the overseas appointment that was the best the navy had to offer. This applied to practically all of a US warship's people, going upward from sailors and marines to petty officers, midshipmen, passed midshipmen,[21] lieutenants, commanders, captains, and through those with the courtesy title of commodore.

However, after studying the navy's officer corps for over two decades, we can recall very few of those holding top level grades whose sense of self--esteem was not impaired in that inland sea by the matter of discipline. In short, that was the backbone of the service, meaning that orders coming from above had to be obeyed instantly and even instinctively from below must at all costs be maintained.

Most of us who have been on conducted tours of *Constitution* and other large sailing warships, after surveying their cramped quarters and low ceilings, have wondered why up to 450 sailors were required to man them. Battle conditions were only part of the reason. The unexpected onslaughts of high wind when the vessel was under full sail required many hands to reef them in; should too few be available, she might turn turtle. Officers were ever aware that disciplinary breakdowns might impose quite literally death sentences for them.

So, for senior and junior officers, their posting to the Mediterranean found discipline to be their potential pitfall. That problem usually did not apply to the sailors and marines, "for their prompt obedience to orders and devotion to duty was reinforced by the application of the colt and cat," at least until they became enraged or soddened by the alcohol that they were able to find on shore and smuggled onto the ship. The midshipmen, typically in their late teens or early twenties, were more to the point. Among them their elders were the worst, for they were marking time until promotion to lieutenants, often long delayed, became reality. They had been in the navy long enough to espy the loopholes in the official regulations and use them for their own selfish advantage. Late in life Elliott was still fretting about his younger colleagues. He informed the president: "With a little grog, a great deal of tobacco, and whipping them when they deserve it, I have never found the least difficulty in managing a crew. It's the young colts of midshipmen I have trouble with."[22]

In reference to *Constitution*'s itinerary, 1835–38, we can think of no more futile endeavor than to dot this text continually with her stops listed in Snow and Gosnell's *On the Decks of Old Ironsides* with some appearing many times. They add up to about eighty! The vast majority of our readers should find adequate our own remarks, buttressed by Martin's short précis in his *A Most Fortunate Ship*. The handful of others who will need Snow and Gosnell's day--by-day itemizations can refer to them to fulfill their research and publication requirements. Moreover, frequent breaks in this story will have to occur when chronology demands such interruptions.

Elliott's sojourn in the Mediterranean was featured by two very long cruises: August 19, 1835, through January 4, 1837, from New York City to Lisbon where Portuguese dock facilities were available, and February 11,

1837, through July 31, 1838, for Port Mahon in the Spanish Balearic Islands, which was at first the US supply depot overseas, later moved to Sicily. Many American commanders there, Rodgers in particular, "thought that the problem [of discipline] emanated from the general depravity at Mahon, which continued to contribute its share of scandal and indiscipline to the fleet for decades."[23] Although the impact of many other officers affected Elliott more than Rodgers, the latter's influence was substantial on the US Navy.

The standard biography of Rodgers the elder has been for almost a century Charles O. Paullin's *Commodore John Rodgers*. It covered his life with reasonable fullness but with many errors of commission and omission, as proven by the need for so much modern research on him by others, ourselves included. Unfortunately Paullin has chosen to portray a Galahad, a paladin, flawless as a naval officer at sea or ashore, so handsome as to attract notice, and a loving and faithful husband. The author admits that Rodgers owned enslaved persons at his Washington, DC, mansion but glosses it over by picturing him as "a master at its best."[24]

A most curtailed mention should be made of a somewhat more balanced image of Rodgers that emerges in an article about Midshipman Samuel F. Du Pont, who served under that commodore for some two years during the mid-1820s.[25] The Mt. Everest of naval disciplinary problems arose when a crew member had been sentenced to death for murder by a court-martial, although even more men had been executed for "mutiny, mutinous conduct, and desertion."[26]

Twice while Elliott commanded the Mediterranean Squadron sailors killed shipmates, once in the frigate *John Adams* in 1836 and again in the frigate *United States* during 1837. Confessions and eyewitness testimonies proved that the facts in each case were so brutal that court-martial death sentences seemed inevitable.

In the first, Thomas D. Allen murdered Thomas Noland near Mahon while they were arguing over when to go back to their ships. While his shipmate was lying on the ground in a drunken stupor, his head was pulverized by a blow from a forty-pound rock, after which Allen admitted his guilt and was sentenced to be hanged.[27]Valle acknowledged his ignorance as to whether the verdict was carried out, but he missed a notation that Allen was hanged in *John Adams* on July 1, 1836.[28]

In the second, John Herring assaulted his messmate Thomas Hyland "while in the grip of a drunken rage." He struck so hard a blow that the other dropped some twenty feet through a hatch and to the bottom of the hold; he died the next day. Herring apparently doomed himself when, told that Hyland was badly injured, he shouted that "he wished that the son-of-a--bitch might die and then he would be hanged." But when he sobered up, he tried to renege on his statement. The same Chaplain Thomas R. Lambert, who with his colleague Lieutenant Charles G. Hunter later cooperated in demanding Elliott's court-martial, came to his aid. They argued that "Herring should not suffer death for an act committed in a drunken stupor and under a false impression, one that he was already doomed to spend the rest of his life regretting."[29]

The chaplain's forceful defense spared Herring the death sentence but at such a cost that he must have deeply lamented dying by inches rather than all at once. The charge of murder had been replaced by manslaughter, but he was to be given the monstrous punishment of four hundred lashes! As the squadron's commodore, Elliott had to review this atrocity, and lowered it, but only to a still frightful three hundred, insisting that the culprit should be flogged "around the fleet at Mahon and his sentence read on each vessel."[30] We have searched in vain for any evidence that this was ever mitigated somewhere along the line to a more bearable level.

Turning with relief to a tolerable subject, some readers may be puzzled as to why "Specific Disciplinary Activities," regarding Etting: Illegal "Extra" Punishment; Lambert-Hunter; and the alleged "Mutiny" in *Constitution,* 1838, does not follow directly. Chronological order, however, dictates that there must be a hiatus before relating Alexander S. Mackenzie's hanging three of his crew in 1842. For that, see below.

A cornerstone of the American navy's labors to maintain order was how the commanding officer reacted to his lower ranks, officers and hands alike. Overwhelmingly, they tended to "go by the book," that is, according to service usages, avoiding as best they could overzealous applications of the cat and colt, without such laxity that would breed apathetic, lazy, or sullen crews. Even those officers known to be martinets could have a solid relationship with their men. As Martin well describes it: "They could be fiercely loyal to a bastard of a Captain who was professionally competent while strictly enforcing official regulations; they found ways of demonstrating their protest of a bullying, incompetent, or erratic leader."[31]

Balanced against Elliott's competence as a naval administrator and adroit diplomat abroad was the flip side of his coin—his incessant quarrels with those inside and outside of the navy. This leads one to agree at least in part with Valle's observation: "There are even a few officers such as Jesse Duncan Elliott and Uriah Phillips Levy [the only Jewish naval officer at that time], whose appearances before naval courts were so frequent that a goodly amount of their biographies could be written solely on the basis of this source."[32]

The *Somers* mutiny is a landmark case in the history of American naval discipline: While commanding the sloop *Somers* in 1842, Captain Alexander

Slidell Mackenzie hanged at sea "three of his men" without the mandatory permission of a court-martial. This became an instant ticking time bomb because one of them was Midshipman Philip Spencer, a rapscallion and the wayward son of no less than John C. Spencer, at that time the Secretary of War in President John Tyler's cabinet.[33] This has been called the only bona fide mutiny in the American naval annals, although some still doubt that the phrase is accurate. A most abbreviated survey of this incident is permissible, since so many books and articles about it have been published already, those by Valle and Admiral Samuel Eliot Morison especially.[34]

Opinions of Mackenzie's decision have differed considerably down to the present. Valle renders a mixed judgment as to the justification of the executions although with a tilt against the captain. He concludes sensibly: "The facts we do know are utterly baffling and include evidence to support either [Valle's own or Morison's] hypotheses."[35]

Elliott and the noted author James Fenimore Cooper may have had nothing directly to do with the *Somers* affair, but each commented most negatively about it. It should be realized that both men abhorred the Perry bloc and its partisans, Cooper after their scathing remarks about the validity of his *History of the Navy of the United States of America*, and Elliott through his embroilment in the Battle of Lake Erie with Perry. (Mackenzie was a Perry brother-in-law and a stout champion of the family).

Cooper led the way in a private letter: "What a miserable business this of the *Somers* case has turned out to be. . . . There was time enough, for he had the question of life or death in *agitation thirty* hours, at least; and to hang a man on circumstantial *evidence*, however strong, without asking him if he could explain these circumstances . . . shows that Mr. Mackenzie is a very fearful sort of Judge!"[36]

Elliott was more graphic, evoking his own seagoing experience in the imposition of death penalties, assailing Mackenzie's handling of a like situation: "That captain should have tried to appeal to Spencer's better nature, recalled to his mind the pain his mother bore . . . subdued him as would a father, and thus touched his finer feelings!" Should he still be incorrigibly defiant, Elliott "would have chained or bolted him down to the deck, secured the arms, prepared for any emergency, have met it, put it down, brought him home, and delivered him up to the Jaws of his country. . . . But alas! instead of this the heart sickens at the tragedy, and morality turns pale when beholding the gross mockery of the press, ay, and the church in giving countenance to the deed."[37]

News of the *Somers* affair produced an immense, immediate, and soon sharply divided national reaction, making it impossible for it to be dismissed without judicial responses. Mackenzie was brought to trial twice, a court of inquiry in December 1842–January 1843, and a court-martial from February to April, demanded by Mackenzie to clear his own name. In both he was acquitted on all charges.[38]

SPECIFIC DISCIPLINARY ACTIVITIES

ELLIOTT *VERSUS* CONSTITUTION'S *PURSER HENRY ETTING*

In 1839 an official investigation disclosed that the official log of *Lawrence* had disappeared after Perry had turned his command of the Erie Squadron over to Elliott in 1813. "Neither the Navy Department nor the National Archives has any present knowledge [of it]; consequently the partial copy in possession of the Historical Society of Newport [Rhode Island] is of considerable historical value."[39] This leads to speculation—had Elliott "deep-sixed" it because of entries damaging to his creditability?

Why that commodore chose to lead off his correspondence with the department while commanding the Mediterranean Squadron in 1835 about Purser Etting poses a conundrum, for it is the strangest, indeed the most outrageous, letter that Elliott ever wrote to Dickerson or any other navy secretary: "There is nothing, I believe, but harmony among those attached to this ship. Should anything of a different character appear, I would recommend that it be *buried in the sea through which we passed* [emphasis added]." This is a heinous remark for the commander of a US man-of-war to make. Dickerson must have reread it with incredulity, for it violated a fundamental rule of the service that everything of note must be entered in the vessel's log. We have no evidence that the subject recurred, although there is a possibility that Dickerson might have mentioned it to other navy secretaries (Paulding, for instance) who recalled it later, perhaps much to Elliott's disadvantage.[40]

Elliott kept stressing the congruent relations between commodore, officers, and men for almost all of 1835. Such harping on the same theme is baffling, for Elliott was engaged already in a venomous altercation with Etting that exploded when that purser, over a month *before* the frigate sailed from New York City to the Mediterranean, circulated an unsigned letter stating that "many other officers" were dissatisfied with their commander and wished to be assigned elsewhere. Etting's plot backfired, however, for Elliott recognized the handwriting, identifying him unquestionably as the miscreant.[41]

As soon as he had spotted Etting's "treachery," Elliott forthwith told Dickerson about it: "I cannot dwell with too much warmth in the attempt which has been made to poison both the Department and the immediate commander."[42] He struck back at his tormentor, challenging his accusation with a flat denial, ordering each officer to reply directly to him by answering two questions: (1) Had any of them conversed with Etting about the commodore's popularity or lack of it? (2) Did any of them think there was an iota of truth in Etting's allegation?[43] What Elliott expected to gain through these interrogations is troublesome to comprehend. Each one of the eighteen officers who responded to the above had to have been aware of the almost total authority that, if desired, the commander of a US warship could inflict upon his juniors. He could make their lives insufferable by repeated snubs; calling attention to their shortcomings, sometimes within earshot of the crew; and assigning them duties more menial than those usual for their rank. Above all, no officer could be oblivious to the fact that promotions and preferred assignments could depend on their captain's final evaluation of them.

ILLEGAL "EXTRA" PUNISHMENT

Maintenance of law and order was the essence of Article XXX of the Articles of War. Seemingly this provision was sufficient when it referred to flogging: "No commanding officer shall on his own authority . . . inflict a punishment on any private [or sailor] beyond twelve lashes with the cat-of-nine-tails [unless altered by a court-martial overruling]."[44] In practice, however, the commander did not have to be a genius to figure out ways around this restriction. While not as painful as the cat, use of colts or canes by officers and petty officers was prevalent and usually legal. More sophisticated, a single case could be separated arbitrarily into as many as three or four charges, so instead of the twelve blows the offender might be given twenty-four, thirty-six, or forty-eight blows with the commander still operating just inside the licit limitation.

Elliott had been absent from *Constitution* when the illegal "extra" punishment of sailor David Floyd had been meted out, but the twenty-four lashes had been ordered by his executive officer. On the commodore's return he learned that Floyd had been guilty beyond doubt of "riotous and mutinous behavior" but save for this one slip was known to be a loyal and excellent seaman. One officer insisted that he be court-martialed on such a serious charge, but Elliott found out the accused could be scourged seventy-five to one hundred times and decided to be satisfied with the original twenty-four. He claimed that "no one understood better than did David Floyd, what he had escaped by my intervention."[45] There is no way of ascertaining how many other officers acted the same without being called before the navy's bar of justice, but there may well have been a great many.

CHAPLAIN THOMAS LAMBERT AND LIEUTENANT CHARLES G. HUNTER VERSUS ELLIOTT

Although two of his foes in the squadron's officer corps had filed separate charges against their commander, they were so closely allied that greater coherence should come from taking up together the cases of Chaplain Thomas Lambert and Lieutenant Charles G. Hunter. Elliott had formed a negative view of each, characterizing Lambert as "unchristian," despite his calling and Hunter as "idle, frivolous, and vexatious in every aspect."[46]

Elliott's first confrontation with Lambert occurred when he ordered him from the frigate *United States* to even more cramped quarters in the schooner *Shark*, effective later that day. Encumbered with a massive sea chest, Lambert had to climb into a boat to traverse a couple of miles to his new post. The commodore swore that the clergyman uttered no word of protest at that time. Instead, Lambert wrote an anonymous letter to the department, calling for his superior's court-martial when he came home.[47]

Here Hunter enters the narrative in circumstances with about as much epic grandeur as opéra bouffe, suggesting that both participants had been inflamed by too much liquor. At Mahon in March 1838 Hunter and Elliott had entries in a horse race before a sizable crowd, at the end of which Hunter jubilantly celebrated his triumph. Elliott, mounted on a donkey, dashed up to dispute the claim, shouting that his opponent had "separated the Honor of an officer from that of a Gentleman," raising the short cane he was carrying as if to strike the lieutenant "had he not been restrained by spectators." Hunter was suspended from duty and confined to his quarters.[48]

Elliott soon detected that Hunter had notified the secretary of the incident and twice attempted unsuccessfully to have him tried for "disrespect and treating with contempt his superior officer." He ordered Lambert, who had some formal training in the law, to study the records for how best to bring Hunter to justice. The entire proceeding was abhorrent to the clergyman who admitted to Elliott that he had dispatched to the department the letter referring to his commander's "villany." The junior-senior relations toward the end of the cruise were well summarized: "Clearly the officers had resolved to blunt their Commodore's disciplinary tactics by a policy of noncompliance with his known and expressed desires."[49]

After his return to New York, the aggrieved Hunter called for aid from Virginia congressman Henry A. Wise, a warm personal friend: "I have demanded the trial of Commodore Elliott for a most violent, unprovoked, and insulting outrage upon my feelings, committed publicly on a race course near Port Mahon . . . in the presence and hearing of several thousand. . . . My wish is, that Commodore Elliott may be brought before a Court of Inquiry for his *general* conduct while commander-in-chief of the Mediterranean Squadron."[50] Wise came through for Hunter with a probably greater impact than the lieutenant had dared hope and against Elliott with telling effect. He not only read in the House of Representatives Hunter's entire letter to him but, within a week, asked why the department had not made public that Hunter had been cleared thoroughly in both of his courts of inquiry? Wise concluded by introducing a resolution calling for the commencement of a full investigation of the commodore's "misconduct" in the Mediterranean, which was adopted by the House on the same day, ensuring that subsequent judicial proceedings about the matter would be practically mandatory.[51]

Elliott's retort to these Hunter-Lambert accusations was unpersuasive. With Lambert, he tramped over the same ground about the latter's resentment arising from his unwelcome transfer from *United States* to *Shark* with no complaint at the time before resorting to his ensuing charge of "degenerate hypocrisy." As he approached Hunter at the races he carried only a small stick—used as an extra spur—offering not the slightest threat to anyone. The commodore focused upon the locale at Mahon before an audience consisting of the island's governor, European military and civil representatives, and ordinary citizens. Hunter had converted "a scene of amusement into one of turbulence, mortification, and shame," thereby bringing acute dishonor to his own Navy.[52]

THE ALLEGED "MUTINY" IN *CONSTITUTION*, 1838

Midshipman Edward C. Anderson presented a dramatic eyewitness account of occurrences aboard that frigate when she terminated her Mediterranean responsibilities at Hampton Roads, Virginia, on July 31, 1838. Earlier that day a majority of the hands had gotten drunk, anticipating that the moment their ship touched shore they were free from naval regulations, as most of their terms of enlistment had expired. Riotous behavior seems to have begun when some of the sailors commenced harassing *Constitution*'s band, after which "much fighting broke out" among the crew. A little later Anderson observed "a crowd of men rushing aft on the quarter deck in pursuit of a black man named Ennis whose head was cut and bleeding, urged on by someone who kept shouting, 'Kill the negro!'" Anderson and two other officers managed to save the fugitive, slapping him into irons "to shield him from the fury of the crew" who wanted to lynch him, and this appeared to have saved his life. Later the officers learned that Ennis was hated because he had knifed one of his shipmates.[53]

For some time Elliott remained aloof in his quarters, expecting that his senior officers would soon restore order. But eventually realizing that they could not, he appeared with Anderson, Lieutenant Oscar Bullus, and another officer. At the forecastle the commodore "stated to the crew that they had broken the regulations of the ship . . . and that discipline must be preserved, that the ship should be taken up to Norfolk in the morning and they should be discharged. But he retreated to his cabin after several in his audience had . . . yelled, 'No!! No! No!' convincing him that nothing might be accomplished until they had slept off their alcoholic debauches."[54] At Elliott's court of inquiry in 1839 Bullus asserted that the commander had been remiss in not quelling "the Mutiny" at Hampton Roads at the cruise's end. In response, Elliott tore into him with the accusation that Bullus, "through fear of the men, whom he had abused, who left the ship in more of a hurry than became an officer of his pretended bravery; for he spoke daringly before the court of his wishes to fire into some hundreds of drunken men, who had become so through his negligence, and because I would not suffer him thus!"[55]

In his *Defence* during his court-martial in 1840 Elliott mustered his choleric resentment about this charge by denying any mutiny in *Constitution* had ever occurred. What had transpired then? "Who doubts, since the evidence thrice repeated before this court, that a very large proportion of the crew of *Constitution*, had, owing to the culpable carelessness of subordinate officers, become intoxicated . . . on that afternoon and night . . . and who doubts that this intoxication was impelled and excited by the conscientious belief that many of their contracts of service having expired, and their feet once planted on their native shore, they were free from the restraints of military discipline, and entitled to set them at defiance ?" Yet "I am gravely charged with having witnessed a *mutiny* , and doing nothing to suppress it! I take issue on both points, and deny, on behalf of the noble crew of *Constitution*, that they ever mutinied, and second, assert it to be incontestably proved, that that which is misnamed a mutiny was by the commander, myself, fearlessly and thoroughly, and judiciously repressed."[56]

Elliott called for sustenance from British Army captain Thomas V. Simmons who had written often on the subject, pointing to the requirements that mutiny must be collective, not individual, and that "a crime of mutiny or revolt, consists not in a mere exhibition of turbulence or violence, but in organized and concerted resistance to lawful authority aiming at subversion for even a brief period. . . . Actual disobedience to some order given is not necessary to constitute the offence of an endeavor to make a revolt. . . . In short, the parties must act together with the intention of mutual encouragement and support."[57] The same opinion was voiced also by US Army lieutenant George A. Prentiss. Elliott added: "It will strike every member of this Court, as tending to derange and confound the scale of punishments . . . if every improper or wanton misbehavior can be exaggerated beyond its real character."[58] It was one of Elliott's most inspiring performances.

LIVESTOCK

Perhaps nothing in Elliott's 1840 court-martial indictment frenzied him more than the specifications against him for carrying animals—primarily horses, jackasses, and mules—home in the venerable *Constitution*, and except for one vital issue, he had a strong argument in his own behalf. He voiced a fierce objection to his characterization of "scandalous conduct tending to the destruction of good morals," or "unbecoming and unofficerlike conduct" for that was "in strict accordance with a wise national policy, long actuating our fellow citizens at large, long sanctioned by the government, and especially useful to . . . a vast body of our countrymen."[59] In reference to the animals brought into the country, "*I* acted on this occasion *with no view to individual benefit* [emphasis added], but was influenced solely by a desire to promote the interests of agriculture and the arts, and thus to promote the views of the Department emanating from the Hon. [Secretary of the Navy] Samuel L. Southard and addressed to the commanders on several stations."[60] Next he leveled his sights on precedent. His orders on departure told him that "it will probably be in your power, while protecting the commercial, to add something to the agricultural interests of the nation, by procuring information respecting valuable animals, seeds, and plants, and *importing such as can conveniently without inattention* to *your more appropriate duties or expense to the government* [emphasis added]."[61] None other than President George Washington had inaugurated this practice, followed by such naval luminaries as Decatur, Chauncey, Bainbridge, Rodgers, George Read, Daniel T. Patterson, and William Crane, all of whom had imported livestock. Not one of them had been "treated with categorical impeachment and censure, much less with imputations of scandalous, immoral, and unofficerlike conduct. Such treatment was reserved to me alone."[62]

Elliott had his herd of twenty-three cared for on a farm near Mahon until June 23, 1838, when he left for America with the animals aboard *Constitution* where (according to him) they were conveniently accommodated in stalls "against the sides [and] were constructed in eighteen hours by the carpenter, and were carefully kept by him unconnected with the guns, their carriages and tackle, and were so slightly fixed, that at a moment's warning, and in less than fifteen minutes, the deck would have been effectively cleared of any obstruction."[63]

When veteran commanders of US men-of-war for many years studied this charge during Elliott's court-martial in 1840, most of them must have been struck by the impossibility of clearing for action a sizable combat vessel in such a brief period of time—hours or more would seem likely. Readers should recognize that for a captain to take any course that would reduce his command's efficacy to resist has to be labeled execrable. This was one of the keenest barbs that would later impale Elliott as to his court-martial convictions (see chapter 12).

The horses, mules, and jackasses taken at Syrian environs, at Mahon, and then at Hampton Roads, Virginia, would be instrumental at Elliott's court of inquiry in 1839 and court-martial a year later. It is simple to conjure up the scene at these ports where the terrified livestock—neighing, braying, bucking, and resisting—had to be transferred forcibly into small boats, amid the shoutings and cursings of the sailors. Midshipman Anderson wrote about such an incident: "The animals were brought aboard *Constitution* . . . and placed mid-ship. . . . There were twenty-three in all. Seven guns on the starboard side of the main deck and the same number on the larboard [port] were disabled. . . . To the best of my recollection the stalls were fastened to the cannon, the upper part to the beams overhead." At Hampton, "the deck was very black after the stalls were taken down, and was covered with a slick, slimy filth, requiring many hours before the mess had been cleansed."[64]

The weak link in Elliott's defense chain was that he had carried too many animals on his man-of-war, and there seems to be no evidence that other officers had so cluttered their gun deck as to make mighty *Constitution* almost a laughing stock of a fighting ship. Perhaps some of his court-martial judges noticed a caustic article that appeared simultaneously in a Washington, DC, suburban paper: "Jesse C. Elliot, who by some freak of fortune, has risen to the rank of Commodore in the US Navy, not contented with abusing his command by his conduct toward his senior officers, has seen fit to convert his ship into a Livery stable, for the purposes of speculating for his own private advancement, at the expense of the comfort of his whole ship's company. . . . The spaces between the guns were fitted up to accommodate twenty [*sic*] jackasses and horses with stabling . . . which would give a large return over cost at home. . . . [He] stopped at Hampton to put out his cargo of cattle, even he perhaps being anxious to conceal the purposes to which the ship had been turned. Had the vessel encountered an enemy in the condition she was, she would have been captured by a sloop of half her guns."[65]

In addition to the well-established assertions that Elliott had seriously interfered with *Constitution*'s ability to do battle, departmental rumors circulated that the commodore had had an ulterior motive for packing his frigate with such a horde of livestock-to fill his own pockets, which, evidently, he did and did well: "I am promised a most bountiful harvest for my Arabians in the Spring. They are out, free of all expense with a return to me promised of 2/3rds from 20 mares each at $75. My other animals are spread from Virginia to New York and west to Missouri and Kansas."[66]

Even after Elliott had been restored to active naval duty in 1843, he returned to the same topic: "I plan to disperse my full-blooded Arabian mare. . . . I wish to sell also two of my jacks. . . . I did not intend to part with any of these animals but necessity compels, and I wish it done. . . . The mares I think will bring . . . $1,200 dollars and the jacks about 1,500 each. They are both jet black and are good foal getters."[67]

Beyond doubt, Elliott was money hungry, for he might have to spend a small fortune on legal fees during his two plus years without naval stipends, 1840–43. Sums that he could wrest from his farm helped a little perhaps, and the above vending of his animals even more. His reinstatement in 1843 restored his service pay, but quite likely his extensive and widely scattered landholdings became the major contributor to his financial recovery. Immediately after noting his "Antiquities Collecting," (see below), he said, "The animals were disposed of as follows (to save space almost all of the recipients' names have been omitted, except when context requires):

A Jack—to propagate on shares [with Elliott]
A Maltese Jenny—in Tennessee
A Jack—to propagate on shares [with Elliott]
A Jack—owned jointly by Com. Elliott [and another].
A Malta Jack and a large bay Arabian horse—belonging to Com. Elliott.
Three Andalusian Hogs—Two broad-tailed Syrian Sheep—Minorca Chickens, Grain, Grass, and Garden Seed—to Mr. T. B. Jacobs.
One Minorca Jack—sent to propagate . . . and belonging to Com. Elliott and T. B. Jacobs.
One Superior Arabian Mare—presented to Mrs. Jacobs.
Four Arabian Mares One Andalusian and three Arabian colts--belonging to Com. Elliott, and propagated on shares.

Of these nine, Elliott owned individually or in tandem no fewer than six, and with the mares and jacks that he valued at between $1,200 and $1,500, his income should have been lucrative.[68]

It is not unlikely that others, after perusing the above evidence, reacted as did James Fenimore Cooper, especially damaging to his friend, as he was known to be a strong Elliott advocate: "Well, what do you think of Elliott's [court-martial] trial? I hear he has been . . . found guilty on the Jack Ass charge. . . . There is certainly a difference between taking on board three or four animals, and taking on board twenty or thirty."[69]

It was a mottled composite between an enlightened aspiration to better the nation's agriculture and greedy personal avarice that confronted his court-martial panel. If Elliott thought that his arguments persuaded the judges of his innocence, he was to be sorely disillusioned.

ANTIQUITIES COLLECTING THROUGHOUT THE CRUISE AND AFTER

When *Constitution* came into one of the scores of ports she entered in the Mediterranean, Elliott occasionally plunged inland to satisfy his zest for

"Antiquities Collecting" (or, more bluntly, looting). He listed "the articles imported by me and presented to the different Scientific, Literary, and Educational Institutions in the United States. . . . A partial glance . . . will show that their estimated value of twelve thousand dollars, is not exorbitant." Evidently Elliott did not have to pay himself for few if any of those itemized; more likely, all that he needed was the permission to export them from the friendly rulers through whose domains he passed.

Elliott particularized all his donations. The most bountiful beneficiaries were the Girard College in Philadelphia—"A Roman Sarcophagus, weighing about 3,500 pounds, and a limb from one of the cedars of Lebanon"; the Medical College of Baltimore—"A Mummy, disinterred in Memphis, Egypt"; the Charlottesville, North Carolina, University—"Two marble balls obtained at the Dardanelles, about eight feet in circumference"; to the Navy Department or government—"Two colossal balls, and a Sarcophagus from Beirut, Syria." The Beirut sarcophagus attracted the greatest attention from American historians at that time and later. Elliott, with a logic-defying leap equal to that of a long jump prize winner, decided that it must contain the remains of the Roman emperor Septimius Severus.[70]

Incredibly, Elliott concluded that it would be ideal for the tomb of President Jackson and his wife!: "Dear Genl., The splendid sarcophagus that I brot [*sic*] with me from the Holy Land is sufficiently capacious to contain the remains of your dear departed wife and your own, and I do hope you will not decline it; your friends here say you should close at once and with your usual firmness."[71]

Jackson must have been thunderstruck by a declaration that he, the apostle of Jacksonian Democracy, should rest in any such edifice, probably mitigated by a realization that Elliott regarded him as a father figure, so he responded with courtesy mingled with an unmistakable rigor: "I have read the whole proceedings of the presentation by you of the Sarcophagus . . . so honorable to my fame, with sensations and feelings more easy to conjecture than by me expressed. . . . But with the warmest sensations that can inspire a grateful heart, I MUST DECLINE ACCEPTING THE HONOR INTENDED TO BE BESTOWED. I cannot consent that my mortal body should be laid in a repository prepared for an Emperor or a King—my republican feelings and principles forbid it—the simplicity of our system of government forbids it. . . . I have prepared a humble depository for my mortal body beside that wherein lies my beloved wife, where, without any pomp or parade, I have requested . . . to be laid, for both of us there to remain until the last trumpet sounds to call the dead to judgment."[72]

After his return home in 1839, Elliott made two presentations not included in the above. Of his two sarcophagi (following Jackson's rejection of any such offering), one was destined for Carlisle College, in Pennsylvania, which he had attended just before his induction into the US Navy in 1804. This would provide for the body of Stephen Girard, the Philadelphia philanthropist. The other he conferred upon "the generous [Englishman] James Smithson," donor of the Smithsonian Institution in Washington.[73]

This work of Elliott to better the scientific, cultural, and educational standards of his nation merits extolment, for nothing in the records seems to demonstrate that he lined his own purse through them. Moreover, they stand in the most contradistinction to the profits he earned for years from sales of the animals he brought back with him in *Constitution.*

THE CREW'S PRESENTATION OF SILVER PLATE TO ELLIOTT

Very likely the genesis of this charge had been the minority report of the House "Special Committee on Commodore Elliott's Case, 22 September 1839," signed by Representatives Charles Naylor and John Chambers. It made up in toto a scalding indictment of Elliott's behavior in the Mediterranean, a silver plate was among the many accusations in it. "He is charged with endeavoring to booster up his reputation and to enrich and sustain himself against the charges of his officers, by procuring to be wrung from the hard-earned pittance of his crew costly presents of plate."[74] Elliott retorted in kind that on January 8, 1837, Boerum wrote him: "A sum of money has been placed in the hands of Lieut. Bullus and myself by the Crew, with the wish that we should purchase a Service of Plate to be presented to you as a testimony of their respect. The amount received [$584.50] has been expended in accordance with that wish; and I now, Sir, in the name of the crew, solicit your acceptance of the Service."[75] The four items of worked silver were "two tureens, a pitcher, and a waiter" and carried the inscription: "Presented as a mark of respect to Commodore J. D. Elliott of the United States Navy, by the Crew of the *Constitution*."[76]

The commodore responded by specifying several instances in which the hands of a US man-of-war had given similar gifts to their commanding officer. He let fly his rage and disgust at those "who are eager to distort and discolor every . . . [illegible] look at this unreal mockery" and "hope to clutch at its airy nothing the substantial dishonor of an American Captain," noting that no other such case had drawn a negative reaction from the department. Elliott swore that on learning of the donation he had informed his officers that he would make up from his own pocket any difference between the $584.50 already collected and the total cost, a matter of only a few dollars.[77] Despite the picayune nature of this specification, his judges found him guilty, which to us is at the very least, highly questionable.

EDWARD C. ANDERSON AND ELLIOTT AND OTHERS

The mandatory business of Elliott's argosy in the Mediterranean was to escort General Lewis Cass, secretary of war, on a diplomatic mission through that inland sea's environs, one of the high points in Elliott's tenure of almost three years in command of that squadron. This entourage would have left Jaffa in what is now Israel and rejoined *Constitution* at Tripoli on the Syrian coast. It consisted of Elliott, Anderson, and Cass with his sizable brood of a wife, three daughters, and a son. A handful of others had been invited to join them.

They were off on a trek to the Holy Land's Christian, Judaic, and Muslim sites in the Syrian and Lebanese interiors, a journey sure to be exhaustive and possibly dangerous. Once there, Elliott had given some sensible advice to his companions. Shipboard security demanded upon the strictest observance of naval law to which civilian rights must be subordinate.[78] Elliott instructed the Cass women, in addition to remaining within eyeshot and earshot of their protectors, that they must dress in masculine clothing, thoroughly clad to avoid any offense to the Muslims they would meet. Turning to the males, Elliott assured them that their nightly libations should be no problem. Despite the Muslim ban on the imbibing of alcohol, most of the "pashas [akin to governors] and other great men ignored them." Recalling that one potentate on an earlier visit to *Constitution* "was so much in his cups that it was with difficulty that he could keep his seat." Until so sodden that he had to be carried away, he had insisted that everyone drink "bottoms up," refilling bumpers as they emptied.[79]

The visitors would have to travel on horses, donkeys, and afoot, to suffer extremes of cold and heat, as the terrain rose to several thousand feet and fell below sea level at the Dead Sea. Moreover, the party was penetrating the heart of Islam where fierce anti-Christian sentiments were sure to be encountered. They were protected only by their own weapons, each carrying "a cutlass and a pair of pistols," as well by similarly armed guards, and occasional detachments of troops supplied by some of those pashas who had given permission for their domains to be entered. Initially we could not understand how Anderson, a lowly midshipman whose commission had not been issued until November 25, 1834,[80] could have snatched this plum assignment from the many scores of officers who had seniority over him serving on "Old Ironsides." But Elliott himself solved the puzzle, giving it a romantic twist. Near the start of their journey he told Anderson that "I owed my good fortune in being selected for the trip entirely to the penchant of Miss Matilda Cass. I therefore determined to be very civil to her on the way and in fact to take her under my special care and protection."[81]

That wily midshipman spent nearly twenty-five closely handwritten pages to describe their itinerary in the Holy Land, but suffice it here to mention only that they rode from Jaffa through Caesaria (Palestine), Mount Carmel (Israel), to Tyre and Sidon, ending in Beirut (the last three in Lebanon).[82]

To terminate the Elliott-Anderson relationship, the two came together again late in the commodore's life. During March 1843 Anderson was in Washington, DC, attending to departmental affairs, and remarks that Elliott was there, up to "some devilment no doubt. He has discovered in the archives the original diagram of the Battle of Lake Erie, which exculpates him from the charges of cowardice in that action and gives him a strong claim upon the justice of his countrymen. He was very much elated [and after showing the diagram to Anderson] he capers about like some very young man, and predicted that the elder's suspension from the service would soon be lifted [that process had just been completed]."[83]

Despite his rapidly approaching death by edema, Elliott drew upon his dwindling energies in a desperate attempt to demonstrate that his Lake Erie vindication was complete, proving that he was entitled rightfully to a preeminent ranking. But he still could not overcome the massive accumulation of his flaws effectually to challenge Perry's number one eminence during the first quarter century of the early navy along the Great Lakes frontier, except for the persistent arguments about this issue that animate American naval literature at present.

THE BUCKSHOT WAR IN PENNSYLVANIA, 1838–1839

Politics in the Keystone State during this so-called war was divided into an almost perfect equipoise between the Democrats and a combination of the Anti-Masons and Whigs.[84] This balance was demonstrated in a vote for a new state constitution during October 1838, "when 113,971 sustained it against 112,759 who opposed it—a slim majority of only 1,212 out of 225,000."[85] In the same election, this time balloting for governor, again no clear majority emerged, with fifty-six Democrats vying against fifty-two Whigs and Anti-Masons. "Each included its own set of eight disputed members without which neither had a legal majority." Furthermore, both blocs threatened to march on Harrisburg to install by force their favorite. The state militia was called out, and their general ordered his men "to arm themselves with buckshot cartridges," hence the name Buckshot War.[86]

Elliott comes into view with a letter to the president of the United States, recalling that in 1839, "I responded to the call of the Chief Magistrate of the State of Pennsylvania . . . to accompany him to the Barracks at Carlisle and assist in urging and advising the Military Officer to put his Dragoons in position for . . . quelling an insurrection . . . [at Harrisburg]. . . . with the power of sustaining him [the governor] in his office. I calmed his fears, having no intention of mixing with the partizans and to appease the one I would quickly give confidence to the other to act a consistent party as a mediator between the parties, this I did."[87] But earlier, Elliott had alluded to the dreaded visage of Navy Secretary Paulding looming on the immediate horizon: "A friend informs me there is some feeling at Washington on the subject of my visit to Harrisburg during the recent excitement [Buckshot War]. I responded to the call . . . approved by General Jackson. . . . I [illegible] the unkind feelings which Mr. Paulding . . . seems to be as if I were almost a stranger to him. My cause at Harrisburg was altogether of a *peace maker* as the accompanying notice will prove. Thus why put on me the severe rebuke[?]"[88]

Elliott's role in these proceedings was hardly consequential, as shown by Philip S. Klein and Ari Hoogenboom's *A History of Pennsylvania*, which, in two-and-a-half pages, does not mention his name. So despite his own foofaraw, the presumption has to be that these events in Pennsylvania would have worked out the same had Elliott remained at home. Nonetheless, the above was part of the commodore's life, and no conscientious biographer of him can afford to dismiss it altogether.

COURT-MARTIAL OF PASSED MIDSHIPMAN CHARLES C. BARTON, 1835–1839

Reminiscent of Elliott's departmental rebuff during his term as Boston Navy Yard commandant concerning Babbit (see. chapter 9), Elliott primed and leveled his guns at a second target, for he abhorred Barton as much as he had Babbit. Throughout most of 1836 Barton launched a sustained onslaught to persuade Secretary of the Navy Dickerson to court-martial his superior and was puzzled why nothing had happened for many months. Not until early 1837 was he told that Elliott had countercharged him with several delinquencies, demanding his court-martial, thereby ensuring that Barton's case would precede Elliott's.

Almost everything forthcoming had emanated from Barton's duel with Passed Midshipman H. P. T. Wood at Smyrna, Turkey, on December 1, 1835. Information about its background is scant, murky, and confusing. Few sources are available about this duel, but one major account of it has been unearthed: Charles O. Paullin's long article, "Duelling in the Old Navy" but with errors and omitting the encounter's result!

"Wood was an officer of the USS *Constitution*, and Barton of the USS *Shark* [each was attached to the *Shark* at that time]. Both were quarrelsome young men. The two seconds were Midshipman James. T. McDonough [for Wood] and William S. Ringgold [for Barton]. Ringgold tried to settle the matter amicably, but Wood insisted upon a fight [Barton was the challenger]."[89]

"The two foes found themselves together, and the consensus of their fellow-officers was anti-Barton, and I regret to say that the rest of the mess followed his example. This, together with other affronts, left Barton with no alternative other than to call him out."[90] No terms for the duel are given, but presumably, they were at the customary ten paces (about thirty feet). Shortly thereafter Barton and his second McDonough were sent ashore for watering duty and Wood, unbeknownst to his immediate superior officer and defying Elliott's instructions to remain in the ship, left to fight his enemy.[91] Shots were exchanged in which Barton was hit in the lower right leg, immobilizing him in agony for a year and a half.

Barton's wound was indeed torturous, and Elliott had the ill fortune to have a most formidable enemy join the fray. Dr. William C. Barton, a USN surgeon, had the medical knowledge to describe the nature of the damage done. Moreover, he was Charles's father, naturally horrified by Midshipman Ringgold's description of what had transpired during the immediate aftermath of the duel. His son's leg was a "comminuted [pulverized] fracture, and shortly after a painful operation for extracting the ball . . . in a condition certainly for not calling for any inhuman aggravation of bodily and mental suffering, nor for any course which might jeopardize his limb or life." Elliott had disregarded "*the protest of the fleet surgeon*, Dr. Thomas J. Boyd, who alone had the right, as he had the capacity, of judging the danger of the course that protest was designed to avert."[92] Elliott demurred from the doctor's final point, accentuating correctly that US naval regulations clarified the relationship between the two officers: "The fleet surgeon is bound to advise with . . . [the captain] on medical and surgical matters," but, "where the good of the service requires, and its discipline is at stake, the fleet surgeon must yield in all cases to the opinions and decisions of the commander-in-chief."[93]

On the day of the duel Elliott had gone ashore at Smyrna and did not return to his flagship until late in the afternoon. Barton had been carried from the dueling ground to *Constitution* under the instructions of Dr. Boyd rather than to *Shark* to which his patient belonged. Already at odds with Barton, the angry commodore forthwith ordered that the invalid be carried from *Constitution* to *Shark*, overriding the protest of the doctor and the frantic appeals of the sufferer.[94]

Elliott explained the reasons why he made this arbitrary decision, swearing that "I knew nothing whatever of the details of the injury, and had a strong reason to believe as a *short time proved* [emphasis added] that Dr. Boyd's feelings exaggerated the danger, and left the removal to the doctors," blaming them for the transfer to the smaller ship: "Surely it was unnecessary . . . to set forth the slinging in a cot, the array of the surgeon, his operations, and the pain he inflicted–the lowering over the side of the frigate, the hoisting over the side of the schooner, and then lowering him down the hatch head foremost, with the accompaniments of excruciating pain, torture, and agony."[95]

The commodore had inserted this to demonstrate his lack of accountability in these distressing circumstances, but stupidly, he had not realized how much further he had validated Barton's case against him. But then the commander turned from this flash of sympathy for Barton to a fiery denunciation of his behavior: "He had violated my positive order [against dueling with Wood]; he had abandoned his post of duty; he had conducted the duel with flagrant publicity, and he had, without the slightest warrant or necessity, avoided *Shark* to which he belonged, to intrude himself into *Constitution*. . . . . The eyes of all the great European fleets were attracted to my ship. It was impossible not to feel and perceive, as the representative chief of our nation in that quarter and at that moment, my conduct was to attest the moral sentiment of the American people, the efficiency of its laws, and the discipline of their navy."[96]

The same Midshipman Anderson, who would enact so prominent a role in accompanying Elliott during *Constitution*'s Mediterranean tour, 1835–38, also had an intimate if brief association with Barton's wound. During Elliott's court-martial at the end of the cruise he testified that "I saw Midshipman Barton brought on board *Constitution*," immediately after the duel. "He was placed in a cot on the starboard side of the main deck between two guns. I held his leg during the portion of the time that the surgeon was performing the operation of extracting the ball, becoming fatigued I was relieved. . . . Mr. Barton appeared to suffer much pain."[97]

Charles C. Barton launched a bare knuckled assault against his superior in three documents: (1) "Manifest of the Charges Preferred to the Navy Department and Subsequently to Congress . . ." [against Elliott], (2) "Refutation of the Recrimination Raised by that Officer," appendix, and (3) supporting evidence. Their combined total was expended in trying to persuade Navy Secretaries Dickerson and Paulding to bring Elliott before a court-martial panel, and through it, Barton eventually achieved his end.[98] But as is so often the case, this package is put together so irrationally that the researcher has no option but to reorganize it into some sensible order, for one charge on page seven does not reappear until page twenty-five.

Barton had been with Elliott in *Constitution* during a hurried diplomatic tour to Europe in 1835. Noticing that Barton had a talent for drawing, on the way home from France, Elliott asked him to paint a couple of sketches for him, which Barton did under the assumption that they were for the Navy Department. Learning that this was not so, he "refused peremptorily" to do any more, after which, "Captain Elliott's treatment of me arose from 'private pique,'" following Barton's reassignment to the Mediterranean on the same frigate.[99]

This picayune spat over art may serve as a springboard to link it to the immeasurably more essential issue of what had happened to Barton in the hours after his confrontation with Wood. It enabled the invalid to build upon the foundation established by Dr. Barton, his father, in his letter to the department in attempting to bring his persecutor to justice by language close to the hysterical: "In this prostrate and aching hour, with my cot tremulous from the thrill of muscular pain and the agony which shoots through the marrow of the bones—in this hour he [Elliott], just after the superadded pain of a surgical operation—as if the thought struck him, 'now is the time to avenge myself on this haughty middie, for his disdainful refusal to paint pictures for me. . . . ' In this hour, Sir, he practiced his cruelty on me!!! . . . I was turned out of *Constitution* as a rabid dog. . . . To the longest day I live I will never forget the bodily agony and mental anguish of that cruel deed."[100]

Barton paused to draw a bead on Elliott's boast of how well he had been treated in *Shark*: "The prison to which . . . [he] sent me when he turned me out of the frigate, was a steerage 16 feet beam, 7 feet 3 inches fore and aft, and 4 1/2 feet between foot deck and overhead beams. . . . In this there messed and slept *five* officers, among whom was my late antagonist! a fit place truly for an extensive wound!"[101]

Turning from the abusive humiliations that had been heaped upon him by his commodore, Barton reverted to a discussion of the duel itself, evoking frowns of bewilderment from the researchers. In his letter of December 5, 1835, to Dr. Barton, Passed Midshipman Ringgold made an eye-opening statement: "When shots were exchanged at the field, Barton, after receiving two fires, his pistol missing fire both times, he had his leg fractured by the second shot."[102]

During early stages of our study, Ringgold's assertion took us aback. If he is correct, from what did Midshipman Wood die? This led to a surmise that perhaps he had succumbed to the lingering aftereffects of another adversary's bullet. Such is a distinct possibility. Captain Charles Gordon, USN, was struck in the stomach while dueling in 1810 and suffered through no less than seven pain-racked years before his merciful release.[103] Further analysis of the data, however, revealed that while Barton was still stricken with his shattered leg, Wood remained with him in *Shark* until January 11, 1836, when Elliott took his entire squadron out of Smyrna.

Barton made an aside while composing a paean to Wood: "He was a desirable companion . . . an excellent sailor . . . generous to a fault. In a word, he was gallant and brave. True, he had been lately my foe—but he was a bold and open one." This noble tribute was sadly marred, however, when Barton tossed off the casual remark that had both been able physically to do so, "a second meeting would have taken place."[104] To terminate Wood's case, when *Shark* arrived at Lisbon in early 1836 he was court-martialed on two charges, both referring to events in Smyrna, almost a year before, which could have ruined him professionally. In the first, Wood was accused of " unofficerlike and ungentlemanly conduct," in that, between November 1835 and early January 1836, he had "run into debt which he had no means of repaying the same, thereby causing . . . the purser of said schooner *Shark* to liquidate the debt from funds designed for the use of the squadron." The second harkened back to December 1, 1835, when Wood did fight and disable C. C. Barton "in the presence of the boat's crew."[105] The passage of many months between the duel and the charge connected with it strongly suggests that the Navy Department was waiting for additional evidence against Wood (his debt) to be found before proceeding against him. When the court sat on February 20, 1836, it ruled quickly that Wood was guilty on the charge "of great indiscretion and imprudence in risking the character of the service by contracting a debt without certain means of repaying it." On the second charge he was also judged culpable and sentenced to a "suspension from duty for six months, and further, that he be dismissed from the Mediterranean Squadron [i.e. from the Navy]." Elliott endorsed both findings.[106]

After his digression about the duel with Wood, Barton went back to his threnody of the woe he had undergone from his tyrannical captain, namely plunging him into dire poverty and then accusing him of desertion for returning to the United States without his commodore's permission. Elliott focused a positive light on the care that he had extended to the invalid within three days of the duel: "Dr. Boyd, who had so strenuously opposed his being taken from the *Constitution,* proposed that he should be carried from *Shark* to the shore; a proposition to which I gave my ready assent, directing comfortable quarters to be obtained for him. . . . He was visited by his companions; he was faithfully nursed; and when at the expiration of about four weeks, the course of duty required the American ships of war to leave that harbour on the 5th of January 1836, he was content, as proven by Dr. Barton himself that his son was 'doing well in every respect [and] left in Smyrna at his own request.'"[107]

Furthermore, Elliott made sure of "adequate pecuniary arrangements for his maintenance and comfort. . . . given an advance of three months' pay," and "I addressed a note to Mr. David Offley, then our Consul [in Smyrna], engaging to honor his drafts at the rate of his legal compensation, of 750. per annum if he remained ill after the first of April following.[108] As commodore, Elliott could not permit such an ailing and immobile officer to remain on a fighting warship—so what more could he have done?

For the many months that the invalid remained at Smyrna, he ripped into his tormentor's account of how carefully his financial support had been planned. Barton stressed that Elliott had to know that a naval officer could not order payment to anyone: that could be done only by *Constitution*'s purser, D. Fauntleroy, who had to justify every penny spent to the auditors of the Treasury Department. This meant that Barton never received his promised advanced pay, nor did Consul Offley "honor his drafts" during that half year. Barton lamented that all he had realized from the latter source was $135, most reluctantly extended in small amounts, all of which had to be repaid. In fact, Offley held back until each sum had been countersigned by Griffin Stith, an American merchant in Smyrna. Barton's destitution was the result: for five months "I have been without one cent, in a foreign country, with a broken and shattered limb . . . [without] friends and acquaintances, save those I made here."[109]

How did Barton survive? Stith, "a noble-hearted man, by no means affluent," supported him, as well as providing the "balm and solace of female tenderness and care. In the bosom of Mr. Stith's family, now returned to the United States and residing in Baltimore, I was nursed and cherished like a son and brother-and gratitude inexpressibly warms me."[110]

Back in America Barton was most complimentary to Secretary Dickerson for rescuing him from poverty and restoring him to some degree to financial and physical stability: "[He] with a degree of feeling and kindness . . . immediately extended to me the evidence of his sympathy, unattended by the slightest token of his displeasure at my return . . . granted immediately my only request that I then made, by directing Commodore Ridgely to receive me into the naval hospital at New York. . . . He subsequently directed Commodore Barron to admit me into the Schuylkill naval hospital [at Philadelphia], and authorized the 4th auditor to pay my passage money . . . and finally placed funds in the hands of Messr. Baring Brothers & Co. of London for the liquidation of [the] surgeon's bill."[111]

Elliott's answer to this accumulating mass of evidence against him was short and feeble. Both he and Purser Fauntleroy had assumed that if any unexpected financial problems confronted Barton, prompt remedial measures would be taken to solve them. Consul Offley was supposed to keep them informed, but he "confesses that Offley had not written because of the pressures of other business." The commodore ended with an ill-timed show of bravado: "Gentlemen you must excuse me for saying that the accusation of casting him off has been too clearly disproved to be now esteemed other than preposterous."[112]

Earlier Barton may have supposed that the matter of his long-term poverty in Smyrna would be the last impediment to be surmounted, but another was emerging simultaneously. In a letter to Dickerson Elliott demanded that his subordinate be court-martialed for desertion: "I directed him, *if able* [emphasis added] to repair to Malta and join his vessel at that place," but in a letter from September 17, 1836, Elliott was told that Barton has "the intention to leave for the United States per the first vessel." This permitted the commodore to inform the secretary that it was a "desertion of his station, and a distinct disobedience of the express orders to him."[113]

Utilizing his "Manifest" as a retort, Barton maundered across a couple of pages prior to concentrating upon his perfect escape clause—Elliott's phrase about coming to Malta, "if able." He shot back the information to the commodore that he was "not in a state to join my vessel. . . . I therefore inform you that I shall proceed to the United States, having been pronounced unfit for duty for one year to come by Dr. Marpurgo of Smyrna, and the surgeons of HBM ships *Tribune* and *Favourite*," enclosing the doctors' confirmatory letters to that effect.[114]

This ordeal over, as he imagined, Barton was unaware that Elliott still had two stones in his catapult to hurl against him for violent outbreaks, justifying his accusation that Barton was "quarrelsome." The first was verbal and applied to John C. Holland, the commodore's clerk at the time but soon named a US Navy purser; the second was physical and concerned a crewmember, "foretopman" George Dennett. Elliott disposed of Holland's cases swiftly, notifying the department that "while we lay in Mahon [in the Spanish Balearic Islands] in October 1835 . . . Barton struck my clerk and mutilated his face; in consequence of which the former was restricted from shore, and a promise obtained from the latter that he could not call Barton out [to duel with him]; if he did I would dismiss him (my clerk) from the squadron."[115] To be expected, Barton's explanation to Dickerson differed markedly: "As regards the personal affair" with Holland, "which Captain Elliott has dragged before the Department . . . [and] Congress, I am bound to defend myself with the expression of sincere regret, Sir, to be obliged, even in self-defense against the sinister insinuations of Captain Elliott to trouble you. The tale is short, and briefly I will tell it. The facts are these: I was grossly insulted by this clerk and I resented the insult on the spot. . . . But [Elliott] first urged me to apologize to clerk Holland, which I decorously but firmly declined." When the commodore persisted, "I then refused in every way and manner to humiliate myself," and ended, leaving the reader to wonder how "gross" had been "the indignity."[116]

Barton's decision to splash about seven times the wordage devoted to sailor Dennett that he had with Holland is comprehensible for no blood flowed in the latter's case, but he felt compelled to stab Dennett with a knife. Overseeing the crew's application to the scores of duties heaped on them was the responsibility of the midshipmen, directed by the lieutenants. Barton found Dennett surly and uncooperative, even edging toward outright defiance. While the men were employed in sweeping the gun deck during February 1835, Barton hailed that sailor, "Why are you on deck?" Dennett replied, "I was sent up by the boat-swain [Robert Whittaker] to make sail." Barton retorted, "Damn your eyes, go down below . . . upon which he took my broom out of my hands, and commenced pushing me in the legs with it." Dennett concluded, "He then raised the broom to strike me, when I took it away from him, and turned to go. . . . I immediately felt a sharp instrument enter my thigh, which proved to be a dirk thrust by Passed Midshipman Barton." Basically Whittaker confirmed Dennett's account.[117]

That was more than sufficient evidence for Elliott: "I immediately inquired into the matter and found that Mr. Barton has, for some trivial cause, in the heat of passion, dirked the man. To avoid a court-martial, I ordered him [Barton] to *Shark*, with strict instructions to his commander not to allow him to visit the shore, apprehensive that some difficulty might arise with the other young gentlemen . . . [of *Constitution*]" and fired it off to the department.[118]

Barton replied hotly, and at length, about Dennett's charge and Elliott's letter, knowing that the secretary would investigate the issue in depth. He insisted that they were a monstrous misrepresentation of the truth. Self-defense had been why he had stabbed Dennett; indeed, his very life was gravely threatened. "I firmly believed then, and do now conscientiously believe but for the *summary punishment* I *inflicted* . . . , though irritated at the contumacy of the man, proceeded with my wits about me, from cool deliberation—*but for this* my scull would probably have been fractured by a blow from a man with a heavy hickory ship's broom, with which he threatened me in a mutinous and resentful manner." Furthermore, "Dennett had the physical strength; I was the weaker one of the two in strife, and I perpetrated this heinous act of self-defense! That was my *act* of cruelty!"[119]

Barton's two concluding points may have caught the favorable attention of the court-martial panel, namely, his lack of alternatives to his assault on Dennett and the written support given to him by his former commanders, all save Elliott.

Suppose as a US naval officer Barton had cried out for aid or, much worse, fled in fear of his life? "Would I not rightly have been held in contempt by the very Dennett and the lookers on of the crew—had fear prevented me from quelling such mutinous behavior as called for instant punishment? . . . The commander of a ship whose sword will not leap from the scabbard to punish the first threatenings of mutiny, will be adjudged by his officers as a craven knight." Barton was totally on target. Personal courage was an absolute for naval and army officers, and had he flinched, he would have been ostracized by his colleagues—"put to Coventry"—soon to be driven from the service.[120]

In singling out Elliott as the one commander who had been dissatisfied enough with his conduct to bring him to a court-martial, Barton provided *fifteen* others who praised him highly, among them such well-known commodores as Barron and Chauncey. Among their compliments were "assiduous," "accomplished," "correct and proper," "irreproachable," "amiable," "exemplary," and "met with my entire approbation."[121] In this narrative Barton's case becomes irrevocably intertwined with Elliott's, necessitating a termination of it in this chapter, to concentrate upon essential chronological material in the chapter that follows. In short, the mélange of Barton's terrible wound by Wood; Barton's strong counterattack against Elliott; the failure of Elliott to provide Barton's service pay, as already pledged; US consul Offley's negligence in Smyrna; the support given the invalid by Stith and family at the same port; the magnanimity of Dickerson, who arranged for Barton's recovery of both health and finances; the highly favorable testimony of all Barton's former commanders, except Elliott; the lack of Barton's alternatives; and more coalesced to exonerate Barton and condemn Elliott during that commodore's court-martial in 1840 (see chapter12).

Twelve

Court of Inquiry, Court-Martial, and Restoration to Active Duty

Some of us who have delved with some depth into the early and mid--nineteenth-century naval history and biography have been impressed by the navy secretaries' brass tacks approach to the particular matter at hand in their letters to officers, curt and to the point, unless the nature of their correspondence required more extensive commentary. We at least have found them often to be distinctive from officers to them that sometimes gave items of purely local interest, attacks on their colleagues, or tidbits of lively naval gossip.

But never have we encountered official missives of such terse and unvarying hostility as those from Secretary Paulding to Elliott. Were they based on some incidents prior to the commodore's departure for Europe? If so, nothing has been unearthed about that possibility. Hence, they must date from Elliott's malfeasances while abroad, namely his harassment of Babbit, his abuse of Barton after the latter's leg had been pulverized during his duel with Wood, the havoc caused in "Old Ironsides" by the livestock leaving New York and arriving back at Virginia, his avid collecting of ancient relics, and the alleged "mutinous" breakdown of the commodore's discipline at Hampton Roads, Virginia.

By midpoint in the cruise, the open and well-publicized ruptures between Elliott and several of his officers had been sure to attract the unfriendly notice of Paulding. The commencement of Elliott's downhill slide toward disgrace came from the secretary's letter to him during the summer of 1838: "The enclosed copy of a communication, recently received from certain officers attached to the frigate *Constitution*, is referred to you for such explanations as may enable the Department more fully to understand the precise nature of the transactions which occurred at the time and on the occasion therein stated."[1] This had to be a crushing blow to Elliott who, already aware of Paulding's animus toward him, had hoped that the controversial nature of the evidence, which balanced the pros and cons to be put forth by both his supporters and enemies, would spare him such an ordeal. This judicial inquest might result in his court-martial conviction, perhaps writing finis to his long years in the service.

Many months later, Paulding was back with a second letter, this the more harmful because it contained specifics relating to the commodore's inability to maintain discipline in what Elliott always called "the alleged Mutiny" at Hampton Roads.[2]

During his interlude Elliott had been centralizing on trying to make sure that the implied direction of his court of inquiry conviction might not lead to his court-martial. He turned to Joel R. Poinsett: "I still feel that you are the only friend [in the cabinet] in whom I could confide and to whom I could rely for *justice* when so unpleasantly situated. . . . I came to the conclusion that if the public interest requires no further proceedings, I should feel better satisfied." Documentation is silent about any moves that Poinsett may have made, but if any, they were inconsequential. The impetus of a court of inquiry to a court-martial had been set, and probably nothing could stop it short of Elliott's plea of guilty to at least some charges, followed by his resignation from the navy.[3]

Elliott may have flinched but should not have been surprised to read: "Sir, a Board of Inquiry . . . has been ordered to convene at the Navy Yard, Phila on 22 April next to investigate certain charges and complaints preferred against you by Officers of the Navy of the U. States together with your official conduct generally while commanding the U. S. forces in the Mediterranean Sea"[4]

Meeting from April 22 to April 27, 1839, Elliott's court of inquiry judges were composed of three commodores, Charles Stewart, presiding; James Biddle and Daniel Todd Patterson; with John M. Read as the judge advocate. Their verdict held by a two to one vote that sufficient evidence existed to require a full court-martial. Stewart was the dissenter and mounted a measured defense of Elliott's comportment; only in the matter of illicit extra flogging was he culpable, and that was much overweighed by his general behavior, concluding "that a Court-martial would not now conduce to the interests of the Navy; but on the contrary it would have a tendency to further weaken the very limited powers of a Commander of an American squadron, abroad; and to render all further efforts to command, abortive."[5] But Biddle and Patterson found Elliott's misconduct sufficient to outvote Stewart, mainly on the grounds of overstocking *Constitution* with animals and the crew's presentation of a silver plate to him, among other things.

Perhaps as equally damaging to Elliott's career prospects as Paulding's cold-blooded maneuverings to expel him from the navy was "The Report of the Special Committee of the House of Representatives," signed by Congressmen Charles Naylor of Pennsylvania and John Chambers of Kentucky. A third member, Francis F. Lyon of Alabama, claiming that as he could not understand the facts in question, at first refused to vote but did so later.

Both Naylor and Chambers had been scandalized by the commodore's behavior during his Mediterranean command, about which they charged him with" the most cruel, inhuman, and brutal conduct toward his officers," as well as "ungentlemanly and unofficerlike" treatment of them. One of the most widely circulated newspapers in the nation devoted the better part of two full columns about the particular activities they found so objectionable, stating that "they *require* investigation." Worse still for the accused, during late February 1839 they introduced such a motion in the House that was quickly adopted.[6] Naylor, Chambers, and Lyon were all Whigs, so politics may have been a factor. Ever since Elliott's administration of the Boston Navy Yard, 1833–35, he had been one of the most notorious protagonists of Jackson and his Democratic Party.[7]

The consequence of this anti-Elliott propaganda created a groundswell of public opinion against him that even had the secretary been more even-handed than the ruthless Paulding, it had made quite certain that his court--martial must be held.

Historian James Fenimore Cooper, who tended to side with Elliott against Commodore Perry about the Battle of Lake Erie, took a roseate view of these proceedings: "Elliott comes out of the Court [of inquiry] well. He is acquitted of everything originally charged, and is only censured for a few light incidental matters. . . . Even Biddle, I am told, acquits him of the Hunter and Barton charges. . . . [Stewart] says that there is no ground for a Court-[martial], and is said to have given a very able opinion. Biddle and Patterson do not agree in particulars, even though they think there should be a Court-[martial]."[8]

Elliott may have tried to appease his dejection about these developments by taking a swat at his gadfly: "Let the world know that to gratify the vindictive passions of J. K. Paulding and others, the country was made to expend a sum sufficient to erect a hospital for a few infirm tars—enough to soothe the hearts of widows and orphans—but yet not enough for Mr. Paulding and his fellow-conspirators to purchase an approving conscience for themselves, or favorable opinions from the meanest."[9]

Elliott reviewed most caustically the navy's judicial system that was treating him so harshly: "The [courts of inquiry] and Courts-martial are not *courts* of *justice*. Their decisions are not according to fact and evidence, but according to professional jealousy and ill-will. . . . These courts should be

. . . abandoned . . . and tried by the civil tribunals of the nation, or before some new courts instituted for the purpose. The officers of the Navy, however competent to judge in ordinary controversies, are the last men to be entrusted with trials of each other."[10] But this jeremiad was ignored, and except for his escape from being cashiered from the service, almost all of Elliott's worst forebodings would transpire.

How to represent the department's indictments of Elliott in detail caused at the onset a brief impasse. But I was delighted to discover in the *Defence of Commodore Elliott*, so as, of course, to negate the material that carried all the prosecution's *Charges* and some of its *Specifications*, enabling the study of the pluses and minuses of both sides at the same time, as specified in this chapter.[11]

Navy Secretary Paulding and Judge Advocate Read had spent months gathering evidence to formulate the widest-ranging enfilade against Elliott in the government's accusations, impressive in number, variety, and ad nauseum repetitions. These arraignments are cited by the prosecution much more fully than need be because almost all are circumstantiated in this chapter, and all the reader will have to do is to refer to them chronologically.

Charge 1: "Oppression and Cruelty and Conduct Unbecoming an Officer," as to Passed Midshipman Charles C. Barton (see chapter 11)
Charge 2: "Using Provoking and Reproachful Words, Gestures, and Menaces, and Conduct Unbecoming an Officer," regarding Lambert/Hunter. Their cases are so similar that we have combined them into this one charge
Charge 3: "Scandalous Conduct, Tending to Be Destructive of Good Morals," part a: the crew's presentation of silver plate to Elliott and part b: livestock that Elliott brought home in *Constitution*
Charge 4: Regarding Barton again
Charge 5: The so-called mutiny at Hampton Roads, Virginia
Charge 6: Silver plate again
Charge 7: Livestock again

Prior to describing charge 8, let us observe that Paulding and Read most likely reviewed their charges against Elliott made in their first seven accusations. They slapped together this hodgepodge of charges in order to dig up anything else, no matter how repetitive the charges were nor whether all the pertinent facts already had been covered most adequately. They would lay down a shotgun barrage, hoping that should one of their earlier arguments have been overlooked, they might strike home with one of their new pellets.

Charge 8: Illegal "extra" punishment

Charge 9: "Unofficerlike Conduct and Disobedience to the Navy rule that strictly enjoins every officer to avoid all unnecessary expenditure of stores belonging to the public," in that Elliott used public stores "for his private use.

Charge 10: Using the public stores again

Elliott must have despaired, at least briefly, as he studied the sheer number of the ten charges and fourteen specifications confronting him. They emanated from the department's hostile view of his activities while commanding the Mediterranean Squadron, 1835–38, especially as to his difficulty with Barton. It appeared most unlikely that he could be cleared on all of them. Still, he garnered all his resources to mitigate against the possibility that he might receive the ultimate punishment—his permanent ouster from the navy—as indeed four of his judges recommended early on (see below). During the several months after his court of inquiry conviction by a slim two to one margin that his court-martial must follow, the prosecution had been assembling its documentation from April 27 through June 22, 1840, to be wielded against Elliott, and he had no option but to do the same, collected for his defense.

Elliott led off well with a "Summary of Charges," which may be epitomized in a single quotation: "Discipline and subordination must be maintained. Their purposes are too vital and paramount to be abandoned; their operations cannot, without the most pernicious consequences, be arrested by frivolity, or relaxed by favoritism. Once waive their necessity;—sanction the idea that regulations are cobwebs to be broken through at pleasure, that rank is entitled to no deference, their commands may be disputed or denied, that the superior officer should silently submit to having his admonitions 'repelled' by flat contradiction, and be content with the 'forbearance' that leave him personally unassailed;—that the settled gradations of authority, with their designated channels of communication are idle formalities; and what will become of the naval system of which [illegible] the American people have been so justly proud?"[12]

But having made such a cogent beginning, Elliott darted off into some sort of an organizational no-man's-land, bypassing altogether the government's affirmations against him. Instead, he came up with his own listing, ranging downward from those he deemed the most important to the least, which could only delve into further chaos. Therefore, at this juncture, for those few readers who might require them for their own purposes, they should refer to the prosecution's *Charges and Specifications* and *Records of General Courts--martial and Courts of Inquiry of the Navy Department, 1799–1867.*[13]

We were elated to discover that the nation's leading weekly newspaper had a short but inclusive one-page numbering of all the allegations against Elliott, giving the verdicts of "guilty" or "not guilty" for each.[14] This enables us to return to Elliott's court-martial charges and specifications that would bring him so much vexation, shame, and financial pain from his service suspension.

By mid-April 1840 the judges had been appointed for the court-martial, and because of the accused's lofty status in the navy, no junior officers sat on the panel. It consisted of five commodores: Jacob Jones (presiding), Lewis Warrington, William M. Crane, John Downes, and Edmund P. Kennedy; and four captains: Charles M. Morgan, David Conner, John T. Sloan, and George W. Storer. From research on my books and articles, all the above are familiar to me, except Storer, and I know of none who had any preconceived opinions for or against Elliott. The latter did, however, have an enemy—Read, the government's prosecutor—but after all, that was the job that he had been employed to perform.[15]

On June 22, 1840, after extended argumentation and split decisions, Elliott's court-martial jurors found him not guilty of five of the ten charges of abandonment of Barton at Smyrna, of failure to suppress the alleged "mutiny" at Hampton Roads, and of wasting public stores.[16]

He was, however, found guilty of the remaining five: of moving Barton from *Constitution* to *Shark*, the crew's presentation of silver plate to the commodore, of importing livestock to America in *Constitution*, and of expending the public stores for his private purposes.[17] The story soon circulated that four of his court-martial panel "voted to break the Commodore [i.e., to cashier him from the Navy altogether]: Jacob Jones, Lewis Warrington, John Downes, and Edmund P. Kennedy."[18]

Elliott's first official notice of his guilt and punishment came from Paulding's incisive letter: "The Naval Court-martial before which you were recently tried at the Navy Yard, Philadelphia, has found you guilty of the 1st, 3rd, 5th, 6th, and 8th charges upon which you were arraigned and sentenced you to be suspended for the term of four years, and that your pay and emoluments be suspended during the first two years of your suspension."[19]

Under the service's chain of command, Paulding passed the verdict up to the president, and John Tyler agreed with it, concentrating upon the accused's single most unforgivable deed: he took on board *Constitution* "so many a number of animals [twenty-three] as to interfere with the accommodation of the men, embarrass the exercise of the guns, and [worst by far] impair her force and efficiency as a vessel of war." But Tyler also found some mitigating details to permit himself to apply a modicum of relief. Previous "commanders of ships and squadrons, had, in pursuance of instructions from the Navy Department, brought to the United States animals of various kinds, without being questioned or censured by the Department. In consideration of these facts and circumstances, the President has thought proper to remit that portion of the sentence of the court which involves the forfeiture of pay during the first two years of Commodore Elliott's suspension."[20]

Elliott's suspension, although eased a bit by the president, threw him into an altered and much inferior life style. He called this to Tyler's attention, for now he had to wrest a living from his farm in Carlisle, Pennsylvania: "In my early life I was somewhat a theoretical Farmer; and from the injustice of which I speak [Paulding's rancor toward him] for the last two years I have been a practical one. This, I find, altogether different from the profession of Arms, which has been my calling since 1804. . . . I feel the pressure still more as my hand is so decayed from the effort of labour in harvesting my small Crop, so much so, that I am compelled to use one of my children in making my letter sufficiently intelligible for your perusal."[21]

Let his biographers, after copying this, exude a sigh of mingled gratitude and regret—the first for his daughter's totally legible penmanship, the second a wistful desire that Elliott's hand was not palsied more often, requiring outside assistance in almost all of his personal correspondence.

As the months dragged by while toiling in the field, Elliott continued on the same theme, notifying his friend Poinsett that: "I wish I could say that I was in possession of a good farm [actually his yield seems reasonably ample]. I own 2/3 of an interest in 23 acres of land in which with much expense . . . made me a comfortable house, and [with] the labor of my own hands and by our man whom I hire, I will make 20 of my 50 bushels of wheat, 200 of oats, 200 of corn, 500 of potatoes, and an acre of turnips, parsnips, cabbage, and celery."[22]

Again: "During my suspension I turned my attention to . . . [pastoral] pursuits, and in the improvement chiefly of the fine sheep and swine I had imported . . . creating a stock admirably suited to the Western country . . . ! presented a few of my best samples to him [Richard M. Johnson, vice president under Martin Van Buren] and was favored by the following acknowledgment: 'Accept my thanks for your kind present of the animals. . . . The specimens of wool are beautiful.'"[23] Toward the end of 1842 Elliott wrote Cooper: "The balance of trade in the purchase and sale of my commodities of my farm bring me much, say 25% and up in sales and 25 more in purchase, that on *meeting* a good offer I have sold my little farm and have made an equally advantageous purchase here [in Westchester, Pennsylvania]."[24] This permitted him to conclude his dirt-farming career on a triumphant note: "Thank God I can plow as good a furrow and throw up as fine a clod as could any man in Pennsylvania!"[25]

On yet another review of this material, we were struck by a conundrum: If Elliott's suspension from the navy had been for four years, with no pay for the first two years but then rescinded by the president, was that not a holiday at full stipends? If so, why did Elliott suffer what he bemoaned as plunging him into a much reduced lifestyle? On August 18, 1993, I telephoned Commander Martin for help. He concluded that because Elliott obviously could not serve on active duty, the best that he could do was to have been placed on half pay, which would explain his sudden descent into poverty. This interpretation fully satisfied us.

These bucolic details having been concluded, even so, the court-martial's verdict was shattering to Elliott. Perhaps others of his closest friends reacted to it as did Cooper, who observed: "I do not like the sentence of Elliott. It is too severe—but then appended the damning *comment—although he could not be acquitted* [emphasis added]." This demonstrates that even as strong a supporter of the convicted as Cooper was, he had to confess that the panel's conclusions had been justified.[26]

As we have seen, the consequences for Elliott were naval and national obloquy, a lower income, and the physical pain of laboring behind a plow. However, a breeze was about to waft through his doldrums, leading to brighter skies, although the disease that would kill him was already underway.

We have been repeatedly affronted by Elliott's conceited self-assurance that he was and always had been impeccably correct in his viewpoints and activities. Indeed, we have been able to unearth precisely one *instance* of Elliott criticizing himself. In a private letter he confessed: "I am always too quick on the trigger, hence I shall reflect more in all my future acts."[27] This pledge, of course, he either would not or could not fulfill. Along with his scrawling calligraphy, these have been the most irksome chores we have had to undertake. In connection with his pen's headlong dash across the page, we might have missed a handful of others, but in no way does that preclude our total assurance that Elliott remained convinced of his perfectibility.

Understandably relieved that his return to the naval roster marked the end of his worst years, Elliott still had some walls to be scaled—citing the information contained in his will of 1829 and its codicil in 1845: his comradeship with Cooper when both he and that author jubilantly hailed the latter's triumphant lawsuit against the editor and publisher William L. Stone; Elliott's questionable decision to honor Cooper with, and distribute widely, medallions for his friend's support in his endless quarrel with Perry about the Battle of Lake Erie; and Elliott's final official posting as commandant of the Philadelphia Navy Yard, 1844–45; the slow but relentless onset of the affliction that would become mortal; and one of the commodore's obituaries, so typical of many others.

Unluckily for his biographers, Elliott was most reticent about his financial situation, unless he was fuming about the cost of monetary penalties imposed upon him by his court-martial conviction and a few other government reimbursement issues. The sources concerning them contain his property listings acquired between 1829 and 1835. On September 4, 1832, Elliott at a public sale bought a "STONE TAVERN HOUSE" on a lot sold by his executor in 1846, a year after Elliott died. In 1835 a new holding was located in midtown Carlisle, Pennsylvania, "with frame buildings and stablings alongside the tavern," denoting a comfortable if not necessarily a well-to-do way of life.

Elliott's will and codicil are valuable in part to probe his changing financial situations but primarily because they reveal detailed mentions of his closest relations. They are provided here in their chronological place rather than to add to chapter 1 about his genealogy and boyhood.

The will led off with bequest "to my beloved wife," Frances Vaughan Elliott, of all his furniture and silver plate (with exceptions), one-third of the estate, and Jacob, "my favorite and trusty slave" (an eye-catching item proving that he possessed more than one); to his only son, Washington Lafayette Elliott, the commodore's gold medal from Congress for his seizure of the two British brigs in 1812, adding that the medal could not be sold to anyone outside of the family, and his "elegant sword," from Congress for the same feat, as well as his personal library, carrying the same restriction as above; to Washington Lafayette, Sarah Ann, and Mary the remainder of the estate, split equally; to his daughter Frances, born after his will of 1829, "one large silver tureen," and an equal share of the legacy with her older siblings; "to my esteemed friend James Fenimore Cooper," Jackson's desk that had been given to the commodore in Boston during 1833; and to his daughter Mrs. Harriet Robinson "the gold snuff box presented to Elliott by Edward Livingston in 1835."[28]

When his holdings came up for probate, Elliott had appointed a single executor who, in his inventory of the estate, valued the lot and buildings at a lowly $485, a wagon at $166, and its harness at $15, all of which were added to $566 worth of property already sold. Without the sword, gold medal, and gold snuffbox, his legacy came to $1,111.47, making the estate total $2,417.47. This sum might be compared to that of the subject of my latest book, *"Mad Jack": The Biography of Captain John Percival*, whose executors listed his estate's value at $28,248.82. Even the latter figure is far overshadowed when Biddle, the subject of my third naval biography, is contemplated in the same context. He was of the opulent Biddle family, among Philadelphia's most elite, and the elder brother of Nicholas Biddle, president of the Second Bank of the United States. James listed his assets at "$46,881 in bonds, stocks, and annuities, in addition to $23,300 loaned to relatives, for a total of $70,181."[29] The best explanation for Elliott's unimpressive holdings is that his legal expenses for defending himself in his court appearances were considerably more than he had anticipated.

Toward the end of the commodore's life, best-selling author Cooper was often his companion. To be sure, the latter had been fighting his own battle against Matthew C. Perry and other Oliver Hazard Perry adherents. It was not, Cooper explained, because he had a close personal and social relationship with Elliott but rather, that circumstances had brought them together, so in defending himself, per se he was defending the commodore as well.[30]

If Elliott already owed a debt of gratitude to Cooper for his past support over the Battle of Lake Erie, it had been much enhanced by his fervent backing of him when that author sued William L. Stone, editor and publisher of the New York *Commercial Advertiser*, for libel in June 1840, although the case was not settled for two years. Stone avowed that Cooper, in volume 2 of his *History of the Navy of the United States of America*, had been guilty of a flagrantly pro-Elliott bias that made any claim to impartiality indefensible in two instances: (1) in capturing the British brigs *Detroit* and *Caledonia* while Elliott commanded US naval forces, he had robbed the US Army officer Towson of his well-merited credit for winning the victory in 1812 (see chapter 2); and (2) at the Battle of Lake Erie a year later, Cooper had been wrong when he championed Elliott in his endless controversy with Perry about which one deserved the more credit for the British fleet's annihilation on Lake Erie in 1813.[31]

After months of legal maneuvering on both sides, an exultant Cooper was able to write Elliott that "the award] was handed in and decides eight points, all in my favor. It decides that Stone has libeled me and is to pay me the $250, agreed on between us in liquidation damages . . . and $50 for my expenses in the arbitration. That the history concerning the British brigs and the Battle of Lake Erie is true. That it was written in a spirit of impartiality. That Stone's review *is untrue*, and not written in a spirit of impartiality. . . . There can be no doubt that this arbitration will be of great advantage to your reputation, for the impression it has produced appears to be profound in New York [where] I had large audiences. I think it is safe to say, that the truth has triumphed, and, as regards the Battle of Lake Erie, *this will be favorable to you as one of the actors, and to me as the historian* [emphasis added]."[32]

This gave Elliott a springboard from which to plunge into the two issues upon which he concentrated during his last months. First, his exceptional decision to glorify Cooper for standing by his side for so long by minting, at his own expense, medallions to be widely distributed (the exact number issued is not given). The second was his declining ability to prolong his already ebbing life.

Elliott's medallions caused Cooper some mortification, but not enough to have made him insist that the entire operation be canceled: "The late Commodore Elliott caused a medal of me to be struck off at the mint. . . . This medal was made not only without my concurrence, but contrary to my wishes, for it seemed likely to bring me into a species of ridicule, as having a medal struck in honor of such a trifling affair. I did remonstrate with Commodore Elliott on the subject, though my opposition was not as earnest, as it otherwise might have been, as the feeling of gratitude it manifested in Commodore Elliott was respectable in him. I had no agency whatever in causing this medal to be struck or presented to anyone."[33] To one of his selected recipients Elliott explained why he had honored his advocate in this unusual way: "Mr. Cooper spurned all but the *facts*, which he obtained by untiring and honest industry, and has recorded on the indelible pages of history, far above the contaminating touch of those who would gladly obliterate them. And for such . . . my own heart urged me to the acknowledgment I make-the medallions, one of which I send you."[34]

Elliott wrote Cooper about their mutual dependence upon each other: "In your defense, that cause and mine being so nearly allied in its maintenance that you were unconsciously my defender, and therefore I am called upon by the impulse of my own feelings to make some expression of the high estimation of the able and impartial manner in which you have defended me and pray you to accept this accompanying memento as a tribute."[35]

There is a picture of both sides of Elliott's medallion to his champion: recto, Cooper' s profile, and inscription, "THE PERSONIFICATION OF HONOR, TRUTH, AND JUSTICE"; verso, "TO J. FENIMORE COOPER, THE OFFERING OF A GRATEFUL HEART FOR THE DISTINGUISHED VINDICATION OF HIS BROTHER SAILOR JESSE D. ELLIOTT."[36]

To conclude the story of the medallions: the commodore was obtuse enough to ask ex-president John Quincy Adams to send one to the Rhode Island Historical Society, aswarm with the Perry family and its sustainers, and Adams did so. In an enclosed statement, Elliott praised Cooper "for the historical justice which he has awarded to the character and conduct of Commodore Elliott in his published writings." The affronted Perryites forthwith rejected the offering because they "could neither adopt nor sanction" what Cooper had written about Perry at the Battle of Lake Erie.[37] Possibly this ludicrous sequence only deepened Cooper's regret that he had been so acquiescent to Elliott when he had had the opportunity to have forbidden him from issuing the medallions, but he had desisted.

Elliott's naval career terminated with his final assignment from the department-to command the Philadelphia Navy Yard, where he served from

December 14, 1844, to December 11, 1845. Of the more than thirty letters that he dispatched to the secretary during this short period, only the following few enlighten us toward the end of his life with more on his characteristics.

In office for a few weeks he complimented himself on the efficiency and harmony of his people: "Every officer in this Yard conducts his duties to my entire satisfaction," but strangely, he coupled this with an admission that Midshipman Timothy W. Fiske had just committed suicide "by swallowing laudanum [opium].[38]

Another Elliott consideration was to cure the "idleness," which was "a very great pity" insofar as the Philadelphia yard was concerned. He suggested that his command should be made responsible for the production of "Hammocks and Bags required for the Navy," as well as "the Sails required for our ships." His exhortations were of course disregarded.[39]

With the Mexican War approaching, Elliott set his goal on a most ambitious project: to command US naval forces against that nation. He was sure that he was the ideal candidate for that chore. He feared that during the hostilities Mexican privateers might cause "heavy losses" to American commerce. He assured Secretary Bancroft that if he were in charge, he would "possess the Castle [San Juan de Ulua] just outside Vera Cruz, to crush that city & shake the foundation of the Capital itself. . . . My familiar knowledge of all the localities induces me to believe, in the event of war, I should be entirely successful."[40]

A welcome glimpse of Elliott's frequently expressed care for his sailors and marines was when he pledged that henceforth he would abstain from inflicting corporal punishment in his command, which he dubbed "degrading to human nature," substituting instead "the discharge of the offender from the service."[41]

Ever the blusterer, Elliott touted his own physical condition with a most bizarre bravado: "My position places me in an attitude of having an old head on young shoulders—permit me therefore to say that the Sword, which I have enjoyed as a gift from the nation, is ready to be drawn from its scabbard in the performance of any sea service which the Executive may see fit to call upon me for."[42]

In our research and writings, seldom have we had to use the word "flabbergasted." Here is an exception: A mere seven months before his death an unrecognizable Elliott emerges in the starkest contrast to his more usual portrayal as a harsh, humorless taskmaster, feudist, and egotist. Cooper is the source for the story in a letter to a longtime friend. He and Elliott had just visited the home of wealthy Philadelphian Joseph R. Ingersoll and family: "I must tell you about Elliott's gallantry. Coming home at two in the morning, he fell in with a party serenading, and he brought them to Ingersoll's house, and gave the ladies, as they assure me, a very delightful serenade. Next day he called, and when the young ladies attributed the serenade to one young

Philadelphian, he came out and claimed his dues."[43] To those of you who have probed Elliott's psyche, his identification as a "serenader" is literally unrecognizable for we have no documentation that he ever attended concerts or recitals nor that he showed the slightest interest in music.

Elliott's finale was darkened by edema, the disease that would be fatal to him. The leading medical authority on illnesses and their treatment described it: "Edema ["dropsy" in that day] usually represents excessive water and sodium in the extra cellular space[,] . . . but it may be caused by cardiac, hepatic, or renal diseases. Initially the problem is evident only by an increase in weight, but later, becomes overt[,] . . . noted first as facial puffing rather than swelling on dependent or lower parts of the body."[44]

Cooper lived close enough to Elliott to visit him and report on his physical worsening. He passed along to others an item received from Commodore William Shubrick: "I had supposed him convalescent. Old officers, however, are sometimes killed off in the service before the breath has left their bodies."[45] Cooper ranged from his ill companion's possible recovery to grave doubts about it: "Elliott is here and in an advanced dropsy, not only of the body and limbs, but of the heart and chest. He cannot survive, I should think, although he seems to think he may."[46] Again: "Poor Elliott can not last long. I went to see him today and found him sensibly weaker. It is plain his family considers his case desperate. . . . I believe he thinks he has no chance in this world. He looks like an emaciated, white-haired old man of seventy."[47]

With his animation rapidly ebbing, on December 8, 1845, he was replaced at the yard by Commander Charles Gauntt, who sent the department news of Elliott's death on the tenth.[48]

Ever since 1812–13 when Elliott burst into the nation's attention, he had been enough of a noteworthy and controversial figure to guarantee that his obituaries would be widespread. The following is typical, highlighting his virtuous accomplishments, while sloughing off his character delinquencies as comparatively unimportant: "He was rude of speech, a plain blunt man, who loved his country and his friends and hated his enemies. He knew little and cared less about drawing room refinements. . . . He never learned the word caution; and to serve a friend or fulfill a duty, he would brave the most imminent danger. . . . He would forget anything but an act of kindness. . . . He was very sensitive, and was elated or depressed by every word of praise or censure. Let his weaknesses and other faults be forgotten. He was a good sailor, a good disciplinarian, a man of undaunted courage and of inflexible honesty; and these are not every-day virtues."[49]

Elliott's assessment as a naval officer and a man in chapter 13 finishes the text. This mandates some dexterity, for attributes contributing to the making of a fine officer may have malefic effects when appraising the man and vice versa.

12.1. Captain Jesse D. Elliott, a lithograph by P. S. Duval, Naval History and Heritage Command, NH 49626

12.2. Jesse D. Elliott family with USS *Constitution* in background, c. 1835. (*Rear, left to right*): Catherine Howell Elliott, Commodore Jesse Duncan Elliott, Washington Lafayette Elliott, Mary Duncan Elliott, Frances Caln Vaughan Elliott; (*front, left to right*): Frances Rebecca Elliott, Sarah Ann Elliott, Harriet Duncan Elliott. Artist unknown. Courtesy of Bill Paine and the William L. Jacobs family.

Thirteen

Jesse Duncan Elliott as a Naval Officer and a Man

It is much easier to deal with Elliott the officer than Elliott the man due to the near complete lack of surviving material relating to his personal life. Therefore, when looking at Elliott the officer one is also seeing Elliott the man. In the surviving material several character traits come to the fore:

Patriotism/bravery
Vanity
Administrative competence
Diplomacy
Inability to compromise
Vindictive grudge carrier

Interestingly, as Elliott's career progressed, and especially as it neared its end, the negative aspects of his personality began to dominate. The result was that Elliott seemed to lose any ability he had to control them. In fact, they came to dominate him and limited his ability to perform his assigned duties.

No American growing up in Elliott's time could avoid the ardent patriotism that existed in the new nation. Elliott was no exception. Early in his career, Elliott was widely regarded as a patriotic and brave officer. His planning and daring seizure of the British brigs at Black Rock show the keen willingness to serve his country that burned within him. Again as commander of the Brazil Squadron, Elliott faced the probability of destruction while asserting the rights of the United States and other neutrals to openly trade on the world's markets.

Even while serving his suspension from active duty, Elliott's patriotism never waned. Not one word of invective or bitterness toward his country survives from this emotionally and financially trying time. Contrast this to his harsh words reserved for the naval court system, his judges, his accusers, and Secretary of the Navy Paulding.

To say that Elliott was vain is an understatement. He never passed up an opportunity for self-aggrandizement, even if the events portrayed were incorrect. It seems his overall goal was to quiet his conscience regarding the events at Lake Erie.

During his first tour in the Mediterranean Sea Elliott painted heroic pictures of himself that show he and his party drew swords, put their backs to the wall, and prepared to fight to the death to preserve American honor. These accounts show Elliott to have been brave and patriotic. They also portray him doing his utmost to serve his country, and both show him to have been brave. Significantly, they also are unsubstantiated. We have only Elliott's word that these events happened as he described.

In later years he was inclined to overstate his physical abilities and condition. This is best seen in his volunteering to lead the US naval forces against Mexico in the 1840s. He claimed he was the most qualified officer for this duty on active service even though in reality he suffered from advanced stages of edema that would eventually kill him. In another instance we see Elliott, while on suspension from active duty, bemoaning the condition of his hands after being forced to take up the plow as a means of supporting his family. One suspects that the physical pain of his blisters and calluses was secondary to the psychological pain of no longer being able to wrest a living from the "gentlemanly profession of arms."

Early and midway through his career, Elliott's abilities as an administrator must be judged quite favorably. Except for the period immediately following the Battle of Lake Erie, he earned high marks for administrative efficiency at every posting. When first sent to Lake Erie, he excelled at organizing and building a base of operations. Later on, his work for the Board of Naval Commissioners and his handling of administrative duties at the Charlestown Naval Yard equally stand out as administrative successes.

Only in two instances do we find him to be lacking in administrative competence. The first is on Lake Erie after being left to command a squadron against no foreseeable threat. In this case we apparently see him succumbing to his feelings of despair and having been cheated of his deserved opportunities. The result is that the base, which first he and later Perry built up, fell into near ruin until the arrival of his replacement.

The second case of administrative failure arises during the course of his Mediterranean cruising aboard "Old Ironsides." At the beginning of the cruise he asked the secretary of the navy to destroy unflattering material sent him by Elliott's crew. By the end of these voyages Elliott would be surrounded by a maelstrom of charges, many including misuse of funds and authority as well as mismanagement of both the ship and his increasingly erratic personal behavior.

In the end, Elliott redeemed himself administratively while on his last posting as commandant of the Philadelphia Naval Yard. By all accounts, the cost-conscious, results-oriented Elliott resurfaced to ably keep track of the myriad responsibilities of a naval yard commander.

Probably Elliott's most consistent successes came in the area of diplomacy. Whether smashing paper blockades off the Rio de la Plata, dining with the leaders of the newly independent Haiti, or chasing pirates, Elliott's command of the Brazil Squadron was one long string of diplomatic successes. Even during his personally disastrous Mediterranean cruising, Elliott time and time again maintained cordial relations with the foreign dignitaries he met.

Elliott's inability to compromise is another recurring theme throughout his career. Following the Battle of Lake Erie, Elliott set off the whole Elliott--Perry feud by refusing to concede that Perry's official report gave him credit for a share of the praise he thought he was due, while also covering up much of Elliott's inexplicable behavior. Elliott returned repeatedly to demand that Perry rewrite his report.

When commanding the Charlestown Naval Yard, Elliott was unable to reverse his position on the issue of the Jackson figurehead. He could not comprehend the 180 degree turn in public opinion that turned his gesture of goodwill into a catalyst for all of the anti-Jackson sentiment in Boston. Rather than wait to affix the figurehead at a more opportune time, Elliott was determined to have the issue resolved in his favor, with the predictably unfortunate results.

Probably no other characteristic is as clearly documented throughout Elliott's life as his ability to carry a grudge. It did not even matter to Elliott if his antagonist died. If anyone who had supported the deceased foe crossed Elliott's path, a cold shoulder was the best to be hoped for.

Without a doubt, the single greatest issue in Elliott's life was his feud with Perry. First with him, and after his death with the "Perry bloc," Elliott hotly defended his role in the Battle of Lake Erie. Only Perry's untimely death prevented him from challenging Perry to a duel. Even after his enemy's death, Elliott divided his peers into those who supported Perry and those who supported himself. He even went so far as to orchestrate the Barron-Decatur duel, which led to the death of Perry's advocate. As we also see in the case of General Towson, decades after the Battle of Lake Erie, Elliott would continue to snipe at and quarrel with the surviving participants who supported Perry. Perry and his supporters were the constant reminders to Elliott of his failure to achieve historical immortality in the service of his country.

13.1. Jesse D. Elliott gold medal and sword awarded by US Congress and gold medal awarded by State of Pennsylvania, painted by John A. Woodside, date unknown, courtesy of Scott E. Rose. Note: reverse of coin on far right (awarded by State of Pennsylvania) depicts October 9, 1812, capture of British ships *Detroit* and *Caledonia* (HOSTIUM SUB MOENIBUS NAVES ET PATRIAE DEDIT. "In spite of enemy opposition he gave ships to his country").

Abbreviations Used in Notes

ASP	American State Papers
CCB	Charles C. Barton
DAB	*Dictionary of American Biography*
DFL	David F. Long
DFL, *Bainbridge*	*Ready to Hazard: A Biography of Commodore William Bainbridge, 1774–1833* by David F. Long
DFL, *Biddle*	*Sailor-Diplomat: A Biography of Commodore Biddle, 1783–1848* by David F. Long
DFL, *GBFR*	*Gold Braid and Foreign Relations: Diplomatic Activities of U.S. Naval Officers, 1798–1883* by David F. Long
DFL, *Porter*	*Nothing Too Daring: A Biography of Commodore David Porter, 1780–1843* by David F. Long
HLNO	*List of Officers of the Navy of the United States and of the Marine Corps, 1775–1900*, edited by Edward W. Callahan
Jarvis, *JDE*	*Biographical Notice* by Russell Jarvis
JDE	Jesse Duncan Elliott
JDE *Speech*	*Speech of Commodore Jesse Duncan Elliott*, also known as the autobiography of Jesse Duncan Elliott
JDE-Towson, *Correspondence*	*Correspondence in Relation to the Capture of the British Brigs* Detroit *and* Caledonia *on the Night of October 8, 1812* by Jesse Duncan Elliott and Nathan Towson
JFC	James Fenimore Cooper

Martin, *AMFS*	*A Most Fortunate Ship* by Tyrone G. Martin
NWR	*Niles Weekly Register*
SN	Secretary of the Navy
YCAL	Yale Collection of American Literature, Beinecke Rare Book and Manuscript Library

Notes

Preface

David F. Long, *Nothing Too Daring: A Biography of Commodore David Porter, 1780–1843*, (Annapolis: US Naval Institute, 1970), 186, hereafter: DFL, *Porter*; *Ready to Hazard: A Biography of Commodore William Bainbridge, 1774–1833* (Hanover, NJ: University Press of New England, 1981), 238, hereafter: DFL, *Bainbridge*; *Sailor-Diplomat: A Biography of Commodore Biddle 1783–1848* (Boston: Northeastern University Press, 1983), 106, hereafter: DFL, *Biddle*; and *"Mad Jack": The Biography of Captain John Percival, USN 1779–1862* (Westport, CT: Greenwood Press, 1993), 105.

Chapter 1

1 *The Name and Family of Elliot(t) and Elliot* (New York: Roots Research Bureau), passim.

2. Jesse Duncan Elliott, *Speech of Commodore Jesse Duncan Elliott, USN, with Appendix and Addenda, Delivered in Hagerstown, Maryland, 14 November 1843* (Philadelphia, G. B. Zieber, 1844). This cumbersome but absolutely vital work is divided into *The Speech*, itself, its *Appendix* and *Addendum*, 55 and 82 pages, respectively. Each segment is not numbered consecutively, requiring separate pagination. Hereafter Jesse Duncan Elliott will be JDE in notes.

3. Robert E. Dunkel to David F. Long, letter, October 17, 1990. Hereafter Long will be DFL in notes.

4. Francis B. Heitman, *Historical Register of the Continental Army* (repr., Baltimore: Regional Publishing, 1967), 215.

5. JDE, *Speech, Appendix,* 1.

6. *Dictionary of American Biography*, vol. 6, 96 (New York: Charles Scribner's Sons, n.d.) (hereafter DAB), and many other dependable authorities.

7. *Washington County Spy*, September 17, 1794. This mill was a textile operation to thicken and strengthen cloth (usually woolen) by pressure, moisture, and heat.

8. Dave Cottingham, "Elliott-Bestor House on the National Register," *Daily*

Mail (Hagerstown), July 7, 1975; and Thomas J. Williams, *A History of Washington County, Maryland· From the Earliest Settlements to the Present Day, Including a History of Hagerstown*, 2 vols. (Baltimore: Regional Publishing, 1968), vol. 1, 236.

9. For the more recent histories of the US wars of the early 1790s that mention Robert Elliott, see Wiley Sword, *President Washington's Indian War: The Struggle for the Old Northwest* (Norman: University of Oklahoma Press, 1985), 85, 91, 250, 264–65, 267; and Richard A. Knopf, ed., *Anthony Wayne: A Name in Arms* (Pittsburgh: University of Pittsburgh Press, 1960, repr. 1975), passim, which contains no less than fifty-six index references to Robert Elliott.

10. Wayne to Elliott and Williams, September 21, 1794, American State Papers (hereafter ASP), *Class II, Claims*, vol. 11, no. 284, September 21, 1794.

11. Elliott to Pierce, October 5, 1794, ASP, *Class II, Claims*.

12. Pierce to Elliott, ASP, *Class II, Claims*.

13. JDE, *Speech, Appendix*, 2. Damon is never identified as to race but probably "servant" is used in the Biblical sense of "bondsman." While living later in Pennsylvania, Jesse owned one and possibly more Black enslaved persons.

14. *Washington County Spy*, November 4, 1794.

15. ASP, *Class II, Claims*, no. 140, 297.

16. ASP, , *Class II, Claims*, 297.

17. Russell Jarvis, *Biographical Notice of Commodore Jesse D. Elliott: Containing a Review of the Controversy between Him and the Late Com. Perry, and a History of the Figure Head of the US Frigate Constitution, by a Citizen of New York*, (Philadelphia, printed for the author, 1835), known hereafter as Jarvis, *JDE*. To repeat an observation made in the preface and to remind readers occasionally throughout, it is not a biography but Elliott's autobiography using Jarvis as a front to hide its real author's identity. After reading hundreds of pages, handwritten and printed, of Elliott' s writing style, word choices, punctuation, and emphases in particular, we are convinced of this beyond doubt.

18. DFL to George Hing, head, Special Collections, phone call, May 30, 1990.

19. Jarvis, *JDE*, 13.

20. Secretary of the Navy (hereafter SN) to St. Clair Elliott, April 2, 1804, Record Group (RG) 45, Secretaries of the Navy to Officers (below Lieutenants), M149, roll 6, p. 356, NA.

21. Christopher McKee, *A Gentlemanly and Honorable Profession- The Creation of the U.S. Naval Officers Corps, 1795–1815*, 164.

22. Jarvis, *JDE*, 12.

23. Jesse and St. Clair Elliott. "Officers' Records," National Archives, Washington, DC, hereafter NA.

24. Until the Civil War the U.S. Navy had no official title higher than "Post Captain." To enable its officers to approximate the status of European admirals, the courtesy rank of "Commodore" was used for those commanding more than one USN warship at the same time.

25. JDE to SN, November 9, 1807, Letters Received by the Secretary of the Navy from Officers [OL], roll 4, no. 143, NA.

26. JDE to SN, May 29, 1808, OL, roll 5, # 22; and JDE to James Barron, December 5, 1808, College of William and Mary Library, sent to me by Dr. William M. P. Dunne, History Department, SUNY, Long Island University, Southampton Campus. An indispensable research tool for anyone working on the eighteenth- and nineteenth-century US Navy is also Edward W. Callahan, ed., *List of Officers of the Navy of the United States and of the Marine Corps, 1775–1900* (New York: L. R. Hammerslay, 1901), known hereafter as *HLNO*.

27. I have done considerable research on the *Chesapeake-Leopard* affair for three of my earlier books, *Porter, Bainbridge,* and *Gold Braid and Foreign Relations: Diplomatic Activities of U.S. Naval Officers, 1798–1883* (Annapolis: Naval Institute Press, 1988), known hereafter as DFL, *GBFR*.

28. William O. Stevens, *An Affair of Honor: The Biography of Commodore James Barron* (Norfolk County Historical Society and the College of William and Mary Library, 1969), 76, 84, 92. It is obvious that Stevens has probed his sources widely and thoroughly, but as he gives no endnote citations, his statements have to be taken on faith. Moreover, he is excessively sympathetic to his subject.

29. Stevens, *Barron*, 70.

30. JDE, testimony, January 18, 1808, in *Proceedings of the General Court--Martial Convened for the Trial of Commodore James Barron, Captain Charles Gordon, Mr. William Hook, and Captain John Hall, of the United States Ship* Chesapeake *in the Month of January 1808* (Washington, DC: J. Gideon, 1822), 145–51.

31. Stevens, *Barron*, 85.

32. Babbit's testimony, January 28, 1808, in *Proceedings*, 171–75.

33. JDE' s testimony, January 29, 1808, in *Proceedings*. Babbit ended his somewhat discreditable life honorably, killed in action against the British early in 1815.

34. JDE, Officers' Records, NA.

35. JDE to his brother-in-law Callendar Irving, December 9, 1809, Princeton University Library.

36. JDE, *Speech*, 3.

37. *Port Folio* 4 (December 1814): 531; and Elliott's son, Washington Lafayette Elliott, to James Fenimore Cooper, February 8, 1846, fills in some details about his siblings, J. F. Cooper Papers, Yale Collection of American Literature, Beinecke Rare Book and Manuscript Library (hereafter YCAL). Washington Lafayette became a lifelong army officer who rose to brigadier general in the Civil War Union service.

38. JDE, "Last Will and Testament," August 19, 1829, Codicil, July 11, 1845, National Archives, Philadelphia Branch. When the NA's facilities in Washington, DC, became overcrowded, local branches were set up.

39. *Port Folio*, 531.

40. JDE, *Speech*, 3.

Chapter 2

1. Our rule has been to exclude, save for brief mention, treatment of 1812–15 activities in which Elliott did not participate, even though many of them may have been pivotal to the course of the war.

2. William S. Dudley, ed., *The Naval War of 1812: A Documentary History*, vol. 1, 1812 (Washington, DC: Naval Historical Center, 1985), 316. Henry Eckford was a most prominent shipbuilder, ably assisted by Noah Brown. Under their direction, Perry's two largest ships, the twenty-gun brigs *Lawrence* and *Niagara* were readied for combat but warned that they were so hurriedly constructed that they could stand no more than one battle. Kenneth J. Hagen, *The People's Navy: The Making of American Sea Power* (New York: Free Press, 1991), 85.

3. Jarvis, *JDE*, 16–17.

4. JDE to Chauncey, September 14, 1812, in Dudley, *Naval War of 1812*, 312–14.

5. JDE to Dobbins, October 2, 1812, in Dudley, *Naval War of 1812*, 321.

6. Dobbins to JDE, October 11, 1812, in Dudley, *Naval War of 1812*, 321–22.

7. Camel lighters are watertight boxes for raising ships. After the box is sunk and attached, the water is forced out so that it floats.

8. Luckily for the Americans that disaster had been averted when Barclay permitted Perry to slip away from Buffalo and slither down to a safer port at Presque Isle, in Erie, Pennsylvania.

9. JDE to SN, October 9, 1812, in Dudley, *Naval War of 1812*, 328–31; and Benson J. Lossing, *The Pictorial Field-Book of the War of 1812 . . . or Illustrations by Pen and Pencil of the History, Biography, Scenery, Relics, & Traditions of the Last War for American Independence* (New York: Harper & Brothers, 1869), 305.

10. Isaac Roach, "Anecdotes," 61, which is a diary written in 1834 of his wartime experiences. Ohio State Museum in Columbus sent a typescript of it. All the following Roach citations are from it.

11. Roach, "Anecdotes," 62; and JDE to SN, October 9, 1812, in "Naval Operations," *State of New York, Oliver Hazard Perry Victory Centennial*, 1916.

12. Lossing, *Pictorial Field-Book*, 285–86n 6.

13. Alfred T. Mahan, *Sea Power in Relation to the War of 1812*, vol. 1 (New York: Charles Scribner's Sons, 1903, 1904, repr. 1960), 355.

14. Howard I. Chapelle, *The History of the American Sailing Navy: Their Ships and Their Development* (New York: Bonanza Books, 1949), 249–50. He is wrong when he says that she carried fourteen-guns.

15. JDE to SN, October 9, 1812, and Sir Isaac Brock to Governor General Sir George Prevost, October 11, 1812, both in Dudley, *Naval War of 1812*, 331, 333.

16. Chapelle, *History of the American Sailing Navy*, 249; and William James, *A Full and Correct Account of the Chief Naval Occurrences of the Lake War between Great Britain and the United States of America* (London, T. Egerton, 1817), 31. A modern commentator asserted that her owner was a "Canadian merchant at [the

town of] Roy," although he also may have been a North West Fur Company employee. Charles W. Elliott, *Winfield Scott: The Soldier and the Man* (New York: Macmillan, 1937, repr. 1979), 50.

17. JDE to SN, October 9, 1812, in Dudley, *Naval War of 1812*, 328.

18. Dudley, *Naval War of 1812*, 331.

19. Towson to JDE, July 6, 1835, JDE and Nathan Towson, *Correspondence in Relation to the Capture of the British Brigs* Detroit *and* Caledonia *on the Night of October 8, 1812* (Philadelphia: United States Book and Printing, 1843), 6. Elliott's and Towson's letters must be regarded warily, for they concerned a dispute between them that became so acrimonious as to come within an eyelash of a duel (see below).

20. Lossing, *Pictorial Field-Book*, 386.

21. JDE to SN, September 9, 1812, in Dudley, *Naval War of 1812*, 329.

22. Roach, "Anecdotes," 63.

23. JDE to SN, September 9, 1812, in Dudley, *Naval War of 1812*, 329.

24. Elliott, *Winfield Scott*, 51.

25. Brock to Governor General Sir George Prevost, October 11, 1812, in Dudley, *Naval War of 1812*, 332.

26. Mahan, *Sea Power*, 355.

27. JDE to SN, October 9, 1812, in Dudley, *Naval War of 1812*, 331.

28. Elliott, *Winfield Scott*, 52.

29. Chauncey to SN, October 16 and 27, 1812, in Jarvis, *JDE*, 18–19.

30. Goldsborough to JDE, October 27, 1812,in Jarvis, *JDE*, 20.

31. SN to JDE, November 2, 1812, in Jarvis, *JDE*, 23.

32. JDE, Records of the Officers, Navy; and Lossing, *Pictorial Field-Book*, 388n1.

33. January 9, 1813, Henry Clay, *Papers of Henry Clay*, vol. 1. *1797–1814*, ed. by James F. Hopkins and Mary W. M. Hargreaves (Lexington: University of Kentucky Press, 1959), 771. Clay seems to have had a personal reason for such extravagant praise. Thirty-odd years later Elliott reminisced about an old schoolmate who might join him in recalling "the charms of our mutual friend and youthful companion, Lucretia Hart. It was to her illustrious husband, Henry Clay . . . to whom I felt under obligation . . . that I presented him the nails intended to hold the British flag aloft through [our] victory," JDE, *Speech*, 9.

34. *Niles Weekly Register*, May 16, 1818, 202–3, hereafter *NWR*.

35. Mahan, *Sea Power*, 30.

36. *NWR*, May 16, 1818, 202–3.

37. SN Benjamin W. Crowninshield to JDE, April 7, 1818, Jarvis, *JDE*, 475.

38. Elliott was comparatively lucky in receiving his bestowal as quickly as he did. James Biddle was voted a silver medal by Congress for his part in USS *Wasp*'s thrashing of HMS *Frolic* late in 1812. It came to him on February 1, 1837, more than twenty-four years later! DFL, *Biddle*, 45.

39. *NWR*, August 21, 1819, 431.

40. Brock to Prevost, October 11, 1812, F. B. Pepper, *Life and Correspondence of Sir Isaac Brock* (London: London: Simpkin, Marshall, 1845), 315.

41. James, *Naval Occurrences*, 83.

42. JDE to SN, October 9, 1812, in Dudley, *Naval War of 1812*, 331.

43. Elliott, *Scott*, 53.

44. ASP, Senate Naval Affairs Committee, Report 517, 2–3.

45. JDE-Towson, *Correspondence*, 7–10.

46. Benjamin Waterhouse to Secretary of War, Honorable Lewis Cass, October 20, 1834, University of Michigan, William L. Clements Library, Lewis Cass Papers, Correspondence, September 30–December 3, 1834.

47. Towson to JDE, July 6, 1835, in JDE-Towson, *Correspondence*, 5–7.

48. JDE-Towson, *Correspondence*, 7.

49. JDE to Towson, July 12, 1835, in JDE-Towson, *Correspondence*, 12, 13.

50. Towson to JDE, July 18, 1835, in JDE-Towson, *Correspondence*, 16–17, 14, 15.

51. JDE to Towson, July 23, 1835, in JDE-Towson, *Correspondence*, 23.

52. JDE to William Holland, *New York Times*, August 11, 1835, in JDE-Towson, *Correspondence*, 25–26.

53. Towson to JDE, JDE to Towson, August 17, 1835, in JDE-Towson, *Correspondence*, 24.

54. Note that this quotation was his own later insertion, in JDE-Towson, *Correspondence*.

55. Canonge to JDE, August 18, 1835, in JDE-Towson, *Correspondence*.

56. James Fenimore Cooper (hereafter JFC) to William and Joseph R. Fry of the *National Gazette and Literary Register*, May 15, 1840, in JFC, *The Letters and Journals of James Fenimore Cooper*, ed. James E. Beard, vol. 4 (Cambridge, MA: Belknap Press of Harvard University Press, 1968), 577.

57. JFC, *Letters and Journals*, 4:40.

58. Chauncey to SN, 4, November 6, 1812, in Dudley, *Naval War of 1812*, 342, 344; and William James, *The Naval History of Great Britain from the Declaration of War by France in February 1793 to the accession of George IV in January 1820*, vol. 6 (London: Harding, Lepard, 1826), 101.

59. Chauncey to SN, October 26, 1812, in Dudley, *Naval War of 1812*, 353.

60. JFC, *History of the Navy of the United States of America*, vol. 2 (New York: G. P. Putnam, 1854), 154–55.

61. Chauncey to SN, November 13, 17, 1812, in Dudley, *Naval War of 1812*, 344–51; and JDE to Messrs [Edward M.] Cox, and Montauduvont, Merchants, New York, November 16, 1812, Chicago Historical Society.

62. Wolcott Chauncey, USA, to JDE, December 19, 1818, in Jarvis, *JDE*, 25.

63. J. S. McPherson to JDE, May 24, 1821,in Jarvis, *JDE*.

64. JDE to JFC, September 11, 1841, YCAL.

65. Francis Mallory to JDE, March 22, 1843, Jarvis, *JDE*, 25.

66. Army Lieutenant Pike had been exploring the Rockies and in 1806 and spotted and tried to climb the peak that commemorates him, *DAB*, 14:599–600.

67. Elliott had gone ashore with the boats and then returned to *Madison*, but realizing that she drew too much water to cross the harbor's sandbar, he went back to *Conquest*.

68. JDE, *Speech*, 4, 5. The American destruction of the public buildings at York was used by the British to justify their similar behavior at Washington, DC, a year later.

69. JDE to naval surgeon R. R. Barton, June 2, 1840, YCAL.

70. Donald R. Hickey, *The War 1812: A Forgotten Conflict* (Urbana: University of Illinois Press, 1989), 199–201.

71. Reginald Horsman, *The War of 1812* (N.Y., Alfred A. Knopf, 1969), 92–94

72. JDE, *Speech*, 5

73. *Port Folio*, December 1814, 354.

Chapter 3

1. Frederick L. Oliver, "Commodore Oliver Hazard Perry of Newport, Rhode Island," *U.S. Naval Institute Proceedings (USNIP)* 80 (July 1954): 777–83.

2. James Fenimore Cooper, "Oliver Hazard Perry," *Graham's Magazine* 43 (May 1843): 269

3. Chauncey to Perry, January 20, 1813, Chauncey Letterbook, William L. Clemens Library, University of Michigan.

4. C. S. Forester, *The Age of Fighting Sail* (Garden City, NY: Doubleday, 1956), 184.

5. Lossing, *Pictorial Field-Book*. The book may be chronologically passé, but it is unique (save for his similar title on the American Revolution).

6. Theodore Roosevelt, *The Naval War of 1812; or, the History of the United States Navy during the Last War with Great Britain*, 7th ed. (New York: G. P. Putnam's Sons, 1898), 261–63.

7. G. T. Altoff, ed. "The Battle of Lake Erie: A Narrative," in *War on the Great Lakes Essays Commemorating the 175th Anniversary of the Battle of Lake Erie*, ed. William Jeffrey Welsh and David Curtis Skaggs (Kent, OH: Kent State University Press, 1991), 7.

8. Lossing, *Pictorial Field-Book*. Lossing's work contains 1,084 pages, illustrated throughout with numerous portraits and drawings amassed by the author during his personal, on-the-spot research in the 1860s, plus exceedingly ample footnotes. To be sure, many of Lossing's conclusions are highly pro-American, and therefore suspect, but in our opinion, no specialist on the War of 1812 can afford to ignore him.

9. Document transcriptions of the War of 1812 in *Northwest*, vol. 4, *Anecdotes of the Lake Erie Area, War of 1812*, transcribed from original sources, by Richard C. Knopf, historical editor and research historian, Anthony Wayne Parkway Board (Columbus: Ohio Historical Society) 1957.

10. Barclay to Sir James Lucas Yeo, September 12, 1813, in *Northwest*, I.

11. Barclay to Sir James Lucas Yeo, September 12, 1813, in *Northwest*, 2.

12. Perhaps an analogy here was the situation confronting Admiral Sir John

Jellicoe at the Battle of Jutland in 1916. Although Admiral Reinhard Scheer's fleet had punished severely the Royal Navy Squadron in the combat itself, the Germans broke off the action and fled to safety. Jellicoe made no attempt to pursue them through uncharted minefields, asserting that he was the one man who could have lost World War I in a single day.

13. G. T. Altoff, "The Perry-Elliott Controversy," *Northwest Ohio Quarterly* 60 (Autumn 1988): 137.

14. Altoff, "Perry-Elliott Controversy."

15. No. 214, Records of the Department of the Navy, Masters Commandant, National Archives, DC1813.

16. Richard J. Cox, "An Eyewitness Account of the Battle of Lake Erie," *Proceedings* (Annapolis: US Naval Institute) 104 (February 1978): 67–74.

17. Altoff, "Perry-Elliott Controversy," 138.

18. Cox, "Eyewitness Account," 62–74.

19. G. T. Altoff, ed., "Samuel Hambleton Diary," Maryland Historical Society.

20. Tristam Burgess, *Battle of Lake Erie with Notice of Commodore Elliott's Conduct in that Engagement* (Providence, 1839), 28.

21. Richard Dillon, *"We Have Met the Enemy": Oliver Hazard Perry, Wilderness Commodore* (New York: McGraw-Hill, 1978), 119–20.

22. Dillon, *"We Have Met the Enemy,"* 126.

23. Altoff, "Perry-Elliott Controversy," 144.

24. Altoff, "Battle of Lake Erie," 5–16.

25. Altoff, "Battle of Lake Erie," 13–14.

26. Altoff, "Battle of Lake Erie," 14–15.

27. Robert Malcomson and Thomas Malcomson, *HMS* Detroit*: The Battle for Lake Erie* (Annapolis, Naval Institute Press, 1990), 126–28.

28. JDE, *Speech*, 7.

29. Dillon, *"We Have Met the Enemy,"* 147. When I reviewed Dillon's book for a professional journal in 1979, I gave it a favorable commentary, but I had to mourn its lack of any scholarly apparatus at all. We conversed by phone, and he confirmed my original speculation that, after the contract had been signed, his publisher reneged on a pledge to include notes and bibliography over the author's frantic objections. Anyone familiar with Perry's career can discern that Dillon understands his subject and how thoroughly he has scoured his sources. I have no hesitation in employing in this biography of Elliott his insights and lucid literary style. But without any proper authentication, by and large *"We Have Met the Enemy"* must be dismissed in favor of those who provide this essential information.

30. Altoff, "Battle of Lake Erie," 14.

31. Altoff, "Battle of Lake Erie," 14–15.

32. Thomas Brownell, affidavit, January 8, 1819, William L. Clements Library, University of Michigan.

33. Dillon, *"We Have Met the Enemy,"* 160

34. Dillon, "*We Have Met the Enemy,*" 149
35. Dillon, "*We Have Met the Enemy,*" 140.
36. Roosevelt, *Naval War of 1812*, 262–74.
37. Roosevelt, *Naval War of 1812.*
38. *NWR*, July 9, 1814, 319
39. Jack Sweetman, *American Naval History: An Illustrated Chronicle of the U.S. Navy and Marine Corps, 1775–Present* (Annapolis: Naval Institute Press, 1984), 36.
40. Altoff, "Samuel Hambleton Diary."
41. *HLNO.*
42. Dillon, "*We Have Met the Enemy,*" 185–86
43. Sinclair to SN, May 2, 1814, in E. A. Cruikshank, ed., *The Documentary History Of Campaigns Upon the Niagara Frontier, 1812–1814*, vol. 8 (Welland, Ontario: Lundy's Lane Historical Society, 1902–3), 262.
44. May 6, 1814, in Cruikshank, *Documentary History*, 328–32.
45. Cruikshank, *Documentary History.*
46. Cruikshank, *Documentary History.*
47. Charles O. Paullin, *Diplomatic Negotiations of American Naval Officers, 1778–1883* . (Baltimore, Johns Hopkins Press, 1912), 108–10.
48. Glenn Tucker, *Dawn Like Thunder: The Barbary Wars and the Birth of the U.S. Navy* (Indianapolis: Bobbs-Merrill, 1963), 451–52.
49. Jarvis, *JDE.*
50. Sweetman, *American Naval History*, 38.
51. Jarvis, *JDE*, 176–77.
52. Gordon never recovered from his dreadful dueling wound in 1810; he was dead within two years of his spirited conduct at Algiers.
53. Tucker, *Dawn Like Thunder*, 453–55.
54. Tucker, *Dawn Like Thunder*, 462–73.
55. Jarvis, *JDE*, 226–27.
56. Jarvis, *JDE*, 227–28.
57. Jarvis, *JDE.*
58. Jarvis, *JDE*, 229.

Chapter 4

1. Altoff, "Samuel Hambleton Diary," November 22, 1813.
2. Charles J. Dutton, *Oliver Hazard Perry* (New York: Longmans, Green, 1945), 216. For total disagreement with Dutton's statement that Perry should have preferred charges against Elliott just after the battle and a further elaboration of this discussion, see a similar idea proposed by James Mills in this chapter.
3. James C. Mills, *Oliver Hazard Perry and the Battle of Lake Erie* (Detroit, John Phelps, 1913), 167.
4. Altoff, "Samuel Hambleton Diary," October 19, 1813.
5. Dillon, "*We Have Met the Enemy,*" 167.

6. Dutton, *Oliver Hazard Perry*, 187–88.

7. Mills, *Oliver Hazard Perry*, 167.

8. *Niagara*'s officers to SN, October 13, 1813, in William W. Dobbins, *History of the Battle of Lake Erie and Reminiscences of the Flagships* Lawrence *and* Niagara (Erie, PA: Ashby Printing, 1913), 124–25.

9. Altoff, "Samuel Hambleton Diary," November 30, 1813.

10. Pierre Berton, *Flames across the. Border: The Canadian-American Tragedy, 1813–1814* (Boston: Little, Brown, 1981), 171.

11. Berton, *Flames across the. Border*, 173.

12. Jarvis, *JDE*, 196–97.

13. Jarvis, *JDE*, 131–32.

14. Jarvis, *JDE*, 132.

15. In re the government's appropriation for and distribution of prize money for the Navy's success at Lake Erie.

16. Dr. Usher Parsons, "Account," Oliver Hazard Perry papers, William L. Clements Library, University of Michigan.

17. Leonard F. Guttridge and Jay D. Smith, *The Commodores* (New York: Harper& Row, 1969), 234–35.

18. Crowninshield to Murray, April 20, 1815, *NWR*, June 5, 1815, 236–37.

19. *NWR*, June 5, 1815.

20. Jarvis, *JDE*, 176–77.

21. Jarvis, *JDE*.

22. Dr. Usher Parsons "Account," Oliver Hazard Perry papers, William L. Clements Library, University of Michigan.

23. O. H. Perry to SN B. W. Crowninshield (no date on the copy in the Perry papers but located chronologically between August 1 and 17, 1818), Oliver Hazard Perry papers, William L. Clements Library, University of Michigan.

24. Oliver Hazard Perry papers, William L. Clements Library, University of Michigan.

25. Samuel Hambleton to Perry, July 15, 1818, Oliver Hazard Perry papers, William L. Clements Library, University of Michigan.

26. JDE to Lieutenant Edward N. Cox, December 28, 1813, Oliver Hazard Perry papers, William L. Clements Library, University of Michigan.

27. Roosevelt, *Naval War of 1812*, 32.

28. William S. Dudley, "Naval Historians and the War of 1812," *Naval History* 4 (Spring 1990).

29. Dudley, "Naval Historians," 57.

30. Michael Palmer, "A Failure of Command, Control, and Communications: Oliver Hazard Perry and the Battle of Lake Erie," *Journal of Erie Studies*, Erie County Historical Society and Mercyhurst College, 17 (Fall 1988), 8.

31. Palmer, "A Failure of Command, Control, and Communications."

32. Palmer, "A Failure of Command, Control, and Communications," 8–16.

33. Palmer, "A Failure of Command, Control, and Communications," 16–17.

34. Palmer, "A Failure of Command, Control, and Communications," 17.

35. Palmer, "A Failure of Command, Control, and Communications," 18.

36. Palmer, "A Failure of Command, Control, and Communications," 20.

37. Often in these wartime years the US Navy sent out several ships under one command (the futile efforts of John Rodgers, the elder, to intercept an expected English convoy in 1812 come to mind), but they were no more than commerce raiders, akin to their Confederate counterparts during the Civil War. In either case their responsibility was not to resist, unless there was no alternative but to scatter and flee.

38. Jarvis, *JDE*, 186.

39. Jarvis, *JDE*, 120–21.

40. Jarvis, *JDE*, 106.

41. Jarvis, *JDE*, 151.

42. James E. Valle, *Rocks & Shoals: Order and Discipline in the Old Navy, 1800–1861* (Annapolis: Naval Institute Press, 1980), 261–62.

43. JDE to JFC, April 25, 1814, YCAL. Elliott's reasoning is suspect because (1) the above is the only accusation of Perry's alcoholism that I have uncovered and (2) the deadly variety of yellow fever during the nineteenth century in the Caribbean tended to spare no one infected, whatever their age or physical condition.

44. Altoff, "Samuel Hambleton Diary," June 19, 1818, William L. Clements Library, University of Michigan.

45. JDE to Commodore Charles Magill, December 11, 1843, Charles Magill Collection, Duke University Library.

46. JDE, *Speech*, 10.

47. JDE to Perry, July 7, 1818, in Jarvis, *JDE*, 207–8.

48. Perry to JDE, August 3, 1818, in Jarvis, *JDE*, 211.

49. JDE to Perry, October 3, 1818, in Jarvis, *JDE*, 213–14.

50. Perry to JDE, October 6, 1818, in Jarvis, *JDE*, 214.

51. McKee, *Gentlemanly and Honorable Profession*, 169–70.

52. JDE to JFC, April 1, 1843, YCAL. Evidently no one called what may have been Elliott's bluff.

53. Timothy J. Runyan and Jan M. Copes, "The Battle of Lake Erie after 175 Years: Commemoration and Controversy," *Inland* 44 (1988).

54. Perry to Benjamin Hazard, June 6, 1819, Oliver Hazard Perry Papers.

55. Altoff, "Perry-Elliott Controversy," 149.

56. Leonard F. Guttridge and Jay D. Smith, The Commodores (N.Y., et al., Harper & Row, 1969), 229–30. This is a trailblazing and eye-opening book. Beforehand, high-level naval officers were portrayed as heroes, with the only criticisms along the line of "He had a quick temper but soon got over it." Here they become recognizable human beings, perhaps talented but otherwise normal. All in the field of early 19th century U.S. naval history are ever in debt to these two authors.

57. Samuel Eliot Morison, *"Old Bruin": Commodore Matthew Calbraith Perry 1794–1858* (Boston: Little, Brown, 1967), 49.

58. Lawrence J. Friedman and David Curtis Skaggs, "Jesse Duncan Elliott and the Battle of Lake Erie: The Issue of Mental Stability," *Journal of the Early Republic* 10 (Winter 1990): 493–515.

59. Friedman and Skaggs, "Jesse Duncan Elliott," 515–16.

60. Christopher McKee, "An Aerial View of Put-in-Bay: United States Historians Scrutinize a Campaign," in *War on the Great Lakes: Essays Commemorating the 175th Anniversary of the Battle of Lake Erie*, ed. William Jeffrey Welsh and David Curtis Skaggs (Kent, Ohio, and London, England, The Kent State University Press, 1991), 90.

61. McKee, "An Aerial View of Put-in-Bay."

Chapter 5

1. Jarvis, *JDE*.

2. Gustavus A. Weber, *The Coast and Geodetic Survey: Its History, Activities, and Organization* (Baltimore, Johns Hopkins Press, 1923), 1; and Joseph Wraight and Elliott B. Roberts, *The Coast and Geodetic Survey, 1807–1957: 150 Years of History* (Washington, DC: Government Printing Office, 1957), 5–7.

3. Weber, *Coast and Geodetic Survey*.

4. Weber, *Coast and Geodetic Survey*, 1; and Wraight and Roberts, *Coast and Geodetic Survey*, 5–7.

5. "Simon Bernard," *DAB*, 2:223.

6. Jarvis, *JDE*, 230.

7. JDE, *Speech*, 15—16.

8. Jarvis, *JDE*, 230.

9. John C. Calhoun, *The Papers of John C. Calhoun*, vol. 3: *1818–1819*, vol. 4: *1819–1820*, vol. 5: *1820–1821*, ed. by W. Edwin Hemphill (Columbia, University of South Carolina Press, 1967, 1969, 1971).

10. Wraight and Roberts, *Coast and Geodetic Survey*, 11.

11. *Calhoun*, 5:599.

12. Jarvis, *JDE*, 229–30.

13. JDE, *Speech, Appendix*, 21

14. Calhoun, *Papers*, 5:601.

15. Calhoun, *Papers*, 5:604.

16. Calhoun, *Papers*, 5:609–10. The reasons for such exact numbers rather than rough approximations for uncertain future requirements are unfathomable.

17. Calhoun, *Papers*, 5:615–16.

18. JDE to SN, August 26, 1820, Captain's Letters, (CL), roll 68, #55, NA.

19. JDE to SN, October 28, 1820, CL, roll 69, #34, 41.

20. These were licenses allowing recipient captains and crews to become privateers, naval auxiliaries, usually splitting the proceeds from captured ships and cargoes between themselves and the issuing country's government. Should a privateer

be captured, these "letters" made their people prisoners of war; without them they could be judged as pirates, subject to execution.

21. JDE to SN, February 22, 1822, CL, roll 78, #26.

22. *NWR*, January 12, 1822, 320. Perhaps I can claim considerable familiarity with this topic. Three times I have had to explore in detail the US Navy and piracy in the Caribbean from 1815 to 1825 for my biographies of *Porter* (203–27) and *Biddle* (93–111), culminating in my *GBFR* (58–67).

23. *NWR*, April 19, 1823, 98.

24. JDE to SN, August 4, 1822, CL, roll 79, #17; and DFL, *Biddle*, 99.

25. DFL, *Porter*, 206–19.

26. DFL, *Porter*, 227–50. For Porter's remaining years, see pages 250–320.

27. DFL, *Porter*, 38.

28. DFL, *Biddle*, 283.

29. DFL, *Porter*, 184.

30. Stevens, *Affair of Honor*, 158–59. This is the definitive life of that officer and based upon many years of solid research. But Stevens has no endnotes to authenticate his citations and is excessively pro-Barron.

31. JDE to Caesar A. Rodney, June 24, 1821, Rodney Papers, Historical Society of Delaware, Wilmington.

32. Brian Garret, my freelance research aide in Washington, DC, to DFL, August 14, 1991, from RG 125, (Records of General Courts—Martial and Courts of Inquiry of the Navy Department, 1799–1867), roll 14 (May 10, 1821–April 13, 1822).

33. Stevens, *Affair of Honor*, 165–67, 169–72.

34. DFL, *Bainbridge*, 265–68; and *Biddle*, 104–5.

35. DFL, *Bainbridge*, 265–68.

36. JDE to Shaw, September 30, 1822, Shaw Papers, Library of Congress, Washington, DC.

37. Guttridge and Smith, *Commodores*.

38. JDE to SN, March 1, 1820, CL, roll 66, #88.

39. JDE to SN, March 12 and 16, 1822, CL, roll 78, #41, 45.

40. JDE to SN, August 4, 1822, CL, roll 79, #17; JDE to SN, February 4, 1823, CL, roll 80, #46.

41. JDE to Rodney, April 8, 1823, Rodney Papers, Historical Society of Delaware.

42. JDE to SN, April 8, 1823, CL, roll 81, #21.

43. JDE to SN, September 8, 1823, CL, roll 85, #34.

44. JDE to SN, September 29, 1823, CL, roll #57.

45. Newton to SN, September 25, 1823. This missive appears to lack identification markings.

46. JDE to Rodney, December 12, 1823, Rodney Papers. Elliott would have shed his disappointment for a sigh of relief after reading about the acute embarrassment that the meticulous Biddle had undergone. The account of his "transporting

[Rodney]; Mrs. Rodney and her maid; nine daughters; a son; and a veritable Matterhorn of luggage to South America; via Europe," is hilarious, although most assuredly not to Biddle himself. When the contents of "Mr. Rodney's Garret and Stable" overflowed the hold and had to be lashed to *Congress*'s decks were itemized and read to John Quincy Adams, "he laughed the tears out of his eyes," although a sense of humor was one of the secretary of state 's least visible attributes, DFL, *Biddle*, 113–15

Chapter 6

1. C. S. Forester, "Bloodshed at Dawn," *American Heritage* 15 (October 1964): 73- 76; DFL, *Bainbridge*, 237–40; and DFL, "William Bainbridge and the Barron--Decatur Duel; Mere Participant or Active Plotter?" *Pennsylvania Magazine of History and Biography* 53 (January 1979): 49–52.

2. JDE to Rodney, October 27, 1821, Rodney Papers, Historical Society of Delaware.

3. Jarvis, *JDE*, 224.

4. *Proceedings of the General Court-martial*, 350. The long refusal of the government to publish the text of Barron's court-martial operated much to his disadvantage. But when they appeared, two years after Decatur's death, they worked a public relations reversal, strengthening Barron's reputation.

5. Stevens, *Affair of Honor*, 76, 84, 92.

6. Alexander Slidell Mackenzie, *Life of Commodore Oliver Hazard Perry: A Commodore in the United States*, 2 vols (Boston: Charles G. Little and James Brown, 1848), 193

7. Allan Westcott, "Commodore Jesse D. Elliott: A Stormy Petrel of the Navy," *U.S. Naval Institute Proceedings (USNIP)* 54 (September 1928).

8. Guttridge and Smith, *Commodores*, 286.

9. Guttridge and Smith, *Commodores*, 148–49.

10. James Barron, August 11, 1842, "The History of a Transaction Which Ought Never to Have Been Occasion For," part 2, Barron Papers, box 11, College of William and Mary Library. This clumsily titled long memorandum shows that Barron's memory remained keen concerning events that had occurred so many years before.

11. Decatur to Barron, June 17, 1819; Barron to Decatur, June 21, 1819, in Stephen Decatur, *Correspondence between the Late Commodore Stephen Decatur and Commodore James Barron, Which Led to the Unfortunate Meeting of the Twenty--Second of March* (Washington, DC: Gales & Seaton, 1820), 5 .

12. Barron to Decatur, June 25, 1819, in Decatur, *Correspondence*, 6.

13. Decatur to Barron, June 29, 1819, in Decatur, *Correspondence.*

14. Alexander S. Mackenzie, *Life of Stephen Decatur: A Commodore in the Navy of United States*, vol. 2 (Boston: Charles C. Little & James Brown, 1846), 315.

15. Susan Decatur to Daniel Smith, January 16, 1821, in Charles L. Lewis, *Romantic Decatur* (Philadelphia, University of Pennsylvania Press, 1937), 215.

16. Barron to Decatur, October 23, 1819, in Decatur, *Correspondence*, 7–8.

17. Decatur to Barron, October 31, 1819; Barron to Decatur, November 3; and Decatur to Barron, December 29, 1819, in Decatur, *Correspondence*, 8–12, 14–25.

18. Decatur to Barron, October 31, 1819, in Decatur, *Correspondence*, 12.

19. Barron to Decatur, November 30, 1819, in Decatur, *Correspondence*, 22.

20. Cochran as Ball's "secretary" is a case study in how an early historian's error can be handed down literally for generations by later authors because no one bothered to check the facts. Not until 1991 did Dr. William M. P. Dunne of the History Department at the Long Island University campus in Southampton, New York, ably assisted by Dr. Donald Sultana of Edinburgh and Malta, prove that Cochran was no more than a minor civil servant in the English government at Valetta. Nor is there evidence that Cochran was "a sure shot" at any distance; apparently his encounter with Bainbridge was his only duel. Small matters, perhaps, but indicative of the digging that should be done to ascertain the truth.

21. Charles O. Paullin, "Dueling in the Old Navy," *United States Naval Institute Proceedings (USNIP)* 35 (1909): 1164–65.

22. Susan Decatur, "Memorial," November 24, 1849, in Lewis, *Romantic Decatur*, 216.

23. Guttridge and Smith, *Commodores*, 271.

24. Guttridge and Smith, *Commodores*, 272.

25. Mary Crowninshield to Benjamin W. Crowninshield, March 11, 1815, Crowninshield Papers, box 8, Peabody Museum, Salem, MA.

26. Crowninshield to Decatur, "early in March" 1815, in Mackenzie, *Life of Stephen Decatur*, 246.

27. Mackenzie, March 24, 27, April 8, 1815, CL, roll 43, #78, 80, 96.

28. Bainbridge to L. W. Tazewell, March 19, 1815, James Lawrence Papers, Miscellaneous Manuscripts, New York Historical Society.

29. Bainbridge to David Porter, April 8, 1815, Bainbridge Papers, Naval Historical Society Collection, folder 3, Washington Navy Yard, Washington, DC.

30. Bainbridge, June 13, 1815, Simon Gratz Autograph Collection, case 5, box 30, Historical Society of Pennsylvania, Philadelphia.

31. Bainbridge, June 13, 1815.

32. G. Henry to John Rodgers, December 12, 1815, John Rodgers Correspondence, roll 11, New York Historical Society.

33. Bainbridge to Porter, September 6, 1815, Bainbridge Papers, Gratz Collection, case 5, Box 30, HSP.

34. Bainbridge to SN, November 15, 1815, CL, roll 47, #45.

35. Susan Decatur, "Memorial," November 24, 1849, in Lewis, *Romantic Decatur*, 215–16.

36. *Poulsen's American Daily Advertiser*, November 18, 1815.

37. *Poulsen's American Daily Advertiser*, November 20, 1815.

38. Guttridge and Smith, *Commodores*, 277. For considerably more detail about this phase of Bainbridge's career, See DFL, *Ready to Hazard: A Biography*

of Commodore William Bainbridge, 1774–1833 (Hanover, NH, University Press of New England: 1981) 188–206.

39. Susan Decatur, "Memorial," November 24, 1849, in Lewis, *Romantic Decatur*, 216.

40. Decatur to Bainbridge, February 10, 1820, in Mackenzie, *Life of Stephen Decatur*, 216. These preparations for the duel were kept secret from Susan, whose first intimation of their meeting was when her dying husband was brought from the field to her home.

41. Decatur, "Memorandum," March 8, 1820, Decatur Letter Book, #809, Decatur Papers, HSP.

42. The modern stereotype of a duel places the combatants back to back to walk the agreed number of paces away from each other, whirling at the signal to shoot. This method was used occasionally, but most participants realized that such an untidy arrangement had too many opportunities to go awry for the seconds to control. The Perry-Heath confrontation was one of the few that followed this procedure.

43. Mackenzie, *Life of Stephen Decatur*, 318.

44. Susan Decatur, "Memorial," November 24, 1849, in Lewis, *Romantic Decatur*, 117.

45. DFL, Porter, 187–88.

46. DFL, *Porter*; and David Dixon Porter, *Memoir of Commodore David Porter of the United States Navy* (Albany, N.Y., J. Munsell, 1875), 417.

47. Porter, *Memoir*, 417. David Porter remained hostile to Elliott for the rest of his life.

48. Porter, *Memoir*, 418; Porter to Hambleton, April 20, 1820, David Porter Papers, 2, Library of Congress, Washington, DC; and Rodgers to Porter, August 7, 1822, John Rodgers Papers, Library of Congress, Washington, DC.

49. Barron, August 11, 1842, "History of a Transaction Which Ought Never to Have Been Occasion For," compiled by College of William and Mary Library, vol. box 11.

50. Hamilton Cochrane, *Noted American Duels and Hostile Encounters* (Philadelphia: Chilton Books, 1963).

51. Susan Decatur to Clay, November 25, 1827, in Henry Clay, *The Papers of Henry Clay*, vol. 6: *Secretary of State, 1827* (Lexington, University of Kentucky Press, 1981), 1316–17.

52. Bainbridge to Porter, March 28, 1820, Rodgers Family Papers, Naval Historical Foundation, LC.

53. Bainbridge to Luther Bradish, March 31, 1820, Bainbridge Papers.

54. Elliott to his confidant Caesar A. Rodney, October 21, 1821, Rodney Papers, Delaware Historical Society, Wilmington; in it Elliot makes the questionable assertion that "Porter stated to him in my presence and that of Dr. Hale of Baltimore that in Barron's account he did not regret what had occurred in the contest with D[Decatur] on the field."

55. Had Susan Decatur been informed about the Elliott-Bainbridge terms set for the scheduled encounter, beyond doubt she would have insisted that they be changed—especially their already drawing a bead on the other—and most likely that would have ensued and, quite possibly, her husband's life would have been spared. Instead, her last forty years became a study in misery. Although she had been bequeathed a fortune, she frittered it away rapidly through extravagance and investments prompted by unwise or corrupt counselors. She had to endure increasingly degraded poverty until dying in a Georgetown convent in 1860, perhaps kept alive so long by her unrelenting hatred of Elliott and Bainbridge, usually referring to them as "my husband's murderers!"

56. Purser Samuel Hambleton, "Memorandum," March 22, 1820, in Mackenzie, *Life of Stephen Decatur,* 411. Bainbridge never again cruised after his return from the Mediterranean in 1821 but did command navy yards in Boston and Philadelphia. During his last years he was racked by constant pain from a variety of diseases, and by the time he died in 1833, he had become a narcotics addict.

57. John S. Barnes, "Memorandum, 1882." in JFC, *History of the Navy*, 180, New York Historical Society.

Chapter 7

1. JDE to SN, December 26, 1825, CL, roll 98, #53; and Jarvis, *JDE*, 232–33.

2. Jarvis, *JDE*, 234–35.

3. JDE to SN, March 5, 1826, CL, roll 101, #65; and Jarvis, *JDE*, 235. This activity was praiseworthy for it enhanced American commerce.

4. DFL, *GBFR*, 145–46; DFL, *Biddle*, 132–35; William L. Langer, *An Encyclopedia of World History*, 5th ed. (Boston: Houghton Mifflin, 1972), 884–85; and Donald W. Griffin, "The American Navy at Work on the Brazil Station, 1827- 1860," *American Neptune* 19 (October 1959): 239

5. JDE to Lobo, April 3, 1826, in Jarvis, *JDE*, 242.

6. Jarvis, *JDE*, 252.

7. Jarvis, *JDE*.

8. JDE to SN, March 5, 1826, CL, roll 101, #65.

9. JDE to Lobo, April 25, 1826, in Jarvis, *JDE*, 244.

10. Lobo to JDE, April 27, May 4, in Jarvis, *JDE*, 245–46.

11. JDE to Lobo, April 3, May 4, 1826, in Jarvis, *JDE*, 247–48.

12. JDE to Lobo, in Jarvis, *JDE*, 257.

13. French Commodore Du Plantys to JDE, June 1, 1826, in Jarvis, *JDE*, 238–39.

14. Austrian Major Chevalier d'Ewald to JDE, July 10, 1826, in Jarvis, *JDE*, 256.

15. JDE to d' Ewald, July 12, 1826, in Jarvis, *JDE*, 255–56.

16. Henry Clay, *The Papers of Henry Clay,* vol. 5: *Secretary of State*, ed. James F. Hopkins and Mary W. M. Hargreaves (Lexington, University of Kentucky Press, 1973), 183–84; Clay, *Papers*, 6:1178–79.

17. Clay, *Papers*, 5:235–36.

18. Clay, *Papers*, 6:1262–63.

19. *NWR*, September 2, 1826, 5–9, and November 19, 1826, 410, 425.

20. *NWR*, November 11, 1826, 164.

21. Jarvis, *JDE*, 258.

22. For a follow-up to the Elliott-Biddle contributions to US diplomacy in lower South America in 1826–27, [see DFL, Biddle, 132–38].

23. Langer, *Encyclopedia of World History*, 854.

24. Jarvis, *JDE*, 259.

Chapter 8

1. Langley, "The Grass Roots Harvest of 1828." *U.S. Naval Institute* 90 (October 1964): 51–59.

2. JDE to SN, 5 Sept. 1827, CL, roll 113, #39.

3. SN to JDE, 11 Sept. 1827, SNL (Secretary of Navy Letters), roll 17, p. 288, National Archives, Washington, DC.

4. Langley, "Grass Roots Harvest," 53, 56.

5. Langley, "Grass Roots Harvest."

6. SN to JDE, September 3, 1829, SNL, roll 18, pp. 354–55.

7. SN to JDE, October 6, 1829, SNL, roll 18, p. 354; and DFL, *Bainbridge*, 120.

8. ASP, *Report of the Secretary of the Navy*, December 1, 1829, vol. 3, 354, 365.

9. Jarvis, *JDE*, 304–5.

10. See chapter 9.

11. Jarvis, *JDE*, 260—72.

12. JDE to Lopez, 26 Dec.; Lopez to JDE, 31 Dec. 1829; JDE to Lopez, 2 Jan. 1830; Lopez to JDE, 31 Dec. 1829; and JDE to Lopez, 4 Jan. 1830, in Jarvis, *JDE*, 275–78. 13 DFL.

13. DFL, *GBFR*, 70.

14. DFL, *GBFR*; and Jarvis, *JDE*, 272–73.

15. Jarvis, *JDE*, 280–81.

16. JDE to Vives, December 12, 1830, in Jarvis, *JDE*, 281.

17. JDE to Vives, in Jarvis, *JDE*, 281–83.

18. This has confused some readers, for that was also the name of JDE's flagship in Mexican waters, c. 1830, until it is realized that there were two *Peacocks*, one British built and sunk and the other American built later. The US Navy Department exulted in embarrassing the erstwhile foe by designating many of its new men-of--war by those they defeated from 1812 to 1815: *Peacock, Guerriere, Levant, Cyane, Frolic, Wasp*, and *Boxer*, for instance.

19. *NWR*, January 30, 1830, 379–80. Clearly it had been a bona fide hurricane.

20. *NWR*, January 30, 1830, 380.

21. The above documentation is from ASP, *Class 6, Naval Affairs*, vol. 3, 868–71.

22. Stephen B. Oates, *The Fires of Jubilee: Nat Turner's Fierce Rebellion* (New York: Harper & Row, 1975), passim.

23. JDE to SN, August 28, 1831, in Jarvis, *JDE*, 286–88.

24. John Boyle, Acting SN, to JDE, September 1, 1831, in Jarvis, *JDE*, 288.

25. *NWR*, September 17, 1831, 26.

26. JDE, *Speech*, 19n; and "Washington Lafayette Elliott," *DAB*, 6:100–101.

27. JDE to SN, December 8, 1831, CL, roll 165, #30.

28. DFL, *GBFR*, 451; and Jarvis, *JDE*, 289–91.

29. Jarvis, *JDE*, 291–92.

30. JDE to SN, April 28, 1832, CL, roll 169, #69; and DFL, *"Mad Jack,"*100–101.

31. *HLNO*, 147.

32. SN to JDE, April 15, 1830, SNL, roll 18, p. 490.

33. SN to JDE and Dallas, April 30, 1832, SNL, roll 21, pp.97–98.

34. SN to JDE, SNL, roll 21, p. 98.

35. JDE to SN, October 23, 1831, CL, roll 164, #76; and SN to JDE, March 12, 1831, SNL roll 19, p. 255–56.

36. SN to JDE, March 13, 1831, SNL, roll 19, pp. 254–55.

37. SN to Dallas and JDE, April 30, 1832, SNL, roll 21, p. 98.

38. It might be noted that JDE never refers to Dallas in his 137-page JDE, *Speech*, *Appendix*, and *Addendia*, published in 1844.

39. SN to JDE, March 17, 1832, SNL, roll 21, 43.

40. DFL, *GBFR*, 89–90.

41. JDE, *Speech*, 17.

42. JDE to SN, August 9, 1831, CL, roll 162, #37.

43. JDE to SN, July 28, 1831, CL, roll 162, #22.

44. JDE to SN, July 12, October 10, 1831, CL, rolls 161, #76, and #164, #18. JDE must have been right in holding a low position of Clack. Although he became a captain in 1838, he was cashiered from the service in 1842, about the harshest punishment for an officer under the Naval Code (*HLNO*, 114).

45. JDE to SN, February 24, 1832, CL, roll 167, #107.

46. The two men had cooperated effectively and cordially during the aftermath of September 8–9, 1812, when Elliott had snapped up the two British brigs near Buffalo.

47. Jackson to SN, September 11, 1832, in Andrew Jackson, *The Correspondence of Andrew Jackson*, vol. 4, *1829–1832*, ed. by John S. Bassett (Washington, DC: Carnegie Institute, 1929), 474.

48. Jarvis, *JDE*, 293, 299.

49. William M. P. Dunne, "Operational History: United States Second Class Sloop-of-War *Natchez*, 1827–1840," unpublished manuscript, July 13, 1988, 12–14.

50. Dunne, "Operational History," 16–18.

51. Clay had been instrumental in arranging the Compromise of 1820 over admitting Maine as a free state with Missouri as a slave state to maintain a sectional balance in the Senate. He would also be prominent in the Compromise of 1850 in which California entered as a free state and the South was appeased by a stringent Fugitive Slave Act.

52. Dunne, "Operational History," 24–27.

53. Lt. Levin M. Powell to Lt. Garret J. Pendergast, March 10, 1833, Powell Papers, New York Historical Society, in Dunne, "Operational History," 29–30.

54. Charles L. Lewis, *David Glasgow Farragut—Admiral in the Making* (Annapolis: US Naval Institute Proceeding, 1941), in Dunne, "Operational History," 24.

55. JDE to SN, February 25, March 3, 1833, in Dunne, "Operational History," 26, 28. To me and my research assistant, M. Lawrence Moberly, the most cheering aspect of this letter is how it was reproduced in the material that came from Dunne. Deciphering Elliott's almost impenetrable handwriting has been the most onerous part of researching his life, and in a mere nineteen lines of it, Dunne found no fewer than thirteen words "illegible." It is heartening for Moberly and me that we were not alone in coping with this agony.

56. JDE, Officers' Records, NA.

57. Jarvis, *JDE*, 298.

58. Count de Choiseul to JDE., January 28–29, February 1; JDE to Choiseul, February 2; and SN to JDE, in Jarvis, *JDE*, 294–98.

59. Lewis, *Farragut*, in Dunne, "Operational History," 34–35.

60. Lewis, *Farragut*, in Dunne, "Operational History."

61. Dunne, "Operational History," 34–35.

62. Jarvis, *JDE*, 299.

63. *House Committee on Naval Affairs, Report* no. 563, ASP, and Class 6, Naval Affairs, vol. 4, 562–76.

Chapter 9

1. Cooper, *History of the Navy*, 3:37.

2. DFL, *Porter* 175–79.

3. Edwin C. Bearss, *Charlestown [Boston] Navy Yard, 1800–1842*, vol. 2 (Washington, DC: Interior Department, National Park Service), 625.

4. Bearss, *Charlestown Navy Yard*, 749–50.

5. *NWR*, September 18, 1831, in Tyrone G. Martin, *A Most Fortunate Ship: A Narrative History of "Old Ironsides"* (Chester, CT: Globe Pequot Press, 1980), 194; hereafter, Martin, *AMFS*.

6. Martin, *AMFS*, 195, 196.

7. Martin, *AMFS*, 196; and DFL, *Bainbridge*, 310–11.

8. Martin, *AMFS*, 195–200, 203–4.

9. DFL, *Bainbridge*, 189–90. For a detailed study of this subject, see Charles O. Paullin, "Naval Administration under the Navy Commissioners, 1815–1842," *U.S. Naval Institute Proceedings (USNIP* 33 (1907): passim.

10. JDE to SN, December 10, 1833, CL, roll 35, #55; and Bearss, *Charlestown Navy Yard*, 628–30.

11. Bearss, *Charlestown Navy Yard*, 634–36.

12. DFL, *"Mad Jack,"* 103–5.

13. Bearss, *Charlestown Navy Yard*, 641–44.

14. Bearss, *Charlestown Navy Yard*, 638–64.

15. Bearss, *Charlestown Navy Yard*, 633, 650, 675, 687–88, 694–95.

16. JDE to SN, August 17, 1835, CL, roll 207, #68.

17. Bearss, *Charlestown Navy Yard*, 648.

18. Bearss, *Charlestown Navy Yard*, 654.

19. Ray A. Billington, *The Protestant Crusade, 1800–1860: A Study in the Origins of American Nativism* (New York: Macmillan, 1938), 58–67.

20. JDE to SN, August 19, 1834, CL, roll 197, #75.

21. Bearss, *Charlestown Navy Yard*, 740–43.

22. Billington, *Protestant Crusade*, 88.

23. JDE to SN, August 25, 1834, CL, roll 197, #93; and Bearss, *Charlestown Navy Yard*, 746–48.

24. JDE, *Speech, Appendix*, 24–25; Billington, *Protestant Crusade*, 87; and JDE Papers, Rosenbach Museum and Library, Philadelphia, #41.

25. JDE, *Speech, Appendix*, 1.844, 24–25; and Billington, *Protestant Crusade*, 87.

26. JDE, *Speech*.

27. Frank L. Mott, *American Journalism, 1690–1960* (New York: Macmillan, 1962), 217.

28. *Boston Morning Post* (in order), June 24, 1833, June 20, 1833.

29. *Boston Evening Transcript*, June 20, 1833; Mott, *American Journalism*, 217.

30. *Boston Evening Transcript*, , June 20, 1833.

31. Jarvis, *JDE*, 309.

32. Jarvis, *JDE*, 311.

33. This account is based largely upon Robert V. Rimini's invaluable *Andrew Jackson and the Bank War: A Study in the Growth of Presidential Power* (New York: W. W. Norton, 1961), 109–53.

34. *Boston Morning Post*, February 21, 1834.

35. *Boston Morning Post*, March 12, 1834.

36. Jarvis, *JDE*, 316–17.

37. Jarvis, *JDE*, 309.

38. Jarvis, *JDE*, 312–13.

39. Jarvis, *JDE*, 319.

40. Martin, *AMFS*, 199.

41. Marion V. Brewington, *Ship-Carvers of North America* (New York: Dover Publications, 1972), figs. 127, 130.

42. Brewington, *Ship-Carvers of North America*, figs. 129, 135.

43. Bearrs, *Charlestown Navy Yard*, 679-83.

44. Bearrs, *Charlestown Navy Yard, 679-83.*

45. *NWR*, July 12, 1834, 329.

46. *NWR*, July 12, 1834, 329.

47. Jarvis, *JDE*, 318-19.

48. Jarvis, *JDE*, 316.

49. JDE to SN, November 19, 1834, Mahlon Dickerson Papers, New Jersey Historical Society, Newark.

50. Matthew C. Perry, *Documents in Relation to Differences Which Subsist between Late Commodore O. H Perry and Captain Jesse D. Elliott* (Washington, DC, 1821), passim.

51. Jarvis, *JDE*, 331.

52. Bearrs, *Charlestown Navy Yard*, 680-81.

53. Bearrs, *Charlestown Navy Yard*, 680-81.

54. Bearss, *Charlestown Navy Yard*, 681.

55. Bearss, *Charlestown Navy Yard.*

56. Brewington, *Ship-Carvers of North America*, figs. 124, 128.

57. Dorothy G. Wayman, "Discussions," *U.S. Naval Institute Proceedings* 55 (1929): 327–28.

58. Jarvis, *JDE*, 318.

59. Jarvis, *JDE*,336.

60. Jarvis, *JDE*, 337.

61. Bearss, *Charlestown Navy Yard*, 677–84.

62. Jarvis, *JDE*, 360. In his long account of the matter Elliott never mentions Dewey's name, probably to deny him any further publicity.

63. Bearss, *Charlestown Navy Yard*, 677.

64. John R. Spears, "Old Ironsides as Sailors Saw Her," *Chautauquan* 31 (July 1900): 377–82.

65. JDE, *Speech*, 8.

66. As noted before, Fitz Hugh had died in battle against the British early in1815.

67. JDE to C. G. Loring, December 4, 1834, in JDE, *Correspondence between Commodore Jesse D. Elliott and Charles G. Loring, Esq.* (Boston, privately printed—almost surely assembled by Elliott himself—1835), 6.

68. I am indebted for help in the mercury treatment and its consequences from Valerie L. Harper, assistant reference librarian; David M. Lean, of the Biological Branch Library; and Professor Samuel C. Smith, of the Department of Animal and Nutritional Science-all at University of New Hampshire. JDE to SN, June 25, 1827, CL, roll 117, #75.

69. Lt. Frank Ellery to JDE, November 24, 1834; and JDE to Loring, December 4, 1834, in JDE, *Correspondence between Commodore Jesse D. Elliott and Charles G. Loring*, 9, 6.

70. See earlier in chapter about Edward Babbit's protest of Elliott's requirement for officers to attend Sabbath services on Sunday.

71. In 1827 JDE had demonstrated an early animus against Edward B. Babbit when he urged vehemently that the lieutenant be denied a requested leave of absence. According to the commodore, Babbit had been granted recently a long

furlough to ship on a merchantman and then a US man-of-war "on a foreign Station to return home, compelling a valuable officer to leave *Cyane* to take his place." To summarize, Babbit treated the Navy as no more than "a convenience." *The Trial of Lt E. B. Babbit on Charges Preferred by Com. Jesse D. Elliott; before a Naval Court-Martial. Assembled at the Navy Yard, Charlestown, 13. October 1834* (Boston, 1835), 61–62.

72. For Loring's statement about Elliott, see *Correspondence between Commodore Jesse D. Elliott and Charles G. Loring*, 10.

73. JDE, *Correspondence between Commodore Jesse D. Elliott and Charles G. Loring.*

74. JDE to Everett, December 16, 1833; and Everett to JDE, in *Correspondence between Commodore Jesse D. Elliott and Charles G. Loring*, 11–14.

75. Captain Joseph Smith, December 3; Captain George Budd, December 2; Passed Midshipman W. C. Spenser, November 24.; Lt. Frank Ellery, December 24; Lt. Uriah P. Levy, December 5; Lt. James Ferguson, December 6; Lt. Edward C. Rutledge, December 11; and Dr. Cornelius Moore, December 31; all in 1834, in JDE, *Correspondence between Commodore Jesse D. Elliott and Charles G. Loring*, passim.

76. JDE to Loring, December 8, 1834, in Jarvis, *JDE*, 348–49.

77. Loring to JDE, December 8, 1834, in Jarvis, *JDE*, 349.

78. Babbit to JDE, December 6, 1834, in Jarvis, *JDE*, 352–53.

79. JDE to Loring, December 10, 1834, in, JDE, *Correspondence between Commodore Jesse D. Elliott and Charles G. Loring*, 13.

80. JDE to Babbit, January 21, 1835, in Jarvis, *JDE*, 356–57.

81. Babbit to SN, January 10, 1834,—misdated December 10, 1835—in Jarvis, *JDE*, 355 .

82. JDE to Babbit, January 21, 1835, in Jarvis, *JDE*, 355–56.

83. *HLNO*, 32.

84. JDE to former SN Levi Woodbury, November 18, 1833, in Jarvis, *JDE*, 357–59.

85. *Trial of Lt E. B. Babbit*, passim.

86. *Trial of Lt E.B. Babbit*, 6. The court-martial's weighty transcript composed no fewer than 120 printed pages.

87. McKee, *Gentlemanly and Honorable Profession*, 169. Although the author does describe at some length the importance of the qualities of leadership in the officer-gentleman, (219, 223–32), he skims over two other characteristics for the advancement and reputation of officers—personal valor and meritorious conduct in battle. As McKee points out, he considered these so obvious as to need no recapitulation, 170.

88. *Trial of Lt. E.B. Babbit.*

89. *Trial of Lt E.B. Babbit*, 7–8.

90. During this time Babbit lived with his brother's widow, Maria, and her two children in a house a half mile across the sprawling navy yard from its docking area.

91. *Trial of Lt E.B. Babbit*, 88–89, 90, 91.

92. *Trial of Lt E.B. Babbit*, 92.

93. *Trial of Lt E.B. Babbit*, , 71.

94. *NWR*, November 8, 1834, 146; and *Daily National Intelligencer*, November 4, 1834, 3/4.

Chapter 10

1. DFL, *GBFR*, 182, based in large part upon Robert V. Rimini, *Andrew Jackson and Course of American Democracy, 1833–1845* (New York: Harper & Row, 1984), 201–18, 230–36, 274–92; John M. Belohlavek, *"Let The Eagle Soar!" The Foreign Policy of Andrew Jackson* (Lincoln: University of Nebraska Press, 1985), 102–26; and Elizabeth B. White, *American Opinion of France from Lafayette to Poincare* (New York: Knopf, 1927), 94–109.

2. DFL, *Biddle*, 170–71.

3. Martin, *AMFS*, 206.

4. Martin, AMFS, 206; and Elliot Snow and H. Allen Gosnell, *On the Decks of Old Ironsides* (New York: Macmillan, 1932), 197–203.

5. Martin, *AMFS*, 206–7.

6. *Boston Daily Evening Traveller*, September 11, 1839, 1–4.

7. JDE, *Speech*, 22–24.

8. JDE, *Speech, Appendix*, 46–48n1; Jesse Erskine Dow, "Old Ironsides on a Lee Shore," *Democratic Review* 1839.

9. *Journal of Commerce* (New York), n. d., in NWR, June 27, 1835, 290.

10. *NWR*, July 11, 1835, 327.

11. *NWR*, July 11, 1835, 327.

12. JDE to SN, December 7, 1835, CL, roll 201, #32, and December 15, 1835, CL, roll 210, #30.

13. Livingston to JDE, December 31, 1835, Jesse Duncan Elliott Papers, #34, Rosenbach Museum and Library, Philadelphia.

14. JDE to SN, January 18, 1836, CL, roll 231, #10.

15. JDE to SN, January 29, 1836, CL, roll 231, #100.

16. The amiable links between Elliott and the Livingstons continued after the family had returned to the United States.

17. JDE to SN Dickerson, October 31, 1835, CL, roll 209, #58.

18. Guttridge and Smith, *Commodores*, 311.

19. The screw propeller was not yet in use.

20. Guttridge and Smith, *Commodores*, 310.

21. Guttridge and Smith, *Commodores*, 312.

22. Guttridge and Smith, *Commodores*, 312.

23. For the warships mentioned above, [see *HLNO*, 726, 727, 730, respectively].

24. Snow and Gosnell, *On the Decks of Old Ironsides*, 207, 297–99.

25. Snow and Gosnell, *On the Decks of Old Ironsides*, 297–99.

26. Midshipman Edward Clifton Anderson journal, in the Edward Clifton Anderson Papers, Southern Historical Collection, Manuscripts Department, University of North Carolina Library, title, 68–69, 135–38, 145–64.

27. Martin, *AMFS*, 208.

28. Martin, *AMFS*, 207. For some reason the author omits the name of the lucky lieutenant.

29. Martin, *AMFS*, 210.

30. Snow and Gosnell, *On the Decks of Old Ironsides*, 297–99.

Chapter 11

1. SN to JDE, May 6, 1836, Mahlon Dickerson Papers, Historical Society of New Jersey.

2. James Kirke Paulding, *The Letters of James Kirke Paulding*, ed. by Ralph A. Aderman (Madison: University of Wisconsin Press, 1962), 219.

3. *DAB*, 14:322.

4. During 1756 in the Mediterranean, Admiral John Byng, of the Royal Navy, was shot for "neglect of duty." This prompted Voltaire to remark sardonically, "pour encouragez les autres." For Barron, see our chapter 2.

5. JDE, *Speech*, 28–29.

6. Amos L. Herold, *James Kirke Paulding: Versatile American* (New York: Columbia University Press, 1926), 129.

7. Herold, *James Kirke Paulding*, 130.

8. *NWR*, September 5, 1840, 145–50.

9. Snow and Gosnell, *On the Deck of Old Ironsides*, appendix B, 297–99.

10. JDE, *Speech*, 35.

11. James A. Field Jr., *America and the Mediterranean World, 1766–1866* (Princeton, NJ: Princeton University Press, 1969), 195.

12. *The New Columbia Encyclopedia* (New York: Columbia University Press, 1975), 1854.

13. JDE, *Speech*, 41.

14. Jose Calvet de Magalhaes, "O Tratado Commercial de 1840," in *Historica das relacoes diplomaticas entre Portugal e os Estados Unidos da America, 1776–1911* (Lisbon: Mem Martins, Publicoes Europa–America , 1991), 124–44.

15. Conversations with Dr. Wheeler, mid-April 1993.

16. DFL, *Porter*, 312–13.

17. Field, *America and the Mediterranean World*, 197–98; and *HLNO*, 261.

18. *NWR*, September 5, 1840, 145–50.

19. Valle, *Rocks & Shoals*, 3.

20. Snow and Gosnell, *On the Decks of Old Ironsides*, 297.

21. Those who had reached that rank were fixed there until retirements or deaths among their superiors created openings for them to advance to lieutenants.

22. JDE to President John Tyler, March 31, 1843, YCAL.

23. Valle, *Rocks & Shoals*, 46.

24. Charles O. Paullin, *Commodore John Rodgers*, (Cleveland: Arthur H. Clark, 1910), 367.

25. James M. Merrill, "Midshipman DuPont and the Cruise of the *North Carolina*, 1825–1827," *American Neptune* 40 (January 1980): 213, 215.

26. Valle, *Rocks & Shoals*, 138–39.

27. Valle, *Rocks & Shoals*, 140–41.

28. Snow and Gosnell, *On the Decks of Old Ironsides*, 297.

29. Valle, *Rocks & Shoals*, 139–41.

30. Valle, *Rocks & Shoals*.

31. Martin, *AMFS*, 248.

32. Valle, *Rocks & Shoals*, 243.

33. Valle, *Rocks & Shoals*, 4

34. For legal definitions of what constitutes mutiny in the US Navy or Army, see "Mutiny at Hampton Roads, VA," 1838, when Elliott was commanding the Mediterranean Squadron.

35. Valle, *Rocks. & Shoals*, 108–10; and Morison, *Old Bruin*, 144–62. Morison takes a stance that Mackenzie and his officers had every reason to fear mutiny after the confessions of young Spencer and the other two culprits and their prospect of a successful piratical cruise. Had only the US Navy been involved, that conclusion might be justified. But by 1842 the British Navy had sent its far-flung squadrons worldwide, and the slightest indication of a black flag afloat would have brought the queen's warships teeming to obliterate it. Morison is silent about this strong probability.

36. JFC to Commodore William Shubrick, November 25, 1842, in JFC, *Letters and Journals*, 4: 87–88, 595.

37. JDE, *Speech, Addenda*, 70.

38. Morison, *"Old Bruin,"* 160–62.

39. Oliver, "Commodore Oliver Hazard Perry," 777–83.

40. JDE to SN Mahlon Dickerson, June 22, 1835, CL, roll 205, #79.

41. JDE to SN, September 3, 1835, "Utmost harmony on Board," CL, roll 208, # 11; and "Utmost harmony prevails," CL, roll 209, #58.

42. JDE to SN, July 7, 1835, CL, roll 207, #22; and July 12, 1835, #34.

43. JDE to SN, July 7, 1835, CL, roll 207, #22; and July 12, 1835, #34.

44. Valle, *Rocks & Shoals*, 80–81.

45. JDE, *Defence of Commodore Elliott at His Philadelphia Navy Yard Court--Martial, 11 May–20 June 1840* (Philadelphia: privately printed, 1840), 23–24.

46. JDE, *Defence*, 22–23.

47. Valle, *Rocks & Shoals*, 190–91.

48. Valle, *Rocks & Shoals*, 190.

49. Valle, *Rocks & Shoals*, 190–91.

50. Hunter to Wise, January 10, 1839, in *NWR*, January 19, 1839, 334. In 1859

Wise was governor of Virginia and refused to commute John Brown's execution by hanging for his raid on Harper's Ferry, Virginia.

51. *NWR*, January 17, 1839.

52. JDE, *Defence*, 21–23.

53. Anderson journal, 134–35.

54. Anderson journal.

55. JDE, *Speech, Appendix*, 60.

56. JDE, *Defence*, 10–15.

57. JDE, *Defence*, 11.

58. JDE, *Defence*, 11.

59. JDE, *Defence*, 6.

60. JDE, *Defence* 6.

61. JDE, *Defence*, 8.

62. JDE, *Defence*, 7.

63. JDE, *Defence*, 8–9.

64. Anderson journal.

65. *Alexandria (VA) Gazette*, nd, in *Portsmouth* (NH) *Journal of Literature and Politics*.

66. JDE to Joel R. Poinsett, nd (probably early 1838), Poinsett Papers, Historical Society of Pennsylvania. Poinsett was secretary of war in Van Buren's cabinet, 1837–41, and part of his responsibilities was to provide livestock for the army. The two men may have done business together, but we have no source to confirm it.

67. JDE to Poinsett., November 25, 1843, Poinsett Papers.

68. JDE, *Speech, Addenda*, 74–75. But when his will was probated shortly after his demise, it was indeed unimpressive (see chapter 13).

69. JFC, *Letters and Journals*, 4:52–53, 586.

70. Research has proven that, rather, it had been the mausoleum for one of the emperor's lesser lights.

71. JDE to Jackson, March 13, 1845, Andrew Jackson, *Correspondence of Andrew Jackson*, vol. 6, ed. by John S. Bassett (Washington, DC: Carnegie Institution,), 381.

72. Jackson to JDE, March 27, 1845, in Jackson, *Correspondence*, 6: 391.

73. Charles Warren, "More Odd Byways in American History," Massachusetts Historical Society, *Proceedings* 69 (1956): 256–57.

74. Charles C. Barton (hereafter CCB), "Manifest of the Charges Preferred to the Navy Department and Subsequently to the Congress against Jesse Duncan Elliott Esq a Captain in the Navy of the United States, for Unlawful Conduct While [Late] Commodore of the Mediterranean Squadron; and a Refutation of the Recrimination Raised by That Officer" (Philadelphia: privately printed, 1839), appendix, xxiii.

75. JDE, *Defence*, 15.

76. JDE, *Defence*, 16.

77. *NWR*, August 18, 1840, 358.

78. SN Dickerson to JDE, October 1, 1836, SNL, roll 25, 272.

79. JDE to Cass, February 5, 1837, Lewis Cass Papers, William L. Clements Library, University of Michigan.

80. *HLNO*, 34.

81. Anderson journal, 134–35.

82. Snow and Gosnell, 299.

83. Anderson journal, 68–69.

84. The Anti-Masons were a political party based upon lower-class suspicions of the privileges enjoyed by the Masonic Order and other secret societies that quickly spread throughout the country. They gained fame in 1831 by the first use of a party convention in place of the former caucus system, and their innovation was almost immediately adopted by other political organizations. Eventually most of these Anti-Jacksonians sided with the Whig Party.

85. Philip S. Klein and Ari Hoogenboom, *A History of Pennsylvania* (University Park: Pennsylvania State University Press, 1980), 148.

86. Klein and Hoogenboom, *History of Pennsylvania*, 149–50.

87. JDE to President John Tyler, July 8, 1842, CL, roll 291, #29.

88. JDE to Joel R. Poinsett [?], 1839, Poinsett Papers.

89. CCB, "Manifest," 10.

90. CCB, "Manifest," appendix; and Midshipman William S. Ringgold to Dr. William C. Barton, December 5, 1835, USN, v.

91. 1st Lt. Benjamin J. Totten to Lt. Ebenezer Ridgeway [Commanding *Shark*], December 3, 1835, USN, iv.

92. Dr. Barton to SN Dickerson, March 22, 1836, USN, v.

93. JDE, *Defence*, 5.

94. CCB, "Manifest," appendix, xiv.

95. JDE, *Defence*, 20–21.

96. JDE, *Defence*, 22–23.

97. Anderson's testimony at JDE's court-martial, May 20, 1840, Anderson papers.

98. CCB, "Manifest," appendix and supporting evidence, passim.

99. CCB, "Manifest," 9–10, 26.

100. CCB, "Manifest," 4, 11.

101. CCB, "Manifest," 15–16.

102. CCB, "Manifest," appendix, v.

103. *HLNO*, 226; Guttridge and Smith, *Commodores*, 453, 454

104. CCB, "Manifest," 20.

105. CCB, "Manifest."

106. JDE, *Defence*, 5.

107. JDE, *Defence*, 19.

108. CCB to SN Dickerson, November 18, 1836, in CCB, "Manifest," supporting evidence, 34–36.

109. CCB, "Manifest," 19.

110. CCB, "Manifest," 21–22.

111. CCB, "Manifest," 7.

112. JDE, *Defence*, 20.

113. CCB, "Manifest," supporting evidence, 35–36.

114. CCB, "Manifest," 39.

115. Dennett's and Whitaker's depositions, 10 Feb. 1837, CCB, "Manifest," appendix, xi–xiii.

116. CCB, "Manifest," 11. Elliott in his twenty-four-page defence makes no mention of Dennett. Luckily for the researcher to permit fuller comprehension of the story, Barton scatters frequent quotations from his commander's correspondence (in order, of course, to negate them).

117. CCB, "Manifest," 7.

118. JDE, *Defence*, 18–21.

119. CCB, "Manifest," 3.

120. CCB, "Manifest," supporting evidence, 41–42.

121. CCB, "Manifest."

Chapter 12

1. SN Paulding to JDE, August 28, 1838, SNL, roll 27, 438. Elliott's reply did no more than to acknowledge receipt of the letter.

2. SN Paulding to JDE, March 26, 1839, SNL, roll 28, 406.

3. JDE to Joel R. Poinsett, December 2, 1839, Poinsett papers.

4. SN Paulding to JDE, March 26, 1839, SNL, roll 28.

5. JDE, *Speech, Appendix*, 56.

6. *NWR*, March 2, 1839, 4.

7. *Biographical Directory of the United States Congress, 1774–1989* (Washington, DC: Government Printing Office, 1989): Naylor, 1558; Chambers, 762; and Lyon, 1403.

8. JFC to wife, September 27, 1839, in JFC, *The Letters and Journals of James Fenimore Cooper*, ed. James E. Beard, vol. 3 (New York: G. P. Putnam, 1853), 428–29, 546.

9. JDE, *Speech, Appendix*, 52.

10. JDE, *Speech, Appendix*.

11. *NWR*, August 18, 1840, 358.

12. JDE, *Defence*, 1–5.

13. *Charges and Specifications*, located at the National Archives in Washington, DC, microcopy no. 273; *Records of General Courts-martial and Courts of Inquiry of the Navy Department, 1799–1867*, case 748, roll 40; Valle, *Rocks & Shoals*, 358.

14. *NWR*, August 18, 1840, 358.

15. *Army and Navy Chronicle*, nd, in *NWR*, April 25, 1840, 114.

16. *NWR*, August 18, 1840, 358.

17. *NWR*, August 25, 401.

18. *NWR*, August 25, 1840, 401.

19. Paulding to JDE, July 6, 1840, SNL, roll 31, 228–29.

20. *NWR*, August 25, 1840, 401.

21. JDE to Tyler, July 6, 1842, CL, roll 291, #29.

22. JDE to Poinsett, June 30, 1842, Poinsett papers.

23. R. M. Johnson to JDE, October 11, 1842, in JDE, *Speech*, 53.

24. JDE to JFC, December 24, 1842, YCAL.

25. JDE to JFC, April 1, 1843, YCAL.

26. JFC to Commodore William Shubrick, October 1, 1840, in JFC, *Letters and Journals*, 4:88, 595.

27. JDE to JFC, June 25, 1842.

28. Merri L. S. Schuman, "A History and Genealogy of Carlisle, Cumberland County, 1751–1835" (Dover, PA: private typescript, 1987), 81, 150.

29. DFL, *Biddle*, 244.

30. JFC to Commodore William Shubrick, October 9, 1843, in JFC, *Letters and Journals*, 4:431–37, 746.

31. JFC to William Fry and Joseph R. Fry, publishers of the *National Gazette and Literary Messenger*, June 23, 1840, in JFC, *Letters and Journals*, 4:47–49, 583.

32. JFC to JDE, June 19, 1842, in JFC, *Letters and Journals*, 4:294, 680.

33. JFC to George Palmer Putnam, December 10, 1847, in JFC, *The Letters and Journals of James Fenimore Cooper*, ed. James E. Beard, vol. 5 (Cambridge, MA: Belknap Press of Harvard University Press,1968), 249, 917.

34. JDE to Albert Gallatin, January 11, 1845, Albert Gallatin Papers, New York Historical Society.

35. JDE to JFC, December, YCAL.

36. JFC to wife, November 30, 1845, in JFC, *Letters and Journals*, 5:844, following p.100.

37. JFC to Putnam, December 10, 1847, in JFC, *Letters and Journals*, 5:249–50, 917; and *NWR*, December 30, 1845, 247–48.

38. JDE to SN George Bancroft, March 26, 1845, National Archives, Philadelphia. To ease the overstrained facilities in Washington, DC, branches elsewhere have been established.

39. JDE to SN John Y. Mason, February 15, 1845, National Archives, Philadelphia.

40. JDE to SN George Bancroft, April 19, 1845, CL, roll 321, #268. Ridiculous! Bancroft knew all about Elliott's physical depletion, and command of the Gulf Squadron went to Commodores David Conner and Matthew C. Perry.

41. JDE to SN, November 16, 1845, CL, roll 325, #37. Numbers thirteen and fourteen are the last letters that Elliott sent to the department.

42. JDE to SN, November 16, 1845, CL, roll 325, #37.

43. JFC to Commodore William Shubrick, May 28, 1845, in JFC, *Letters and Journals*, 5:33, 806.

44. Robert Berkow , ed., "Edema," in *Manual of Diseases and Therapy* (Rahway, NJ: Merck, 1987).

45. JFC to Commodore William Shubrick, May 28, 1845, in JFC, *Letters and Journals*, 5:50–53, 816.

46. JFC to wife, November 30, 1845, in JFC, *Letters and Journals*, 5:100–101, 844.

47. JFC to wife, in JFC, *Letters and Journals*, 5:106–7, 847. A few days later Elliott was dead.

48. Gauntt to SN George Bancroft, December 11, 1845, National Archives, Philadelphia.

49. A typical Elliott obituary: *North American* (Philadelphia), December 16, 1845, provided by the Chester County, Pennsylvania, Historical Society, sent to me by Richard Winslow III, the authority on the maritime history of Portsmouth, New Hampshire, and surrounding areas.

Works Cited

"Alexandria Gazette." *Portsmouth (NH) Journal of Literature and Politics*. Portsmouth, NH.

Altoff, G. T., ed. "The Battle of Lake Erie: A Narrative." In *War on the Great Lakes Essays Commemorating the 175th Anniversary of the Battle of Lake Erie*, edited by William Jeffrey Welsh and David Curtis Skaggs, 5–16. Kent, Ohio: Kent State University Press, 1991

———. "The Perry-Elliott Controversy." *Northwest Ohio Quarterly* 60 (Autumn 1988): 135–62.

———, ed. "Samuel Hambleton Diary." Maryland Historical Society. Baltimore, MD.

American State Papers. *Class II, Claims*. Vol. 11,Wayne to Elliott and Williams. September 21, 1794.

Anderson, Edward Clifton. "Edward Clifton Anderson Journal." University of North Carolina Library. 1813–82, Title, 68–69, 135–38, 145–64.

Army and Navy Chronicle, 1940, 114.

Barnes, John S. *Memorandum, 1882*. in *History of the Navy of the United States of America*. Vol. 1, Part 3. By James Fenimore Cooper. New York: G. P. Putnam, 1859.

Barron, James. "The History of a Transaction Which Ought Never to Have Been Occasion For." Compiled by College of William and Mary Library. Vol. Box 11. August 11, 1842.

Barton, Charles C. "Manifest of the Charges Preferred to the Navy Department and Subsequently to the Congress against Jesse Duncan Elliott Esq. a Captain in the Navy of the United States, for Unlawful Conduct While [Late] Commodore of the Mediterranean Squadron; and a Refutation of the Recrimination Raised by That Officer" Philadelphia: privately printed, 1839.

Bearss, Edwin C. *Charlestown [Boston] Navy Yard, 1800–1842*. Vol. 2. Washington, DC: Interior Department, National Park Service, 1984.

Belohlavek, John M. *"Let The Eagle Soar!" The Foreign Policy of Andrew Jackson*. Lincoln: University of Nebraska Press, 1895.

Berkow, Robert, ed. *Manual of Diseases and Therapy*. Rahway, NJ: Merck, 1987.

Berton, Pierre. *Flames across the Border: The Canadian-American Tragedy, 1813–1814*. Boston: Little, Brown, 1981.

Billington, Ray A. *The Protestant Crusade, 1800–1860: A Study in the Origins of American Nativism*. New York: Macmillan, 1938.

Biographical Directory of the United States Congress, 1774–1989. Washington, DC: Government Printing Office, 1989.

Boston Evening Transcript. 1833.

Boston Morning Post. 1833–34.

Brewington, Marion V. *Ship-Carvers of North America*. New York: Dover Publications, 1972.

Burgess, Tristam. *Battle of Lake Erie with Notice of Commodore Elliott's Conduct in that Engagement*. Providence, 1839.

Calhoun, John C. *The Papers of John C. Calhoun*. Vol. 3: *1818–1819*. Edited by W. Edwin Hemphill. Columbia: University of South Carolina Press, 1967.

———. *The Papers of John C. Calhoun*. Vol. 4: *1819–1820*. Edited by W. Edwin Hemphill. Columbia: University of South Carolina Press, 1969.

———. *The Papers of John C. Calhoun*. Vol. 5: *1820–1821*. Edited by W. Edwin Hemphill. Columbia: University of South Carolina Press, 1971.

Callahan, Edward W, ed. *List of Officers of the Navy of the United States and of the Marine Corps, 1775–1900*. New York: L.R. Hammerslay, 1901.

Calvet de Magalhaes, Jose. "O Tratado Commercial de 1840." In *Historica das relacoes diplomaticas entre Portugal e os Estados Unidos da America, 1776–1911*), 124–44. Lisbon: Mem Martins, Publicoes Europa–America , 1991.

Chapelle, Howard I. *The History of the American Sailing Navy: Their Ships and Their Development*. New York: Bonanza Books, 1949.

Chautauquan, July 1900, 381.

Clay, Henry. *The Papers of Henry Clay*. Vol. 1: *1797–1814*. Edited by James F. Hopkins and Mary W. M. Hargreaves. Lexington: University of Kentucky Press, 1959.

———. *The Papers of Henry Clay*. Vol. 5: *Secretary of State*. Edited by James F. Hopkins and Mary W. M. Hargreaves. Lexington: University of Kentucky Press, 1973.

———. *The Papers of Henry Clay*. Vol. 6: *Secretary of State, 1827*. Edited by James F. Hopkins and Mary W. M. Hargreaves. Lexington: University of Kentucky Press, 1981.

Cochrane, Hamilton. *Noted American Duels and Hostile Encounters*. Philadelphia: Chilton Books, 1963.

Cooper, James Fenimore. *History of the Navy of the United States of America*. Vol. 3. New York: G. P. Putnam, 1853.

———. *The Letters and Journals of James Fenimore Cooper*. Edited by James E. Beard. Vol. 3. Cambridge, MA: Belknap Press of Harvard University Press,1964.

———. *The Letters and Journals of James Fenimore Cooper*. Edited by James E. Beard. Vol. 4. Cambridge, MA: Belknap Pres of Harvard University Press, 1968.

———. *The Letters and Journals of James Fenimore Cooper*. Edited by James E. Beard. Vol. 5. Cambridge, MA: Belknap Press of Harvard University Press,1968.

———. "Oliver Hazard Perry." *Graham's Magazine* 43 (May 1843): 269.

Cottingham, Dave. "Elliott-Bestor House on the National Register." *Daily Mail*, July 7, 1975.

Cox, Richard J. "An Eyewitness Account of the Battle of Lake Erie." *Proceedings* (US Naval Institute) 104 (February 1978): 62–74.

Cruikshank, E.A., ed. *The Documentary History of Campaigns upon the Niagara Frontier, 1812–1814*. Vol. 8. Welland, Ontario: Lundy's Lane Historical Society, 1902–3.

Daily National Intelligencer. November 4, 1834, 3–4.

Decatur, Stephen. *Correspondence between the Late Commodore Stephen Decatur and Commodore James Barron, Which Led to the Unfortunate Meeting of the Twenty-Second of March*. Washington, DC: Gales & Seaton, 1820.

Dictionary of American Biography (DAB). Vol. 6. New York: Charles Scribner's Sons, n.d.

Dillon, Richard. *"We Have Met the Enemy": Oliver Hazard Perry, Wilderness Commodore*. New York: McGraw-Hill, 1978.

Dobbins, William W. *History of the Battle of Lake Erie and Reminiscences of the Flagships* Lawrence *and* Niagara. Erie, PA: Ashby Printing,1913.

Dudley, William S. "Naval Historians and the War of 1812." *Naval History* 4 (Spring 1990).

Dudley, William S., ed. *The Naval War of 1812: A Documentary History*. Vol. 1. Washington, DC: Naval Historical Center, 1985.

Dunkel, Robert E. Letter to David F. Long. October 17, 1990.

Dunne, William M. P. "Operational History: United States Second Class Sloop-of--War *Natchez*, 1827–1840, Including a Chronology of the Nullification Crisis." Unpublished manuscript, July 13, 1988.

Dutton, Charles J. *Oliver Hazard Perry*. New York: Longmans, Green, 1945.

Elliott, Charles W. *Winfield Scott: The Soldier and the Man*. New York: MacMillan, 1937.

Elliott, Jesse Duncan. *Correspondence between Commodore Jesse D. Elliott and Charles G. Loring, Esq*. Boston: privately printed, 1835.

———. *Defence of Commodore Elliott at His Philadelphia Navy Yard Court-Martial, 11 May–20 June 1840*." Philadelphia: Mifflin & Parry, 1840.

———. *Speech of Commodore Jesse Duncan Elliott, USN with Appendix and Addenda, Delivered in Hagerstown, Maryland, 14 November 1843*. Philadelphia: G. B. Zieber, 1844.

Elliott, Jesse Duncan, and Nathan Towson. *Correspondence in Relation to the Capture of the British Brigs* Detroit *and* Caledonia *on the Night of October 8, 1812.* Philadelphia: United States Book and Printing, 1843.

Field, James A., Jr. *America and the Mediterranean World, 1766–1866.* Princeton, NJ: Princeton University Press, 1969.

Finnie, David H. *Pioneers East: The Early American Experience in the Middle East.* Cambridge, MA: Harvard University Press, 1967.

Forester, C.S. *The Age of Fighting Sail.* Garden City, NY: Doubleday, 1956.

———. "Bloodshed at Dawn." *American Heritage* 15 (October 1964): 73–76.

Friedman, Lawrence J., and David Curtis Skaggs. "Jesse Duncan Elliott and the Battle of Lake Erie: The Issue of Mental Stability." *Journal of the Early Republic* 10 (Winter 1990): 493–516.

Griffin, Donald W. "The American Navy at Work on the Brazil Station, 1827–1860." *American Neptune* 19 (October 1959): 239.

Guttridge, Leonard F, and Jay D Smith. *The Commodores.* New York: Harper & Row, 1969.

Hagen, Kenneth J. *The People's Navy: The Making of American Sea Power.* New York: Free Press, 1991.

Heitman, Francis B. Historical Register of the Continental Army. Repr., Baltimore: Regional Publishing, 1967.

Herold, Amos L. *James Kirke Paulding: Versatile American.* New York: Columbia University Press, 1926.

Hickey, Donald R. *The War of 1812: A Forgotten Conflict.* Urbana: University of Illinois Press, 1989.

Horsman, Reginald. *Matthew Elliott: Indian Agent.* Detroit: Wayne State University Press, 1964.

———. *The War of 1812.* New York: Alfred A Knopf, 1969.

Jackson, Andrew. *The Correspondence of Andrew Jackson.* Vol. 4, *1829–1832.* Edited by John S. Bassett. Washington, DC: Carnegie Institute, 1929.

———. *The Correspondence of Andrew Jackson.* Vol. 6, *1839–1845.* Edited by John S. Bassett. Washington, DC: Carnegie Institute, 1933.

James, William. *A Full and Correct Account of the Chief Naval Occurences of the Lake War between Great Britain and the United States of America.* London: T. Egerton, 1817.

———. *The Naval History of Great Britain from the Declaration of War by France in February 1793 to the Accession of George IV in January 1820.* Vol. 6. London: Harding, Lepard, 1826.

Jarvis, Russell. 1835. *Biographical Notice of Com. Jesse D Elliott: Containing a Review of the Controversy between Him and the Late Commodore Perry; and a History of the Figure Head of the U.S. Frigate Constitution, by a Citizen of New York.* Philadelphia: privately printed, 1826.

Klein, Philip S., and Ari Hoogenboom. *A History of Pennsylvania.* University Park: Pennsylvania State University Press, 1980.

Langer, William L. *An Encyclopedia of World History*. 5th ed. Boston: Houghton Mifflin, 1972.

Langley, Harold D. "The Grass Roots Harvest of 1828." *U.S. Naval Institute* 90 (October, 1964): 51–59.

Letters Received by the Secretary of the Navy from Officers. National Archives, Washington, DC.

Lewis, Charles L. *David Glasgow Farragut: Admiral in the Making*. Annapolis: US Naval Institute Proceeding, 1941.

———. *Romantic Decatur*. Philadelphia: University of Pennsylvania Press, 1937.

Long, David F. *Gold Braid and Foreign Relations: Diplomatic Activities of U.S. Naval Officers, 1798–1883*. Annapolis: Naval Institute Press, 1988.

———. *"Mad Jack": The Biography of Captain John Percival, USN 1779–1862*. Westport, CT: Greenwood Press, 1993.

———. *Nothing Too Daring: A Biography of Commodore David Porter, 1780–1843*. Annapolis: US Naval Institute, 1970.

———. *Ready to Hazard: A Biography of Commodore William Bainbridge, 1774–1833*. Hanover, NH: University Press of New England, 1981.

———. *Sailor-Diplomat: A Biography of Commodore Biddle 1783–1848*. Boston: Northeastern University Press, 1983.

———. "William Bainbridge and the Barron-Decatur Duel; Mere Participant or Active Plotter?" *Pennsylvania Magazine of History and Biography* 53 (January 1979): 49–52.

Lossing, Benson J. *The Pictorial Field-Book of the War of 1812 . . . or Illustrations by Pen and Pencil of the History, Biography, Scenery, Relics, & Traditions of the Last War for American Independence*. New York: Harper & Brothers, 1869.

Mackenzie, Alexander S. *Life of Stephen Decatur: A Commodore in the Navy of United States*. Vol. 2. Boston: Charles C. Little & James Brown, 1846.

Mackenzie, Alexander Slidell. *Life of Commodore Oliver Hazard Perry: A Commodore in the United States*. 2 vols. Boston: Charles G. Little and James Brown, 1848.

Mahan, Alfred Thayer. *Sea Power in Relation to the War of 1812*. Vol. 1. New York: Charles Scribner's Sons, 1903.

Malcomson, Robert, and Thomas Malcomson. *HMS* Detroit: *The Battle for Lake Erie*. Annapolis: Naval Institute Press, 1990.

Martin, Tyrone G. *A Most Fortunate Ship: A Narrative History of "Old Ironsides."* Chester, CT: Globe Pequot Press, 1980.

McKee, Christopher. "An Aerial View of Put-in-Bay: United States Historians Scrutinize a Campaign." In *War on the Great Lakes Essays Commemorating the 175th Anniversary of the Battle of Lake Erie*, ed. William Jeffrey Welsh and David Curtis Skaggs, 90. Kent, Ohio: Kent State University Press, 1991

———. *A Gentlemanly and Honorable Profession: The Creation of the U.S. Naval Officer Corps, 1794–1815*. Annapolis: Naval Institute Press, 1991.

Merrill, James M. "Midshipman DuPont and the Cruise of the *North Carolina,* 1825–1827." *American Neptune* 40 (January 1980): 213, 215.

Mills, James C. *Oliver Hazard Perry and the Battle of Lake Erie.* Detroit: John Phelps, 1913.

Morison, Samuel Eliot. *"Old Bruin": Commodore Matthew Calbraith Perry 1794–1858.* Boston: Little, Brown, 1967.

Mott, Frank L. *American Journalism, 1690–1960.* New York: Macmillan, 1962.

The Name and Family of Elliot(t) and Elliot, passim. New York: Roots Research Bureau.

"Naval Operations." *State of New York, Oliver Hazard Perry Victory Centennial.* Albany: J. B. Lyon, 1916.

The New Columbia Encyclopedia. New York: Columbia University Press, 1975.

Niles Weekly Register. Baltimore: Franklin Press, May 16, 1818.

———. July 9, 1814, 319.

———. June 5, 1815.

———. January 12, 1822, 320.

———. April 19,1823, 98.

———. November 19, 1826, 410, 425.

———. September 2, 1826, 5–9.

———. November 8, 1834.

———. June 27, 1835, 290.

———. July 11, 1835, 327.

———. September 5, 1840, 145–50.

North American (Philadelphia). December 16, 1845.

Northwest. Vol. 4, *Anecdotes of the Lake Erie Area, War of 1812.* Transcribed from original sources, by Richard C. Knopf, historical editor and research historian, Anthony Wayne Parkway Board. Columbus: Ohio Historical Society, 1957.

Oates, Stephen B. *The Fires of Jubilee: Nat Turner's Fierce Rebellion.* New York: Harper & Row, 1975.

"Officers' Records." Jesse Duncan Elliott and St. Clair Elliott. National Archives, Washington, DC.

Oliver, Frederick L. "Commodore Oliver Hazard Perry of Newport, Rhode Island." *U.S. Naval Institute Proceedings (USNIP)* 80 (July 1954): 777–83.

Palmer, Michael A. "A Failure of Command, Control, and Communications: Oliver Hazard Perry and the Battle of Lake Erie." *Journal of Erie Studies* (Erie County Historical Society and Mercyhurst College) 17 (Fall 1988): 8–20.

Paulding, James Kirke. *The Letters of James Kirke Paulding.* Edited by Ralph A. Aderman. Madison: University of Wisconsin Press, 1962.

Paullin, Charles O. *Diplomatic Negotiations of American Naval Officers, 1778–1883.* Baltimore: Johns Hopkins Press, 1912.

———. "Dueling in the Old Navy." *U.S. Naval Institute Proceedings (USNIP)* 35 (1909): 1164–65.

———. *Commodore John Rodgers*. Cleveland: Arthur H. Clark, 1910.

———. "Naval Administration under the Navy Commissioners, 1815–1842." *U.S. Naval Institute Proceedings (USNIP)* 33 (1907).

Pepper, F. B. *Life and Correspondence of Sir Isacc Brock*. London: Simpkin, Marshall, 1845.

Perry, Matthew C. Documents in Relation to Differences Which Subsist between Late Commodore O. H. Perry and Captain Jesse D. Elliott. Washington, DC, 1821.

Porter, David Dixon. *Memoir of Commodore David Porter of the United States Navy*. Albany NY: J. Munsell, 1875.

Port Folio. December 1814, 531.

Proceedings of the General Court-martial Convened for the Trial of Commodore James Barron, Captain Charles Gordon, Mr. William Hook, and Captain John Hall, of the United States Ship Chesapeake . . . *in the Month of January 1808*. Washington, DC: J. Gideon, 1822.

Rimini, Robert V. . *Andrew Jackson and the Bank War: A Study in the Growth of Presidential Power*. New York: W. W. Norton, 1961

———. *Andrew Jackson and Course of American Democracy, 1833–1845*. New York: Harper & Row, 1984.

Roosevelt, Theodore. *The Naval War of 1812; or, the History of the United States Navy during the Last War with Great Britain*. 7th ed. New York: G. P. Putnam's Sons, 1898.

Runyan, Timothy J., and Jan M. Copes. "The Battle of Lake Erie after 175 Years: Commemoration and Controversy." *Inland* 44 (1988).

Schuman, Merri L. S. "A History and Genealogy of Carlisle, Cumberland County, 1751–1835." Dover, PA: private, 1987.

Snow, Elliot, and H. Allen Gosnell. *On the Decks of Old Ironsides*. New York: Macmillan, 1932.

Spears, John R. "Old Ironsides, As Sailors Saw Her." *Chautauquan*, T. L. Flood, Meadville, PA. 1890.

Stevens, William O. *An Affair of Honor: The Biography of Commodore James Barron*. Norfolk County Historical Society and the College of William and Mary Library, 1969.

Sweetman, Jack. *American Naval History: An Illustrated Chronicle of the U.S. Navy and Marine Corps, 1775–Present*. Annapolis: Naval Institute Press, 1984.

The Trial of Lt E.B. Babbit on Charges Preferred by Com. Jesse D. Elliott; before a Naval Court-martial. Assembled at the Navy Yard, Charlestown, 13. October 1834. Boston, 1835.

Tucker, Glenn. *Dawn Like Thunder: The Barbary Wars and the Birth of the U.S. Navy*. Indianapolis: Bobbs-Merrill, 1963.

Valle, James E. *Rocks & Shoals: Order and Discipline in the Old Navy, 1800–1861*. Annapolis: Naval Institute Press, 1980.

Warren, Charles "More Odd Byways in American History." Massachusetts Historical Society, *Proceedings* 69 (1956): 256–57.

Wayman, Dorothy G. "Discussions." *U.S. Naval Institute Proceedings* 55 (1929): 327–28.

Weber, Gustavus A. *The Coast and Geodetic Survey: Its History, Activities, and Organization*. Baltimore, Johns Hopkins Press, 1923.

Westcott, Allan. "Commodore Jesse D. Elliott: A Stormy Petrel of the Navy." *U.S. Naval Institute Proceedings (USNIP)* 54 (September 1928).

White, Elizabeth B. *American Opinion of France from Lafayette to Poincare* (New York: Knopf, 1927), 94–109.

Williams, Thomas J. *A History of Washington County, Maryland from the Earliest Settlements to the Present Day, Including a History of Hagerstown*. Vol. 1. Baltimore: Regional Publishing, 1968.

Wraight, Joseph, and Elliott B. Roberts. *The Coast and Geodetic Survey, 1807–1957: 150 Years of History*. Washington, DC: Government Printing Office, 1957.

Index

Page numbers in italics refer to images.
JDE refers to the subject, Jesse Duncan Elliott.